Organizing Schools for Improvement

Organizing Schools for Improvement
Lessons from Chicago

Anthony S. Bryk, Penny Bender Sebring, Elaine Allensworth,
Stuart Luppescu, and John Q. Easton

The University of Chicago Press Chicago and London

Anthony S. Bryk is president of the Carnegie Foundation for the Advancement of Teaching and was founding senior director of the Consortium on Chicago School Research, University of Chicago.

Penny Bender Sebring is founding codirector of the Consortium on Chicago School Research, the Urban Education Institute, University of Chicago.

Elaine Allensworth is codirector for statistical analysis at the Consortium on Chicago School Research, the Urban Education Institute, University of Chicago.

Stuart Luppescu is chief psychometrician at the Consortium on Chicago School Research, the Urban Education Institute, University of Chicago.

John Q. Easton is director of the Institute of Education Sciences, U.S. Department of Education, and was executive director of the Consortium on Chicago School Research, University of Chicago.

The University of Chicago Press, Chicago 60637
The University of Chicago Press, Ltd., London
© 2010 by The University of Chicago
All rights reserved. Published 2010
Printed in the United States of America

19 18 17 16 15 14 13 12 11 10   6 7 8 9 10

ISBN-13: 978-0-226-07799-4 (cloth)
ISBN-13: 978-0-226-07800-7 (paper)
ISBN-10: 0-226-07799-3 (cloth)
ISBN-10: 0-226-07800-0 (paper)

Library of Congress Cataloging-in-Publication Data

Organizing schools for improvement : lessons from
Chicago / Anthony S. Bryk . . . [et al.].
     p. cm.
    Includes bibliographical references and index.
    ISBN-13: 978-0-226-07799-4 (hardcover : alk. paper)
    ISBN-10: 0-226-07799-3 (hardcover : alk. paper)
    ISBN-13: 978-0-226-07800-7 (pbk. : alk. paper)
    ISBN-10: 0-226-07800-0 (pbk. : alk. paper)
    1. School improvement programs—Illinois—Chicago—Case studies.
    2. School management and organization—Illinois—Chicago—Case
studies.   3. Educational change—Illinois—Chicago—Case studies.
    4. Public schools—Decentralization—Illinois—Chicago—Case studies.
    5. Education, Urban—Illinois—Chicago—Case studies. I. Bryk, Anthony S.
  LB2822.83.I3074 2010
  371.2'090977311—dc22   2009010635

CONTENTS

ACKNOWLEDGMENTS

Organizing Schools for Improvement: Lessons from Chicago represents a significant strand in the cumulative body of research produced by the Consortium on Chicago School Research at the University of Chicago (CCSR). The study and this book are the culmination of more than a decade of data collection and analysis, school visits, and discussions with colleagues, members of the CCSR Steering Committee, Chicago educators, policy makers, reformers, and other scholars.

We benefited greatly from the diligence and resolve of the CCSR research staff, which organized the massive survey administrations of thousands of students and teachers and hundreds of school principals. Despite tight time lines, the staff cleaned and prepared data, developed numerous measures, and documented survey procedures.

Among the many people who assisted us, we want to single out for special recognition R. Matthew Gladden, who formulated the conceptual outline and defined and analyzed the unique variables we used to explore community social capital and social problems in chapter 6. Matt persevered with his insightful and careful analyses, even as we paused to attend to the needs of other studies. We deeply appreciate his contribution. In addition, Yeow Meng Thum conducted lengthy and complex analyses of test scores to create the value-added indicator.

We also are indebted to Donald Moore, who at an early stage identified key themes in the literature that helped to shape our conceptual framework. Similarly, we thank BetsAnn Smith, who helped us draft the *Path to Achievement* document for the Chicago Public Schools (CPS). It was here that the idea of five essential supports first saw print. We also acknowledge the late Fred Hess and the Chicago Panel on Public School Finance, who had a major influence on this research, and provided initial support for developing our value-added indicators of academic improvement. Stephen Raudenbush gave us access to data from the Project on Human Development in Chicago Neighborhoods, which was so vital for understanding the communities surrounding the schools. In addition, he reviewed a draft of the 2006 CCSR report, *The Essential Supports for School Improvement,* which was the first description of our findings; his key questions about our theoretical framework and empirical evidence led us to fine-tune and clarify our argument. Charles Payne was an active "critical friend" throughout this work. He challenged our ideas, pushed us to refine our conceptualization, and provided critical independent validation evidence for many of the organizational indicators used in this research.

Arie van der Ploeg, who has been a valued colleague and friend, also reviewed the earlier report and provided excellent suggestions. Barbara Eason-Watkins examined the prologue and helped to build awareness within the CPS of the earlier report. She gave us much-needed encouragement at a point when the end seemed far away.

We appreciate the kindness of Richard Lock in sharing neighborhood crime data from the Chicago Police Department. And we are grateful to Chapin Hall Center for Children at the University of Chicago for the data on child abuse and neglect. These data sets were invaluable in probing the impact of community context.

Over the years, the CCSR Steering Committee has contributed enormously to our research questions and our interpretations of results. This group of Chicago educators, administrators, school reformers, and scholars has generously given its time and talents to help us make sense of our findings and communicate them in fair and clear ways. Deliberations in Steering Committee meetings significantly influenced our thinking and the way we wrote the book, and we are grateful to the committee members for pushing us further.

None of this would have been possible without the cooperation and involvement of CPS leaders. They provided us with test scores and administrative data, and they encouraged teachers and students to participate in the surveys. On two separate occasions, thousands of teachers administered the survey to their students and also completed their own lengthy questionnaire. Schools allowed researchers to visit classrooms and professional development sessions and talk to most anyone they could. To their credit, school system leaders' desire for evidence to accelerate their reform agendas outweighed concerns about possible negative publicity.

In constructing more than seventy figures, Shari Grace created images that clearly convey a genuine understanding of the concepts and the evidence behind them. She patiently and promptly made revisions until they were perfect.

We also extend our thanks to Sandra Dantzler for conscientiously making corrections, and copying and assembling more drafts of the book than we care to remember. Often this work spilled over into evening hours so that we could meet deadlines. Alina Kelly, Drew Dir, Gabriel Molina, and Marisol Mastrangelo also provided excellent editorial assistance in making figures, assembling appendixes, proofreading text and illustrations, and tracking down references and notes.

Our project team at the University of Chicago Press was extraordinary in its support and professionalism. John Tryneski and Elizabeth Branch Dyson provided valuable feedback and enthusiastically championed our project within the Press. We are particularly grateful to the two anonymous readers who examined our manuscript twice and offered suggestions to make it more accessible to readers ranging from practitioners to quantitative researchers. Sandra Hazel, our manuscript editor, assiduously removed errors in the text and shaped it to better express what she knew we were trying to say. No detail was too small to escape her scrutiny. Anne Summers Goldberg deftly managed the overall, complex process; Maia Wright transformed a plain manuscript into a beautiful, pleasing book. Jamie Solock coordinated the important final step of production, and Rob Hunt worked closely with us to determine how best to reach the educators, policy makers, and researchers working on the pressing problems of urban school reform, to make them aware of the book.

Finally, we have been fortunate, indeed, to have the steadfast support of the John D. and Catherine T. MacArthur Foundation, the Joyce Foundation, and the Spencer Foundation. They provided long-term funding for us to pursue this agenda of the factors that matter most for improving student achievement in Chicago public elementary schools. Their commitment was philanthropy at its best. They believed in the power of the ideas that we sought to vitalize in the Consortium on Chicago School Research, trusted that we could bring this mission to life, and personally supported us as we pursued a sometimes difficult and uncertain path. There is no way to fully express our gratitude for their confidence in and support for our endeavor.

I am from streets with buildings
that used to look pretty.
From safe walking trips to
Mr. Ivan's family grocery store,
where now stands a criminal sanctuary.
I am from a home and garage
illustrated with crowns, diamonds,
upside-down pitchforks, squiggly
names and death threats.
I am from a once busy, prosperous
and productive community;
where the fathers and mothers
earned a living at the steel mills,
and the children played
Kick the Can and Hide and Go Seek
until they could play no more.
I am from here.

Ms. Sparks, Sixth-Grade Teacher, Hancock Elementary School[1]

Like many teachers, Ms. Sparks grew up in the neighborhood where she now works. Neither she, nor her parents, nor any members of her extended family, however, live there any longer—some time ago all escaped the violence and general decay for safer and more prosperous communities. The housing stock in Oak Meadows is now worn and dilapidated; many buildings were burned out in the late 1960s and '70s and subsequently torn down. Neighborhood fixtures like dry cleaners, retail stores, and gas stations are long gone.

The main building for the Herbie Hancock Elementary School[2] was built around 1900. Although over one hundred years old, it retains the architectural flourishes that were common in public buildings of the time. A "new building" was added in the early 1960s to accommodate the growing student population in Oak Meadows. It is a low, nondescript structure that could have been commissioned by most any bureaucracy. It would have fit just as comfortably in a cold-war-era Eastern European city as on the South Side of Chicago.

As Bonnie Whitmore took up the principalship at the Hancock School in 1989, she inherited a very troubled school community. Gangs roamed freely in the neighborhood, and the crime rate there was among the highest in the city. Maintaining order at Hancock had been a high priority. On more than one occasion, neighborhood conflicts had spilled right through the front doors of the school itself. Although the Local School Council had appointed Bonnie with enthusiasm, some worried aloud that what the school really needed was "a man who could wear the pants and show everyone who was in charge."

Whitmore's predecessor, Mr. Martin, sequestered himself most of the time in his office, where he dealt with the school's myriad day-to-day operational problems. Up through the late 1980s, little beyond this was expected of administrators at schools like Hancock. Keeping things under control and avoiding major crises were their main priorities. District administrators generally gave positive evaluations to principals like Mr. Martin, who kept order in their schools. In truth, however, Martin had basically "retired on the job."

The accumulated organizational neglect was quite obvious as one moved out into classrooms and around the school. Teacher quality was highly variable. Some teachers were quite good, but many others were deeply entrenched in their old ways of doing things, even though their students were obviously not learning. In general, teachers were left to "do their own thing" in their classrooms regardless of the ultimate results. As a group, the faculty was cantankerous and divided. Middle- and upper-grade teachers in the old building looked down on the primary-grade teachers in the new building whom they judged as not having to work very hard. Little interest in or support for meaningful change could be found anywhere. Not surprisingly, in 1990 Hancock's standardized test results placed it among the one hundred worst elementary schools in Chicago in both reading and math.

Six Years Later: Hancock on the Move

It is an unusually nice late spring afternoon in Chicago as Hancock's teachers gather in the cafeteria after school for a regularly scheduled professional development session.[3] After welcoming remarks from the principal, a teacher leader offers a brief overview of the day's activity, and teachers quickly move around the room to form small work groups. As they systematically review stacks of student papers, teachers begin to outline a set of observations about the strengths and weaknesses of their students' written work. They focus on identifying shared problems that students appeared to be having in understanding and writing about the key ideas in some common instructional units that they are attempting to teach. As a group, they begin to brainstorm about how their instructional efforts might be improved and draw up some preliminary recommendations to be forwarded to a schoolwide curriculum committee. At the end of the meeting, the principal announces that eleven of their colleagues have been accepted into a special citywide program that will prepare them for the arduous journey toward possible certification from the National Board for Professional Teaching Standards. Clearly, profound changes have occurred at Hancock, and even more appear on the horizon.

After a period of steady decline, enrollment at Hancock began to increase during the early 1990s. By 1996, the school served more than one thousand students, from pre-kindergarten through eighth grade. Grades 6 through 8 formed a middle school that served students graduating from Hancock's lower grades as well as those coming from other elementary schools in the area. Some sixty-five teachers now formed the faculty.

Renewing this faculty had been a chief concern for Bonnie Whitmore. Before her tenure at Hancock, Bonnie had developed a reputation in her previous principalship as a no-nonsense educator. She held high standards and expected the same from the entire school staff. Several teachers who had been at Hancock for a number of years chose to leave early on in Bonnie's tenure, feeling they would be more comfortable at a school where their instructional practice might receive less critical scrutiny. In turn, Bonnie invested heavily in the professional development of those who chose to stay on as well as the new teachers whom she hired.

One of these new teachers was Patricia Sparks. Although she came to Hancock with limited professional experience, Patricia threw herself into the various professional development opportunities at her new school. She worked hard to incorporate into her lessons both the subject matter content and the new pedagogy that she learned about in school-based workshops. Over time, she joined an emerging cadre of strong teacher leaders within the school.

At the same time that Bonnie was advancing the professional development of her staff, she also worked hard to nurture a collegial spirit among the faculty and camaraderie around their collective efforts toward school improvement. Using her own personal funds, she organized monthly staff breakfasts that created opportunities for relationship building and professional development.

The end result of this concerted focus on professional capacity building was a very different faculty. Gradually, teachers deepened their subject matter and pedagogical knowledge, and felt increasingly comfortable talking about their practice and their efforts to improve it. They were encouraged to take courses and attend conferences and professional meetings, and then develop workshop sessions at Hancock where they might share with colleagues what they had just learned. Eventually, the expertise of several teachers, who had been quite active in these professional development activities, became widely recognized. These individuals now took on significant leadership roles within the faculty and larger school community.

A number of important structural changes, introduced in the early 1990s, were key in supporting these developments. Working with her faculty, Bonnie introduced common planning periods for each grade level. To create more time for professional development, Hancock added a few minutes to each school day, and once a month released students early to allow teachers to participate in ongoing professional development and to continue their improvement planning. Bonnie also allocated substantial discretionary resources for securing extra teacher substitutes to free up her regular staff, so that they could observe other teachers' classrooms and work with outside staff developers.

Instructional improvement efforts focused initially on literacy. Developing students' reading and writing skills is the single most important goal of elementary education. This work engages a substantial amount of time and effort from almost all members of an elementary school's faculty, and was a strategic choice for where best to begin.

After extended opportunities for discussing their own instructional practices, teachers came to recognize the incoherence in instruction across Hancock's classrooms and grades. Subsequently, the faculty agreed to adopt a common literacy framework, Pat Cunningham's Four Blocks.[4] Grade by grade, teachers sought to systematically build skills in phonics, word study, vocabulary development, and writing while offering students a rich exposure to literature, and to meaningful discussions about the ideas encountered there. Moreover, teachers nurtured a "love of reading" through a supplemental Links to Literacy program that recognized each book read by a student with a colorful paper link posted on hallway bulletin boards.

Instructionally embedded assessments represented another central reform element. Teachers at Hancock agreed to conduct assessments every five weeks that provided common data on each student's progress as a reader and a writer. The content of these assessments evolved, based on teachers' analyses of their students' annual standardized test scores and more general discussions about student learning at the school. For example, when the results from a new state assessment showed weaknesses in students' narrative writing skills, teachers went to work. Professional development time was set aside to study the new narrative writing rubric developed by the Illinois Department of Education, and then teachers used this rubric to analyze their own students' work. As the faculty reviewed these results with the school literacy program coordinator, they planned additional workshops to further hone their skills in this instructional domain.

Along the way, Hancock also made good use of a wide array of external resources available through various universities, cultural organizations, and social agencies in the Chicago area. A couple of years into their instructional reform efforts, teachers became concerned about weaknesses in their students' mathematics learning. Two faculty members from a local university spent over two years helping Hancock's teachers to diagnose gaps in mathematics instruction at the school and improve the alignment in the mathematics curriculum across the grades. Although it took some time, math test scores eventually did rise. For the teachers at Hancock, initiatives like this gave real meaning to the phrase "all students can learn." With time, effort, and the right support, they learned that much more was really possible. Increasingly, they saw the efficacy of their efforts in action. As one teacher noted, "We don't feel we're any different from any other school anyplace else. Our kids, given the opportunity, can do it."[5]

Outside resources also proved especially helpful as the school sought to address the numerous academic, personal, social, and health-related needs of the students and families that Hancock served. While instructional improvement was the school's primary concern, staff quickly realized that these other problems, left unattended, could seriously impede their students' learning. Assembling a first-rate social services support team and accessing external program services that extended well beyond the meager ones offered by the school system itself was another key piece in the school's reform agenda. In general, social and academic supports for student learning form one of the most fragmented and incoherent programmatic areas in large urban school systems. Locating, accessing, and coordinating the contributed services from various universities, hospitals, and neighborhood and citywide social service agencies—and making all of this actually work for the students at Hancock—took considerable ingenuity and commitment.

Reconnecting to families and supporting them in the education of their children was still another reform strand that emerged. The school initiated Even Start, a state-funded program that brings parents and children in pre-kindergarten through second grade together for a variety of activities, including reading and computer use. Hancock became a site for a parental GED program and offered job search classes. To capitalize on the presence of many grandparents in the community, it started the Grandparents Club. A Real Men Read program was also launched to enlist adult male role models from the neighborhood to come into the school to read stories to children. The staff was constantly looking for new and more effective ways to reach out to parents and strengthen their ties to the local community. Even though some of these activities felt frustrating to teachers, as parents did not always reciprocate their efforts, they nonetheless knew they had to keep trying.

In short, principal Bonnie Whitmore catalyzed an impressive array of changes at Hancock Elementary School. She took the lead in articulating a coherent vision of reform for her school community. She pushed for curriculum alignment and greater pedagogical coherence, classroom by classroom and grade by grade. She envisioned Hancock as a community of professional practice, where school improvement was everyone's job. She introduced the idea of continuous assessment of students' performance, and maintained focus on the key issues affecting individual students' learning and studying evidence about whether learning was actually occurring. Finally, Bonnie opened the school to outside expertise as a resource for improvement,[6] and she championed the difficult work of strengthening ties to parents and the local community.

Despite having been a principal for many years, Bonnie never lost touch with her identity as a teacher. As she stated, "I knew the times [as a teacher] when I was not supported and allowed to do the things that I felt would really benefit children. As an instructional leader, as a principal, I'm always a teacher, too." She also knew that while she might be able to envision reform, it would take the engagement of many individuals throughout her school community to make it happen. She explained:

> I can't be the leader of everything, and there are leaders within school, people with strengths and talents. As the overall leader, I have to allow these other leaders to emerge . . . I look at myself more as a facilitator than someone who's in charge of something, because we're all part of this.[7]

However, when the situation demanded it, Bonnie could also be quite authoritative. Those who resisted reforms at Hancock became an increasing focus of her attention. As the chairperson of the first Local School Council (LSC) noted, "The older regime doesn't much care for Mrs. Whitmore." Although encouraging teachers' instructional improvement efforts, facilitating teachers' work, and supporting it with resources were key elements in Bonnie's leadership style, those who did not come on board with the emerging reforms knew that they had to leave. Eventually, most did, of their own accord.

In 1997, Bonnie Whitmore was among twenty-two school principals who won a School Leadership Award from the Chicago Principals and Administrators Association. Her choice came with considerable justification. Hancock ranked as one of the most improved schools in both reading and mathematics in the city of Chicago.

Alexander Stands Still

Less than two miles away in a neighborhood directly adjacent to Oak Meadows stands Alexander Elementary School.[8] It is a pale-yellow, concrete-block building that serves about five hundred students from pre-kindergarten through eighth grade. Like Hancock, the neighborhood surrounding Alexander is very poor. Directly across the street from the school is an abandoned building, which students must pass every day on their way to school. In clear view of the school are broken windows, partially burned buildings, garbage, and debris. Not far away, one can occasionally see clusters of older men who gather during the day to socialize and drink.

As school reform began in 1989, most of Alexander's faculty had been at the school for a very long time, many teachers for more than twenty years. They wistfully recalled the halcyon days when the community was different, students seemed to care about school, families were stronger, and teaching was a respected and enjoyable profession. All of these things had changed, and none for the better, during their tenure at this school.

Like Hancock, Alexander began the decade among the worst one hundred schools in Chicago in terms of its students' reading and math achievement. Unlike Hancock, however, it remained so six years later.

Issues of order and safety were chronic concerns in this school community. The sounds of gunfire were not uncommon, and much local crime stemmed from the use and sale of illegal drugs. Parents often kept their children from playing outdoors unless they could be present. Fear of victimization also meant a real reluctance to attend evening meetings at Alexander. One parent told of the time she was on her way home from a meeting when bullets whizzed by her. She ran back to the school as if it were a "foxhole." Another, who was a candidate for the LSC, refused to attend an evening candidates' forum unless provided with a bulletproof vest. Yet if meetings were held during the day, working parents could rarely attend.

Given the dangers of the streets, the school was always locked, and a security guard was on full-time duty. Several years earlier, Alexander had opted for a "closed campus" and a shortened day. This meant that teachers had no lunch hour and left early with the students at 2:30 p.m. This constrained schedule limited teachers' interactions with one another, and helped maintain their isolation as the norm. As one teacher explained:

> I go in my classroom, teach my children, bring them to lunch, take them to gym and the library and go home. I don't get involved. I've learned not to get involved in situations where I have no control. I don't know how long before I'll be retiring. I mean I care, but I prefer going home . . . I feel I have given my time.[9]

Betty Green, the principal of Alexander, grew up in Chicago, attended Chicago public elementary and high schools, graduated from a local teachers' college, and received her master's degree from a local university. In her early twenties, she had begun working as a teacher at Alexander. She became a counselor and finally the principal there in the mid-1980s. When LSCs were formed in 1989, each council had to choose the principal for their school. The Alexander council refused to consider anyone else. Betty Green was their choice to lead reform in their school community.

Under her leadership, Alexander became a safer and more orderly place. She courageously confronted and chased gang members away from the school grounds several times and eventually got them to agree to stay away. She was able to get a play lot built so the preschool children would have a place to romp around. Inside the building, arguments, cursing, and occasional fistfights among parents and teachers had ceased. Norms of civil conduct had been established, and for the most part, folks now got along with one another. Betty had become "mom to the school community," and this meant a lot to parents and teachers alike.[10]

Betty worked actively with her first LSC, encouraging parents and teachers to initiate change. She also sought to expand teacher participation in instructional improvement. Toward that end, she initiated a professional personnel committee, called the first meeting, and recommended possible projects. But like the LSC, this committee never jelled as a functional work group. Teachers, as was also true of the parents, felt uneasy about their

new leadership roles, having grown accustomed over the years to just doing what Betty asked of them. They worried that taking a more active role
might reignite conflict across the school community and, more important,
jeopardize their personal relationship with Mrs. Green. All of this posed a
major dilemma for Betty. Without her direct personal involvement, reform
objectives were unlikely to be accomplished; but with it, teachers and parents would remain dependent on her—and there was far too much work
for just one person to shoulder.

Like the Hancock School, Alexander launched a wide array of initiatives
to connect to parents, strengthen ties to the local community, and improve
instruction. The school began workshops and GED classes for parents, offered after-school tutoring, created smaller classes for primary students
funded by Title 1, and launched a program for gifted students. Although
each of these initiatives began with considerable enthusiasm, few took
root, and virtually all were moribund within a couple of years.

Even more troublesome, there was little evidence of an overall plan
toward which all these initiatives and people were working. The idea of
a comprehensive improvement strategy seemed highly foreign to Alexander's leaders. As the assistant principal responded when asked to characterize a good school: "Off the top of my head, that's hard for me to say . . . I
haven't graduated to that level of thinking yet . . . I'm used to having not. It's
hard for me to think of a good school when I've been here for so long."[11]

Alexander did initiate a partnership with a local university to focus on
comprehensive school change, which included a major effort to strengthen
instructional practice in both literacy and math. This work got off to a very
promising start the first year, with active faculty participation and some
genuine instructional leadership emerging from the school's literacy coordinator and a few other teachers. Their growing expertise, and the changing school community relationships which ensued, however, threatened
Betty's traditional role as the "school mom." Tensions arose with the university partner, as its efforts were challenging established norms at Alexander. While the partnership persisted for several years, the initial promising
developments were stunted, and little of value emerged from this work.[12]

Alexander's efforts to engage parents in the school community also
proved difficult. There was a small core of reliable volunteers, but most
parents appeared largely apathetic. Many were very young, in their early
twenties, having had their children when they were just in their mid- to
late teens. Extreme poverty pressed down hard on these young parents,
sapping their energy and dashing most shreds of hope. Betty Green understood that many simply could not respond in a sustained, effective fashion.

The enduring problems that they confronted fostered widespread malaise and depression. When she asked parents why they did not come to the school, they often talked about "the stress and how they weren't coping very well, just living day to day. And they weren't sure how to help their children at home."[13]

For those who were able to get involved at Alexander, the school sometimes operated as an agent of adult social mobility. Perhaps through a job at the school or some adult training activity, or by securing a GED, these parents now had opportunities to better themselves, and many moved up and out of the Alexander community as soon as they could. As the LSC chair explained, "The area is so transitory that sometimes you get your hands on some [parents] that you find are really interested . . . and by the time you have them where you want them . . . then, they're gone."[14]

In sum, a complex community dynamic of disorder, concerns about human safety, and high transience among neighborhood residents combined to exacerbate the problems of reform at Alexander Elementary School. Building and sustaining a collective capability to support comprehensive change just seemed overwhelming. In many ways, the sense of isolation, resignation, and hopelessness found in the community infused the school itself. Although some individuals tried very hard to improve opportunities for the children at Alexander, doubt remained widespread that this school could actually be fundamentally different.

Intriguing Questions

How did Hancock beat the odds? Why did Alexander fail to do so? These two schools appeared quite similar and like dozens of other Chicago schools. The per-pupil fiscal resources supplied by the central administration were virtually identical. In terms of student test scores, the two schools started out in 1990 about the same. Less than two miles apart, the two schools serve adjoining neighborhoods that appeared similar on most sociodemographic characteristics. Both schools serve only African-American children, virtually all of whom were considered low income by federal standards. Many parents were unemployed. Census data from 1990 tells us that in both neighborhoods, about half the men aged sixteen and older did not work. Similarly, about half the households in each neighborhood received public aid of some kind, such as food stamps or Aid to Families with Dependent Children (later replaced by Temporary Assistance to Needy Families), and each school had more than a few children whose family was homeless.

But over time, these two schools did become quite different places. And, change processes like this occurred literally hundreds of times during the early and mid-1990s across the city of Chicago. What, then, accounts for the varied educational outcomes that emerged among these schools?

The cases themselves offer some intriguing suggestions. Differences in principal leadership style and the engagement of both parents and school staff in the work of improvement are obvious. The sustained focus on instruction and professional capacity building at Hancock also stands out as notable. While on the surface the two school communities look demographically similar, more subtle differences in local history and community may have also played a role here. Student mobility, for example, was somewhat higher at Alexander than Hancock.

Ideas such as these represent interesting conjectures, largely grounded in a post-hoc and somewhat anecdotal comparison of the developments in two specific schools. In the pages that follow, we seek a more systematic analysis. We strive to understand the internal workings and external conditions that distinguish improving elementary schools from those that fail to do so. In so doing, we aim to establish a comprehensive, empirically grounded theory of practice—in this instance, the practice of organizing schools for improvement—that teachers, parents, principals, superintendents, and civic leaders can draw on as they work to improve children's learning in thousands of other schools all across this land.

**A RARE OPPORTUNITY TO LEARN
ABOUT SCHOOL IMPROVEMENT**

An Unprecedented Reform in a Highly Disadvantaged Context

The early 1990s was a period of extraordinary ferment and great optimism about schools in Chicago. The Chicago School Reform Act of 1988 had changed all the rules. It devolved significant resources and authority to newly formed Local School Councils and mandated these leaders to reform their schools. Contrary to what has since become the accepted wisdom about how best to advance large system change, the Reform Act deliberately constrained the power of the central bureaucracy to interfere with local initiative. Rather than centrally developed plans for the improvement of its schools, Chicago chose a very different course: democratic localism as a lever for change.

At base here was a simple but powerful belief. If local school professionals reconnected with the parents and communities they were supposed to serve, and if everyone were empowered to reform their schools, together they could be much more effective in solving local problems than some impersonal bureaucracy. These distant institutions were the source of the problem; solutions had to be found elsewhere. Now, the citizens of a city had been directly commissioned to improve their schools. Nothing like this, on this scale, had ever been tried before.[1]

No explicit blueprint for improvement was set out in the 1988 Reform Act. Rather, it charged school community leaders to develop their own plans to improve student learning. Not surprisingly, a diverse array of approaches ensued. From a research perspective, the Chicago public school system from 1990 through 1996 represented an extraordinary natural experiment in school change. Local School Councils chose principals who brought very different leadership styles to their efforts. School community leaders attacked a broad set of problems in highly diverse ways, pursuing different solutions and implementing each with varying intensity and duration. Schools started in different places and had different local resources on which to draw. We also now know that student learning improved dramatically in some schools, such as Hancock, but failed to do so in others, such as Alexander. Taken together, these conditions provide an opening to learn more about how the base resources present in school communities condition their capacity to make fundamental changes in their structure and operations, and how changes in these key organizational features in turn link to improvements in student learning. In short, Chicago's decentralization reform afforded an extraordinary opportunity to assemble a large longitudinal database with which we could examine and test empirically key propositions about how schools work and how their operations might be improved to enhance student learning.

The Chicago School Context

The dismal performance of the Chicago Public Schools (CPS) through the 1970s and 1980s has been well documented. Few observers write about the CPS without recounting the famous quote of the then secretary of education William Bennett, who in 1988 labeled these schools "the worst in the nation." Though arguably other major urban school districts had equally severe or even worse problems, no one could dispute the basic facts. The CPS was plagued by astronomically high dropout rates, extremely low student achievement, constant labor strife, unstable leadership, and a wholesale lack of political and public support.

This school system decay accompanied a major economic and social transformation in the city of Chicago during the second half of the twentieth century. Middle-class and white flight began in the 1950s and escalated in the 1960s. Between 1967 and 1987, Chicago lost 325,000 jobs, most of them in the manufacturing sector.[2] The 1980s saw a marked increase in the concentration of poverty in public school enrollments, and the dwindling numbers of white and affluent students who remained in the city increasingly chose to attend private schools.[3]

These trends combined to create a public school system with an extraordinary concentration of poor and minority students. By 1990, nearly 9 out of 10 CPS students were from a racial minority, with 57 percent being African-American and 28 percent Latino. More than 8 out of 10 African-American elementary students were enrolled in racially isolated

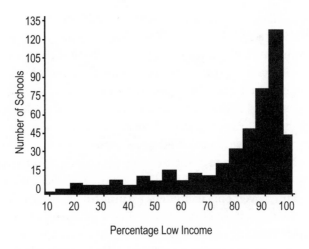

Figure I.1. Concentration of low-income students, Chicago
public elementary schools, 1994.

schools where more than 80 percent of the student population was African-
American.

Equally troubling, a very high percentage of CPS students lived in poverty. According to the 1990 census, 40 percent of Chicago's families who
enrolled children in its public schools had incomes below the federally
defined poverty line.[4] The vast majority of CPS elementary students met
the federal educational definition for low income, with 82 percent eligible
to receive a free or reduced-price school lunch in 1994. As figure I.1 shows,
in 1994 more than 200 Chicago elementary schools had more than 90 percent of their students receiving a free or discounted lunch. In fact, there
were more schools in this category (91 to 100 percent) than in any other. In
comparison, only 21 percent of students in the rest of Illinois were deemed
eligible for a free or reduced-price lunch.

To put all of this in perspective, if we were to relocate one of Chicago's
"more affluent" and integrated schools in almost any other district in the
state of Illinois, it would immediately rank as that district's most disadvantaged school. When we think about Chicago's modal school—racially isolated, with a 100-percent African-American student body and a low-income
enrollment exceeding 90 percent—there is literally no relevant comparison school in most other districts in Illinois. Not surprisingly, neither the
CPS, nor most other districts for that matter, were prepared to provide, or
even knew how to provide, the necessary educational and social supports
so that all these students would actually learn.

Primer on Chicago's School Reform

The Illinois legislature passed a school reform bill in the spring of 1988, which the governor signed in December of that year. Public Act 84-1418 radically decentralized the Chicago public school system, moving authority away from the central office to the approximately 575 individual schools. The legislation also transferred significant resources to these local schools. By the end of the phase-in period in the mid-1990s, the average elementary school received about $500,000 in discretionary funds. These monies could be used for a wide range of purposes, including hiring additional staff, buying new equipment and materials, purchasing new programs, and securing more professional development time and services.

Each school community elected a Local School Council (LSC), composed of the principal, two teachers, six parents, and two local community members (high schools also had a student member). LSCs were granted the authority to select and evaluate their school's principal, who was now employed under a four-year performance contract; and to approve the annual school improvement plan and budget that guided the use of their discretionary fund. To this day, Chicago remains the only large school district in the nation where local school communities have the authority to select, evaluate, and replace their principals. Compensating in part for their loss of tenure, principals gained increased authority over their own buildings and the right to hire teachers of their own choosing, without regard to system seniority considerations; they also were given primary responsibility for developing their school's annual improvement plan and budget.

In 1995, the Chicago Public Schools experienced another reform jolt with the passage of a second major piece of state legislation, authorizing a mayoral takeover of the school system. The mayor was granted the authority both to appoint a small Reform Board of Trustees, replacing the previous school board, and to directly appoint a Chief Executive Officer for the CPS to replace the system's former schools superintendent. De facto, all senior appointments in the CPS have subsequently been vetted through the mayor's office.

Beginning in 1996, the new CEO developed a number of high-stakes accountability initiatives and centrally planned improvement efforts that came to define phase 2 of Chicago school reform. While most of the provisions of the 1988 decentralization remained in the 1995 legislation, and in fact still remain in place today, the introduction of centrally mandated reforms marks the end of the natural experiment in local school improvement that the 1988 legislation had precipitated.

Early Findings on Reform Initiation

Three of us were coauthors of an earlier volume, *Charting Chicago School Reform: Democratic Localism as a Lever for Change* (hereafter referred to as *Democratic Localism*).[5] This book examined the creative chaos that ensued as fundamental structural change was initiated in a major urban public school system. Our investigation focused on detailing the logic of the reform, probing its critical assumptions, and testing this logic against evidence of what was actually happening in the schools.

In general, a process of institutional change, as intended by the 1988 reform, can be divided into two major components. First is an *initiation phase*, where attempts to challenge a dysfunctional status quo are mounted. If successful, this melds into a second, *sustaining phase*, where individual roles, rules, and responsibilities are reshaped under a reordered authority structure. The evidence that we had assembled by 1993 clearly indicated that profound changes were being initiated in many of Chicago's schools, but also that this challenge of the status quo was still evolving.[6] While it was too early to make judgments about sustaining effects, substantial evidence was now in on the initiation phase.

Democratic Localism concluded that Chicago had been successful in catalyzing significant reform in a large number of its school communities. A combination of quantitative and qualitative evidence documented that expanded democratic participation had emerged in a diverse array of contexts, and where this local enablement had taken hold, fundamental organizational changes were being advanced, including efforts to improve instruction. Widespread institutional change had been initiated at the elementary school level.

More specifically, our book told a "story of three thirds." Of the elementary schools most in need of improvement, roughly one-third were self-initiating, actively restructuring schools; another third were engaged in similar processes, but struggling; and a final third showed no visible signs of meaningful change. These schools were left behind by reform.

The top group clearly appeared to be headed in the right direction. They had developed effective local governance, which was focusing on systemic school improvements. The Hancock case described in the prologue is an exemplar of such a school community. The middle group consisted of schools more like Alexander, in that they tried to undertake similar initiatives, but floundered with the implementation. Moreover, the overall strategy guiding the selection of new activities was not always clear. Worthwhile new efforts appeared side-by-side with other activities of dubious value.

The bottom third of schools remained largely unaffected by the reform. A small number of these were plagued by serious conflict, and meaningful improvements were unlikely to emerge until this fighting ended. For the bulk of them, however, neither teachers nor parents had become actively involved, and principals had consolidated their power around maintaining a dysfunctional status quo. The social contexts were so stable that nothing consequential had happened or was likely to emerge so long as these schools were left on their own.

Of significance, successful reform initiation had occurred across a broad cross section of communities, largely without regard to class or race. While we worried about the one-third of schools left behind by reform, and offered specific recommendations for subsequent policy action, any observer had to be impressed by the promising start that had occurred in many school communities. Everything that we knew then about improving urban schools, and more generally about organizational restructuring, suggested that if schools in the top group stayed the course, and if at least some of the middle-group schools joined them, a broad base of improvements in student learning should eventually materialize across the city.

But, could school communities actually sustain these efforts over several more years? Put somewhat differently, would the basic changes initiated in the first few years actually crystallize in a reorganization of how teachers work in classrooms and engage parents and their local community? And, ultimately, was the overall logic of decentralization correct: if all of this occurred, would improvements in student learning actually follow?

A Shifting Focus to Student Outcomes

Over the long term, the primary standpoint for judging any school reform is very clear: have substantial improvements in student learning occurred? Judging the short-term efficacy of major institutional change efforts, however, is much more complicated. These are not simple programs from which we should expect direct and immediate effects on students. In fact, student outcomes might actually look worse in the short term as established routines are discarded, and experimentation with new, untested practices emerges.[7]

A major corporate restructuring can serve as the proper analogy here. In the short term, a corporation may well show a string of deficits in its bottom line as it goes about fundamentally reorganizing its operations. The most immediate concern is whether the intended changes are actually occurring and whether the organization appears to be developing in ways that portend profitability.

This analogy proved prescient for Chicago during the early 1990s. Through 1992, we saw little evidence of any significant changes in the city's standardized test scores, even though our field studies and survey data suggested that the initiation of reform was productively moving forward in many communities. We banked heavily on the latter in predicting what would happen next. Alas, the evidence of the impact on students did subsequently materialize.

Systemwide Trends

In 1990, only 24 percent of Chicago elementary school students scored at or above the national average in reading comprehension,[8] and only 27 percent in mathematics. Systemwide, student test scores declined slightly in 1991, bottoming out in 1992 and then starting an upward trajectory over the next several years. By 1996, 29 percent of students were at national norms in reading; the comparable figure for mathematics was 31 percent. Although these statistics were far from acceptable, at least Chicago finally seemed to be making progress.

Substantial Variability in Improvement

In general, we would expect a decentralization reform, absent strong central support and guidance as was the case in Chicago during the early 1990s, to produce varied consequences. In this regard, the wide differences among school communities in their reform initiation processes were not surprising. Similarly, we expected substantial variation in school achievement trends to emerge over time as well.[9] Figures I.2 and I.3 illustrate this, presenting the trends in the Iowa Tests of Basic Skills reading and math assessments for the quarter of schools with the most improved scores and for the quarter with the least improvement over the period 1990 through 1996.[10]

Among the 118 most improved schools in reading, about 37 percent of the students scored at or above national norms in 1996, whereas in 1990 only 22 percent had done so. The substantial improvement in this group of schools largely materialized over the four-year period of 1993 through 1996. Among the 118 schools with the least improvements, the trend was essentially flat, with 24 percent of students scoring at or above national norms in both 1990 and 1996.

Trends in math scores displayed the same patterns. The 117 most im-

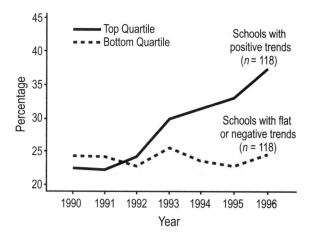

Figure I.2. Percentage of students scoring at or above national norms in reading, 1990–96.

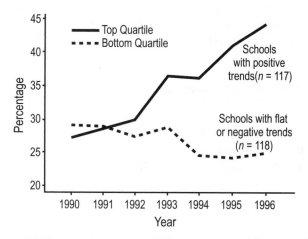

Figure I.3. Percentage of students scoring at or above national norms in math, 1990–96.

proved schools made great gains, moving from 27 percent of their students scoring at or above grade level to 42 percent. Since having 50 percent of students reach national norms was an objective set out in the 1988 Reform Act, these Chicago schools were actually approaching the legislatively established performance standard. In the least improved schools, in contrast, math scores actually declined, from 29 percent at or above grade level to 25 percent.[11]

Interestingly, although these two groups of schools look quite different in their seven-year achievement trends, if one looks at their data only through 1992 (that is, the information available to us when we first produced our "State of School Reform" analysis, which eventually became *Democratic Localism*), the two sets are indistinguishable. The nonimproving schools actually started slightly higher in 1990 than their improving counterparts. Although the rank order had reversed by 1992, we would not have been able to identify these two groups from the test score data available up to that point.

Thus, among a group of over 200 schools enrolling over 150,000 students, which basically started out about the same, a substantial number improved but others did not. These results bring to the fore the core concern motivating this book: what did the improving schools actually do to realize these gains in student learning? In *Democratic Localism* we began to sketch a theory of comprehensive school development. As the results on student learning began to emerge, it became clear to us that greater attention to this concern was now warranted. Were we on the right track back in 1993 in describing the essential features of improving schools, or was all of this just coincidental?

Organizing Schools for Improvement

A comparison of the experiences at Hancock and Alexander schools offers one entry into this topic. As sketched in the prologue, the two schools suggest a number of features that might well be key to successful improvement. Hancock, for example, clearly benefited from stronger principal leadership. Bonnie Whitmore facilitated and sustained the engagement of both parents and faculty in a sequence of improvement initiatives. For several years, the school community sustained focus on a few major problems: building professional capabilities among staff; strengthening the ties among teachers, parents, and the local community, focusing the efforts of all adults on creating a more engaging and supportive environment for students; and enhancing the core of instruction so that it more effectively addressed what their students really needed to learn.

While all of this seems commonsensical, the actual orchestration of these various changes was quite complex. In essence, the reform story at Hancock involved multiple strands of activity, advanced in a highly integrated fashion, that eventually cumulated in substantial improvements in student learning. In contrast, Alexander initiated some activities in virtually all these domains, but none were sustained through to fundamental organizational change.

Stepping back a bit, the comparative analysis of school development cases, like those sketched in the prologue, provides rich details for articulating a theory of action for organizing schools for improvement. But are the generalizations that stories like this suggest in fact warranted? Might there be other schools that did all the right things, like Hancock, but where student learning did not improve? Similarly, might there be other schools where student learning improved, but where few or none of the features salient in our actively restructuring schools were actually present?

To address questions of this sort, we need to explicate specific propositions about the core features of school improvement, as suggested by the observations presented above . Then, we need to assemble a body of empirical evidence about the base state and subsequent developments in each of these key elements in the organization and operation of schools, and how all of this in turn links to trends in student outcomes. Chapter 2 offers our elaboration of such a conceptual framework of essential supports. We then proceed in chapters 3 and 4 to test the adequacy of this theory against extensive data on school development and student learning.

Revisiting the Influence of School Community Context

Proponents of Chicago's 1988 decentralization argued that all school communities had untapped resources to leverage reform. Reformers trusted that parents' common desire to secure a quality education for their children would be sufficient to catalyze positive change and make schools more responsive to the needs of their students.

Not all community leaders endorsed this view, however. Some worried about the historic neglect of their schools and the larger changes that had been occurring in their communities. Just one year earlier, William Julius Wilson had published his seminal book, *The Truly Disadvantaged: The Inner City, the Underclass, and Public Policy,* in which he and his colleagues documented the increasing concentration of poverty in inner-city Chicago.[12] A deteriorating local economy and the flight of middle-class whites and blacks had left some neighborhoods with high levels of joblessness, welfare dependency, family deterioration, violent crime, and drug addiction. These larger contextual changes substantially reduced the institutional resources in some communities while multiplying the problems that their leaders had to confront. Being "empowered" to improve local schools under such circumstances had led some to charge that the new law was deliberately designed to fail so that the conservatives could sweep in with a school-voucher policy.[13]

As noted earlier, our evidence on the initiation of reform did not offer much credence to these concerns. Both the survey data from teachers and principals that we had collected in 1991 and 1992 and the results from a synthesis of independent case studies in over twenty elementary schools indicated that a school's ability to initiate meaningful organizational and instructional changes appeared unrelated to the socioeconomic and racial composition of their student body.

By 1994, however, as results emerged from our second round of surveys, a somewhat different picture began to take form. As before, improving schools could be found in virtually every neighborhood in Chicago without regard to race or social class. In contrast, the most negative reports about reform tended to cluster in schools whose enrollments were predominantly African American and where 90-plus percent of the students were low income. Subsequently, data from student achievement trends bore this out as well. A distinct and troubling pattern of inequity in school improvement had emerged. Clearly, a closer look was warranted.

Problems with Traditional Educational Indicators of Disadvantage

Both in popular media and in academic policy analyses, student populations in urban schools tend to be described in terms of two basic statistics: percentage minority and percentage low income, with the latter based on the federal definition of a student's eligibility for a free or reduced-price lunch. These statistics are widely used because they are the only common data on student background that is routinely collected by most school systems. Unfortunately, such data are not very useful for characterizing differences among school communities in Chicago, where the modal school is nearly 100 percent minority and 100 percent poor. While some of these schools improved, others did not. Did all these schools really share the same basic context resources and confront similar improvement problems?

In order to take more seriously the concerns raised about community context and its potential effects on school improvement, we needed to turn to other data sources. Using students' home and school addresses,[14] we were able to create a more detailed account of the socioeconomic characteristics of the neighborhoods around schools and where students live based on information obtained from the 1990 U.S. Census, 1994 data on public aid recipients, and 1994 Chicago public housing information.[15] We combined these data into an overall socioeconomic status index that included school community information on employment status, poverty rate, household education levels, proportion of students receiving free or reduced-price lunches, and percentage of families receiving public assistance and living in public housing. (See appendix A for details.)

A Previously Unrecognized Subclass:
The Truly Disadvantaged School Community

As expected, this new indicator documented that school communities are much more varied in their socioeconomic features than suggested by the traditional percentage low-income statistic. The schools that clumped together in figure I.1 with 90- to 100-percent low-income enrollments became more differentiated as this additional information was brought to bear (see figure I.4). Of special significance, our composite indicator identified a distinct subset of 46 schools quite different from the rest of the school system. These schools served neighborhoods characterized by extreme rates of poverty. On average, 70 percent of residents living in the neighborhoods around these 46 schools had incomes below the poverty line, and the median family income in 1990 was only $9,480.[16] In 6 out of 10 of these schools, more than 50 percent of the students lived in public housing.[17]

Moreover, virtually all these schools had predominantly African-American enrollments. This consolidation of socioeconomic disadvantage and racial segregation is vividly displayed in figure I.4. Within an overall school system where disadvantage is normative, these places stood out as

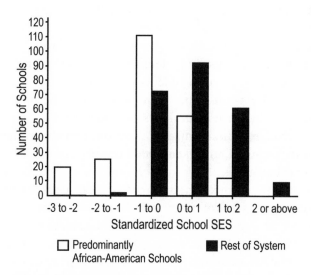

Figure I.4. Consolidation of disadvantage: Race and social class in the CPS.

truly extreme. They were the educational manifestation of the larger institutional downturns described by Wilson—truly disadvantaged schools within truly disadvantaged communities.

It is now clear that many of these schools failed to improve under decentralization. Typically, at least some change efforts were initiated in each school, but in many instances they failed to culminate in real differences for students. This finding still leaves open the question of why. Race and poverty are merely demographic descriptors. What was it about these school communities that actually made them especially hard to improve?

Our findings on this account form the basis for chapters 5 and 6. In brief, they tell a complex story about extraordinary human needs and modest base capacities to sustain meaningful improvement. Some schools were disadvantaged by structural features, including large size and relatively high student mobility. Some began with weak relational trust across the school community that proved impervious to change. Many confronted an extraordinary concentration of student needs, including students who were homeless, in foster care, or living in contexts of neglect, abuse, and domestic violence. Finally, features of the community itself played a role.

Probing Deeper: Communities' Social Resources for Supporting Institutional Renewal

Moving beyond the gross characterization of neighborhoods by race and class, an emerging strand of social research over the last decade has brought attention to the quality of social relationships that exist in communities and the impact that this has on everyday life in neighborhoods as well as on their capacity to solve local problems. For example, researchers have found that communities where residents know and trust their neighbors and are willing to intervene if they witness fights, vandalism, or truancy have lower crime rates than other neighborhoods with the same levels of concentrated economic disadvantage.[18] Our book provides evidence that the social resources within neighborhoods also play a significant role in the reform of their schools.

One key resource in this regard are viable local institutions such as neighborhood clubs, political organizations, and churches. Such institutions can foster dense networks of community residents who know and trust one another and share a history of collective action. These intra-community social resources can be appropriated to tackle new local challenges, such as when Chicago school reform turned to local control.[19] In addition, the task of improving schools may at times require support from external entities, such as political leaders, businesses, and nonprofit organizations. A vital local institutional base can also help effect these extra-community connections.[20]

Correspondingly, just as positive social relationships across a community may facilitate reform, negative ones may inhibit its success. Democratic localism as a lever for change banks on the willingness of parents and other community members to join with one another to solve the problems of their local schools. Yet the fear of victimization associated with safety concerns may well impede the formation and sustenance of such voluntary associations. On this point, all forty-six of the truly disadvantaged school communities that we identified struggled against very high crime rates. On average, one in every ten residents in these neighborhoods was assaulted each year. Statistics like this make it likely that either a family member or a close neighbor had been a recent victim.

As we detail in the pages that follow, reforming truly disadvantaged schools proved especially nettlesome. Our findings represent a challenge to the prevailing political rhetoric that all schools can improve in their effectiveness. To be sure, we fervently want to *believe* these claims. But, we also now *know* that all schools do not start in the same place, and those that are truly disadvantaged have enormous barriers to overcome.

Data for This Study

This study draws on the extensive longitudinal database about Chicago and its public schools assembled by the Consortium on Chicago School Research (CCSR) at the University of Chicago. The conceptual design for this database emerged from prior CCSR fieldwork detailed in *Democratic Localism*. Key in this regard was a synthesis conducted by the CCSR of two independent longitudinal field studies, carried out during the first four years of school reform. These two studies examined twenty-two elementary schools that varied geographically as well as in terms of the racial composition of students, their income levels, and their prereform student achievement levels. The observations gleaned here were subsequently corroborated (and critiqued) by other researchers involved in field studies at that time. In addition, the conceptual design benefited greatly from insights generated by our colleagues in the Center for School Improvement at the University of Chicago, who were directly involved in local school reform activities during this period.[21]

Student Outcome Data

The outcome measures in this study are based on annual individual student test scores in reading and mathematics on the Iowa Tests of Basic Skills from 1990 to 1996, and on school reports of average daily attendance over this period. The development of these indicators is further detailed in chapter 1 and appendix B. These data were made available to the CCSR by the Chicago Public Schools.

School Administrative Records

Other CPS information supplemented these test scores in important ways. Most important are administrative records from the CPS Comprehensive Student Information System. These records contain basic registration information about students, such as birth date, race, gender, home address, school attended within the CPS, and grade level. The CCSR data archive contains two annual "snapshots" from these *master files*—one from the fall and one from the spring of each academic year. Since the files contain records of all transitions from grade to grade and from school to school, we can accurately track student movements. We use these data to calculate student and school mobility rates, categorize schools according to their racial and ethnic composition, determine the length of students' enrollment within specific schools, and match characteristics of students' residential communities to their schools. The combination of test score files and master files provides the necessary data to create our key outcome of interest, a value-added index of school improvement, and to assess trends in this key indicator over time.

Periodic CCSR School Surveys

The vast majority of our explanatory variables come from a series of CPS principal, student, and teacher surveys that the CCSR conducted beginning in 1991. We rely especially on teacher and student surveys from the spring of 1994, since this data collection occurred at approximately the midpoint in our study period (1990 to 1996). We supplement the 1994 surveys with information on the initiation of reform from the 1991 (teachers) and 1992 (principal) surveys; and with data on the sustained effects of decentralization in 1997 (principal, teachers, and students).

General content. The survey series, Charting Reform, was initiated in 1991 and sought ongoing, systematic data about school communities, local responses to the decentralization reform, and the varied impact that the reform was having on adults and students across the city.

Beginning in 1994, the scope of the surveys expanded to collect much more detailed information about teachers' professional work. These surveys inquired about instructional practices, opportunities for continued learning, and the development of professional collaboration and community. Like the earlier 1991 survey, these surveys also explored teachers' perceptions of the school environment, their participation in school governance, and the involvement of parents and community in school life. Also beginning in 1994, a student survey was administered in conjunction with the teacher survey. These surveys inquired about students' experiences in school, their motivation and engagement with learning, their educational and career aspirations, their perceptions of the school environment, and their relationships with teachers. Students were also asked to furnish their views about classroom instruction to enrich the overall descriptions available in the CCSR archive about teaching and learning in the CPS.

The 1997 surveys built on the 1994 study and contained many of the same items. Additional items were added to improve measurement of some key concepts—especially those related to teachers' work lives.

Response rates. The 1991 teachers' survey, Charting Reform: The Teachers' Turn, was the first study undertaken by the Consortium on Chicago School Research. A total of 12,708 teachers (70 percent) in 401 schools completed the survey. In the companion survey of principals in 1992, over 90 percent responded to our requests for information. In 1994, 266 of the 477 elementary schools in the CPS participated in the teacher survey, the student survey, or both. We received individual surveys from some 13,000 sixth-grade students, 13,800 eighth-grade students, and 6,200 teachers. An analysis of these data indicated that they were highly comparable to the entire population of schools in the CPS.[22]

The response rates in 1997 were higher than for any other CCSR survey project. Of the 477 elementary schools in the system, 422 (or 88 percent) participated in the student survey, the teacher survey, or both. In total, 21,900 sixth graders, 19,700 eighth graders, and 10,300 elementary school teachers responded to the surveys. A response rate analysis again assured us that these data were representative of the entire Chicago public school system.[23]

Other Data Sources

Since this book investigates both the organizational characteristics of schools and the social context of school communities, we sought out additional data resources to help us better understand the latter phenomenon. As described earlier, we added to the CCSR archive data from the U.S. Census, public aid data, Chicago public housing data, and crime statistics from the Chicago Police Department.

We were also exceptionally fortunate to be able to take advantage of two other innovative research endeavors occurring in Chicago during the 1990s. First, through the Project on Human Development in Chicago Neighborhoods (PHDCN), we gained access to unique information about the 363 microneighborhoods that constitute the city of Chicago, based on interviews, surveys, and videotapes collected by the PHDCN. This information provided real depth for our analysis of the social resources in the city's different school communities.[24] Second, through collaboration with the Chapin Hall Center for Children, we gained access to its extensive longitudinal database on the public social services provided to all children and families in the city of Chicago. These data proved extremely helpful as we sought to examine the concentration of students living in exceptional circumstances in various Chicago school communities and the effects that this might have on a school's capacity to improve.[25]

CHAPTER 1 DEVELOPING APPROPRIATE OUTCOME INDICATORS

We articulate in this book a theory of practice about organizing urban schools for improvement and then systematically test it against data on school change. To do this requires good measurement of the degree to which student outcomes actually improved in each school. For the purposes of this study, we developed three such indicators: the first focuses on trends in student attendance, and the second and third are based on trends in students' reading and math test scores.

Attendance Trends

The necessity of attending school is rarely questioned. Compulsory attendance dates to colonial times, when political leaders sought to assure that children would gain an education to prepare them for their eventual roles as citizens in a new democratic society.[1] Today, regular school attendance is seen as essential to support each child's development along multiple dimensions—intellectual, physical, social, and occupational. A deep research base supports this view. We know, for example, that students who regularly attend class, and are actively engaged in classroom activities, perform better on standard measures of achievement.[2] Similarly, research shows that student achievement, particularly for students from low-income families, can regress during the summer months, when they are typically not in school.[3]

Improving student attendance was a specific goal of the 1988 Reform Act, although here, too, schools were left to decide how best to address this concern in their local community. Unlike student achievement, average elementary school attendance did not improve across the CPS under

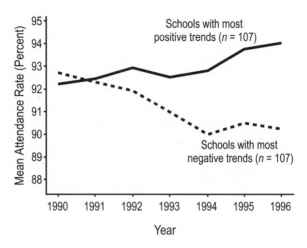

Figure 1.1. Attendance trends for improving and nonimproving schools, 1990–96. Note: The attendance rate for each school was calculated during the spring.

decentralization. The systemwide attendance rate over this period hovered around 92.5 percent. To put these statistics in context, a good elementary school might report an average daily attendance in the 95- to 96-percent range. (It is virtually impossible for any school to achieve a much higher rate, given occasional student illness and various family emergencies that might keep students out of school.) In contrast, an elementary school that reports attendance around 90 percent or lower would likely be a troubled place.

Like the basic test score trends reported in the introduction, individual schools varied in their attendance trends over this period. (See figure 1.1.) The top quartile of schools, with the most improved attendance from 1990 to 1996, began with an attendance rate of 92.2 percent and ended the period in 1996 with an average rate of 93.8 percent. A number of schools in this group had crossed the 95-percent threshold and "topped out" in terms of improvement on this indicator. In contrast, in the bottom quartile of schools, average attendance actually declined from 92.8 percent in 1990 to 90.5 percent in 1996. As we document in chapters 3 and 4, many of these schools had serious problems.

Descriptive statistics of the type just presented are useful for telling the basic story of what happened under reform. Such statistics can prove problematic, however, when we need a precise indicator of the efficacy of each individual school's reform efforts. For example, the simplest way for a school to improve its attendance is to enroll "better" students. With considerable demographic changes occurring across Chicago during the period of our study—gentrification forcing poor families out from some neighborhoods, new immigrants reconstituting other neighborhoods, and the demolition of some high-rise public housing projects changing still others—a school's attendance rate could easily change for reasons other than genuine organizational improvements.[4]

To remove the effects associated with these spurious factors, we computed an adjusted attendance trend for each school, which controlled for changes over time in the composition of students enrolling there.[5] The end result was a better outcome indicator of the degree to which each school actually improved its effectiveness at reducing absenteeism (rather than just enrolling different kinds of students). We use this indicator in chapters 3 and 4 to identify the top and bottom quartile of schools in the CPS in their attendance trends and to analyze what these schools did differently to affect this.

Improving Academic Productivity in Reading and Mathematics

During the period of our study, the Chicago Public Schools administered a nationally norm-referenced assessment, the Iowa Tests of Basic Skills (ITBS), every year to almost all students in grades 3 through 8 and to most students in grades 1 and 2 as well.[6] Annual CPS reports detailed how students fared in reading and math achievement. The results from these tests were typically reported by CPS as "percentage of students at or above grade level." (The school data trends presented in the introduction were based on these CPS reports.) In this metric, an improving school is one where the percentage of students performing at or above grade level is increasing each year.

Problems with Public Statistics for Judging Improved School Productivity

While there is simplicity about descriptive statistics that makes them appealing for public reporting purposes, they, too, can be quite misleading as evidence of systematic school improvement. We detail some of these problems in the section below and proceed to identify "A Better Approach" based on value-added indicators anchored in a content-referenced measurement scale. Of necessity, the discussion below is somewhat technical. The reader less interested in such details might simply jump ahead to the section that immediately follows it.

Percentage of students at or above national norms: a weak statistical indicator.
The "percentage at or above national norms" is a threshold indicator and
as such is highly sensitive to the test score results for the subset of the
students whose academic achievement is near the cutoff, or threshold.
Improvements by students who have very low achievement levels (for example, movement from the 10th to the 30th percentile) and those with
very high achievement levels (for example, movement from the 70th to
the 90th percentile) have no impact whatsoever on a school's standing
as measured by the percentage at or above national norms. It is only the
achievement of students near the cutoff that really counts. The percentage
at or above indicator could show a large "school improvement effect," for
example, if an intervention were narrowly targeted on students just below
the threshold, even though the vast majority of students in the school
were left unaffected.[7] Such an indicator violates a very basic equity consideration: the progress of all students should count in judging a school's
improvement (or lack of improvement).

Technically speaking, the percentage of students at national norms is
not a "sufficient statistic." There is more information present in the data
than has been captured by this particular indicator. In this regard, the
school mean achievement is a better overall statistic, since the data for all
students influence the end result.[8]

The need to focus on improvements in learning, not just status. It would be tempting to form a test score trend based on the yearly mean achievement in
each school, and use this as the basis for school improvement analyses.
Such a trend indicator, however, can be problematic, especially in urban
contexts with high student mobility rates. A school may be adding a lot to
student learning, but if the school has a continuous influx of new, weak
students (for example, a school in a neighborhood that is a port of entry
for immigration), annual test score reports may seriously underestimate
these positive effects.[9] On the other side of the ledger, if a school begins
to attract a more capable student population, its achievement trends
are likely to improve for reasons unrelated to increased organizational
productivity.

In order to make a valid inference about changes in a school's performance, we need to answer two questions: How much are children learning during the period in which they are enrolled at that school? and Are
these learning gains improving over time as new cohorts of children move
through the school? Formally, we seek to estimate the "value-added" that a
school contributes to student learning. In an improving school, we would

expect to see increasing value added over time as a school's reform initiatives really take hold.

The nonequivalence of grade equivalents. Since a value-added analysis directs attention to trends in student learning over time, it requires evidence on test score gains for children as they move across grades and years. A problem arises, however, in that norm-referenced test statistics, such as grade equivalents or percentile ranks, are not actually designed to make such comparisons. That is, a focus on student learning gains requires an analysis of data from the different forms and test levels, which might be administered to students over time.

The basic problem is that the same student can achieve different results, depending on the particular form and level of the test he or she may have taken. To document this, we undertook an experiment with twenty-four groups of Chicago students to whom we randomly administered two different levels and/or forms of the ITBS at one sitting.[10] We found a significant bias in half these comparisons. For example, students who took level 9 of form H (given to third graders in Chicago in 1991) on the same day that they took level 8 of form G (given to second graders in Chicago in 1990) were seven times more likely to record a higher grade equivalent on level 9, form H than on level 8 of form G.

These inconsistencies in norm-referenced scores are particularly problematic when examining student learning over time. To measure how much a student has learned, for example, in third grade of the 1990–91 school year, it is necessary to compare that student's results at the end of third grade with his or her results at the end of second grade the previous year. This involves calculating a difference between the form H, level 9 results and the form G, level 8 results discussed above—an appropriate calculation only if all the information share a common scale. Consequently, for the purposes of our research, it became necessary to create a new ITBS test score scale that would allow us to make more valid judgments about improvements in student learning that might actually be occurring in the CPS.

A Better Approach

In response to these various concerns, we developed an *academic productivity profile* that summarizes each school's contributions to student learning and how this value-added may change over time. In order to make the information in this profile meaningful, we first had to transform students' reading and mathematics test scores into an equated, *content-referenced scale* so that data could be aggregated across the different test forms and levels administered in the Chicago Public Schools from 1990 to 1996. The basic elements of our approach are sketched out below. Appendix B provides further technical details.

A content-referenced scale. In order to put all the ITBS results on a single scale that would allow us to make valid comparisons across time, we conducted a series of Rasch analyses.[11] These analyses used data from four separate studies that we undertook to equate the eight levels and six different forms of the ITBS used in Chicago between 1989 and 1996.[12] Equating the different levels within a form, called *vertical equating,* is a relatively straightforward procedure, as each of the levels of the ITBS used between the third and eighth grades shares one-third to one-half of its items with those in adjacent levels. Simultaneous calibration of all the levels together automatically puts them all on the same scale. This is referred to as "common-item equating." In addition, through *horizontal equating* we were able to link test forms, which do not share items. This is accomplished by having groups of students take two different forms of the test in the same administration. We refer to this as "common-person equating." In our studies, each horizontal-equating group consisted of between 150 and 450 students. In addition, since levels 7 and 8 (used in grades 1 and 2) do not share items with any adjacent levels, it was necessary to use common-person equating for these levels as well.

A key benefit of a Rasch analysis is that both the test scale scores and the item difficulties are placed on the same scale. As a result, any student's test score can be interpreted in terms of what that student knows and can do, rather than just how he or she ranks relative to other students in a national sample. In general, a child with any given scale score is likely to answer correctly those items clustered around that point on the scale, and even more likely to answer correctly the easier items (for example, those with lower scale difficulty), but less likely to answer correctly the more difficult items. Such a content-referenced scale is especially useful when we seek to assess student learning over time, as it allows us to calculate the amount gained in each subject (reading and math) compared with the previous year.[13]

An academic productivity profile. In developing a productivity profile for each school, we sought to focus directly on the amount students learn each year and whether these learning gains increase over time. According to this standard, improving schools should show greater learning gains at the end of our study, the 1995–96 academic year, than in the base period of 1990–91.

We can display the information for judging the changing productivity of any school through a set of grade-level visualizations for that school. Figure 1.2 illustrates this for one grade from a randomly selected Chicago school. The overall data on test score results for each grade in each school are represented as a trapezoid that is built up out of two distinct pieces of evidence. The bottom line forming the trapezoid captures the input trend. It reflects any changes that may be occurring over time in the average achievement of students entering that particular grade. Notice that in our example, the input trend is slightly declining over time. In contrast, the top line captures the output trend for the grade, that is, how the average end-of-year achievement may be changing. Interestingly, the output trend in our example is moving up rapidly, even though students are entering this grade a bit further behind each year (that is, the slight downward trajectory previously referenced in the input trend).

Our central concern—the trend in student learning gains over time—is captured in the overall shape of the trapezoid. When academic productivity is improving, as is the case in our illustrative example, the trapezoid appears to spread apart over time. In contrast, in the context of declining productivity the trapezoid would appear to be converging over time. Finally, a perfect parallelogram (that is, where both the input and the output trends are parallel) would represent zero change in productivity for a grade over the seven years of our study. In this instance, whatever changes in student outcomes may be occurring simply mirror identical changes in the average prior achievement that students are bringing to that grade.

While displays such as figure 1.2 are helpful for visualizing the overall performance of a school, we needed to summarize this graphical information in an overall numerical index in order to conduct statistical analy-

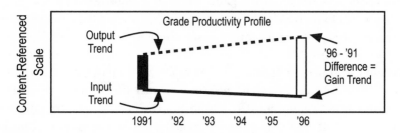

Figure 1.2. An illustration of a grade productivity indicator.

sis on these data. Since preliminary analyses suggested that variability in the gain trends among grades depended to some degree on the prior achievement of students entering that grade during the base year (1990), the learning gain recorded in the base year (1990 to 1991), and the input trend, we decided to compute a summary indicator that adjusted for or held these other three components constant. In so doing, we are, in essence, comparing the gain trend for a particular grade in a given school to all other schools' grades that are just like it—that is, grades that started with the same achievement level in 1990, had the same learning gains that first year, and had similar input trends over time. An improving school grade by this criterion has a stronger gain trend than others that started in the same place and experienced similar input trends. We computed this adjusted gain trend for each grade in each school for both reading and mathematics and then averaged them across grades, separately by subject, to form two overall indicators of change in academic productivity in each school, hereafter referred to simply as the *school's productivity trend indicators.*[14]

As a final step, we identified the top and bottom quartile of schools in the CPS based on these two composite indicators. The result was two distinct groups of schools with quite different productivity patterns in each subject. As was the case in *Democratic Localism,* we again excluded from our analyses about 15 percent of the Chicago elementary schools that were initially high achieving (that is, at or above national norms in 1989), leaving 390 schools that should have been focused on improving student learning. The excluded group consisted primarily of magnet schools, which benefited from selective student admissions procedures and were under little pressure to improve in the early 1990s.

Figures 1.3 through 1.6 illustrate the end result of this process. Presented here are aggregate profiles for the top- and bottom-quartile schools on changes in academic productivity in reading and mathematics, respectively.[15] The percentages appearing below each grade productivity trapezoid are the extent to which the test gains at the end of our study, 1996, exceeded (or were less than) what they were in that grade during the base period of 1990. We refer to this percentage as the *Learning Gain Index,* or LGI.[16] This statistic provides a direct measure of a school's changing productivity in student learning in each grade. For example, the elementary schools in the top quartile on the LGI in reading averaged a 10-percent improvement in student learning gains at grade 5 from 1990 to 1996. (See figure 1.3.) Top-quartile schools for mathematics averaged a 30-percent improvement in student learning gains at the same grade level. (See figure 1.4.)

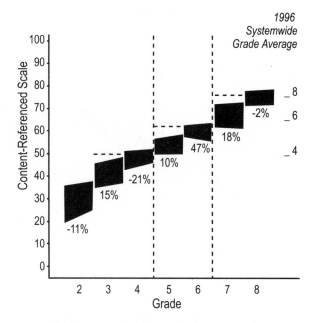

Figure 1.3. Reading productivity profile for top-quartile improving schools, 1990–96.

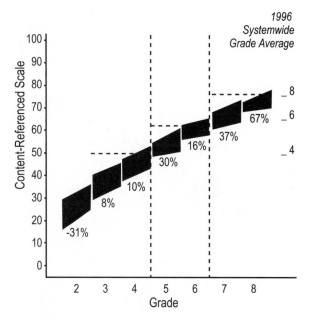

Figure 1.4. Mathematics productivity profile for top-quartile improving schools, 1990–96.

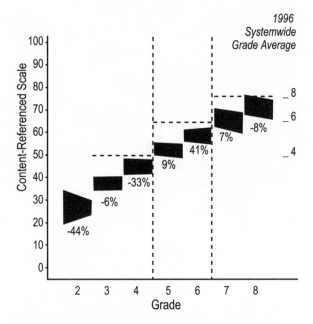

Figure 1.5. Reading productivity profile for bottom-quartile nonimproving schools, 1990–96.

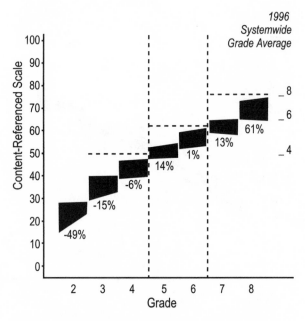

Figure 1.6. Mathematics productivity profile for bottom-quartile nonimproving schools, 1990–96.

Our First Look at Overall Trends in Academic Productivity over Time

Armed now with good indicators of improvement for each Chicago elementary school, we are poised to investigate the different patterns of productivity changes that occurred across the CPS under decentralization. One obvious place to begin is with the LGIs presented in figures 1.3–1.6. Clearly, some schools moved substantially ahead over the course of our study. Aggregating the LGIs across grades 2 through 8 indicates that reading productivity among the top quartile of schools improved by about 8 percent overall. This means that annual student learning gains in this subset of schools were on average about 8-percent greater in 1996 than when reform began in 1990. For improving schools in mathematics, the learning gains were about 20-percent greater in 1996 than in the base period. It is important to recognize in this regard that these represent average improvements *per grade* in student learning. Accumulated over the eight years of instruction that a child might receive in one of these elementary schools, this translates into an extra half year of learning in reading and over 1.25 years more learning in mathematics.[17] Unfortunately, not all schools fared as well.

To explore this further, we computed the same overall LGIs in both reading and mathematics for our full analytic sample of 390 Chicago public elementary schools. Figure 1.7 provides box plots[18] of these improvement

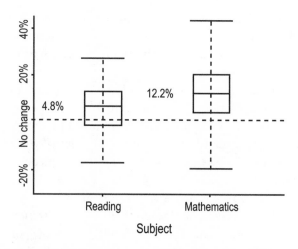

Figure 1.7. Broad-scale improvement in student learning gains under decentralization; distribution of percentage productivity improvements, 1990–96.

indices. The average Chicago elementary school improved productivity in reading by 5 percent and improved in mathematics by 12 percent between 1990 and 1996. Over 80 percent of the elementary schools showed at least some improvement in mathematics learning, and close to 70 percent improved in reading (that is, these schools had positive LGIs).

These data provide compelling evidence that the Chicago decentralization reform generated a broad base of academic improvements in many, but not all, elementary schools. Although far from sufficient in size, these results do indicate that wide-scale gains in student learning had materialized by 1996. Moreover, it is important to recognize that these test score improvements occurred absent a high-stakes accountability system, such as was introduced into Chicago post-1996. This fact increases our confidence that the observed test score gains represent genuine school improvements. In contrast, interpreting test score trend under a high-stakes, test-driven accountability reform is much more complicated. Considerable evidence has accumulated, for example, that the incidence of cheating, "gaming the tests," and student exclusions from the testing program all increased post-1996 with the advent of the new accountability regime.[19] In order to understand fully how much schools actually improved under such circumstances would require much more complex analyses in an effort to take into account and adjust for the influence of these extraneous factors.

Revisiting the Outcome Results for the Hancock and Alexander Schools

We conclude this chapter with a look at the three outcome indicators for the Alexander and Hancock schools introduced in the prologue. Recall that strong principal leadership at the Hancock School fostered the development of a vigorous professional community that was both actively reaching out to parents and sustaining a focus on improving instruction. In contrast, reform efforts at Alexander remained fragmented, suffering from both poor coordination and a lack of follow-through.

In 1990, the average daily attendance at Alexander was 92.4 percent; at Hancock it was slightly lower, 92.1 percent. By 1996, Hancock had effected some improvement in attendance to 92.6 percent, even though its upper grades had begun to receive increasing numbers of weak students from other neighborhood schools. At Alexander, in contrast, attendance went in the opposite direction, declining almost a full percentage point over this period. So, regardless of the fact that Alexander had actually started out a bit better, it ended up six years later in a significantly worse position.

Similar patterns emerged in the LGIs. Students at Alexander witnessed no improvement in mathematics over this period, and were actually learning about 9-percent less in reading in 1996 than in 1990. In contrast, Hancock students' learning gains were 19-percent greater in mathematics, and nearly 10-percent greater in reading. These results placed Hancock solidly among the top quartile of elementary schools in Chicago in terms of improvements in academic productivity. In contrast, the results at Alexander were typical for the nonimproving schools reported in figures 1.5 and 1.6. This evidence simply confirms what we alluded to in the prologue. Although in 1990 these two schools started out in similar places, they had become quite different in their institutional effectiveness by 1996. We now turn our attention to examining more systematically what happened at these two schools and many others like them across the city, to produce such different results for the children.

It is customary in books of this sort to present the "framework or theory chapter" as if the organizing ideas for the research had sprung forth in a pure intellectual form from the solitary reflections of some author(s)—with other relevant academic citations dutifully acknowledged, of course. In truth, our framework has a social history as well as an intellectual one, and understanding this is key to comprehending the final form that these ideas have taken. So we begin by returning to the early days of school reform in Chicago and describe how the framework detailed in this chapter took root in the fertile soil of the Chicago School Reform Act of 1988.

The Social Life of an Idea: The Evolution of a Framework for School Improvement

Although passed by the Illinois legislature in the spring of 1988, the initiation of the Reform Act was delayed until the fall of 1989. Most of the 1989–90 academic year was taken up with organizing for Local School Council elections and then the creation, by these newly elected LSCs, of bylaws and various operating procedures. Half the councils were authorized to offer a performance contract to their principal in the late spring of 1990; the other half had this authorization deferred until the spring of 1991. From the perspective of initiating substantive local change, we mark the LSC's opportunity to hire its own principal as the start of reform in each school community.

Thus, by the spring of 1992, some schools were two years into this process, but others just one. Regardless, the reform legislation itself was four years old, and increasingly a question was being raised: Is this reform actually working? In this context, the Steering Committee of the Consortium on Chicago School Research (CCSR) urged us to undertake a broad-based assessment of the state of the reform, which we eventually published the following spring. This was a most unusual project. Although the core of the work was carried out by CCSR staff, individuals from multiple institutions participated in the undertaking. In addition to original CCSR data collection and analyses, the report included a synthesis of independent field study results conducted by other groups, and several members of the Steering Committee were actively involved in helping to frame the overall study.[1]

This research was exceptionally timely. Although, as noted earlier, the report told a "story of three thirds," with some school communities clearly moving forward, others struggling, and still others moribund, the local policy community generally interpreted our findings as validating the 1988 legislation. Even so, the report also brought public attention to a set of system-level problems impeding further improvements. In our view, Chicago had achieved about as much reform as could be expected from local schools left to their own devices. More constructive action from the central administration was required to support a deepening of these local efforts. For one, a more robust system of assistance for local school development was needed; and second, a viable process of central accountability had to be formulated to identify troubled schools and jump-start reform in these communities.

The CCSR's public convening efforts concerning these findings coincided with a decision by the Chicago Public School Board to conduct a national search for a new superintendent. This search brought Argie Johnson to Chicago from New York City. Although Johnson's superintendency was limited to two years, as she was immediately replaced by Mayor Richard M. Daley upon his takeover of the school system in the summer of 1995, her brief tenure led to a period of glasnost within the central office. A number of "nontraditional professionals" were drawn into that office through the encouragement and support of a business-civic group, Leadership for Quality Education. In one of the first efforts anywhere to bring private management consultants into the processes of central office redesign, the firm of CSC Index, whose principals, Michael Hammer and James Champy, had just published *Reengineering the Corporation,* were recruited to guide this effort. As part of these larger system-level initiatives, two of us, John Easton and Tony Bryk, took leaves of absence from our respective institutions, the

Chicago Panel on School Policy and the University of Chicago, to join in this work. Easton took on the responsibility for rebuilding the research, assessment, and analysis capacity for the school system, with support from Bryk, who also acted as a general advisor to Argie Johnson on larger district reform issues. The framework of the *essential supports for school improvement* came to life in this unusual context of institutional change.

One of Johnson's first initiatives as superintendent was to formulate an intervention plan for nonimproving schools. She invited a group of Chicago reformers and school stakeholders, including teachers, principals, and LSC members, to help formulate a systemwide improvement agenda.[2] CCSR associates participated in these meetings and took a major role behind the scenes in crafting what eventually became the conceptual guide for a range of subsequent reform activities.

The original guide was significantly influenced by prior research on effective schools,[3] other ongoing CCSR research in Chicago, direct experiences in school intervention of our sister institution, the Center for School Improvement at the University of Chicago,[4] and sustained conversations with the many local stakeholders assembled by the CPS. Key intellectual contributions came through the federally funded National Center on School Restructuring (CORS) at the University of Wisconsin, where Bryk was a coprincipal investigator. The center, under the leadership of Fred Newmann, was actively investigating the processes of organizational restructuring that had been initiated in many U.S. schools in the early 1990s. Emerging ideas from the work at CORS influenced the evolution of the essential supports and vice versa: early results of Chicago's reform also shaped the final CORS findings.[5]

Taken together, a grounded theory of school organization and its improvement emerged from this rich mix of traditional academic pursuits and practical improvement activities. More specifically, we sought to develop a "theory of practice" that effectively serves two masters. First, it should afford clinical guidance to practitioners—directing their efforts toward the core aspects of school improvement that merit their attention. Lacking such clinical validity, a framework of essential supports would be of little practical utility. Thus, the essential supports aim to provide local school leaders with a guide for analyzing their own school's operations and reform efforts, and to shape a public agenda for ongoing policy discussions about how best to advance such improvements.

Second, the framework should be anchored in organizational theory and provide analytic traction for efforts to examine its validity empirically.

In this latter regard, an effective theory identifies the critical elements that combine to form the overall framework, guides the development and refinement of measures for each of these core elements, and directs attention to specific interrelations that we should find among measures of these elements and their relation to valued student outcomes. Absent such an evidence base, the framework lacks empirical warrant for its use in guiding school improvement.

Finally, we note that the development of this framework of essential supports was itself an evolutionary process. Our ideas continued to evolve as we gathered additional field data, developed survey items, analyzed both of these, and shared results (and engaged in extensive discussions) with the CCSR's Steering Committee and the interested public.

Framework Overview

Schools are complex organizations consisting of multiple interacting subsystems. Each subsystem involves a mix of human and social factors that shape the actual activities that occur and the meaning that individuals attribute to these events. These social interactions are bounded by various rules, roles, and prevailing practices that, in combination with technical resources, constitute schools as formal organizations. In a simple sense, almost everything interacts with everything else. A key in theory formation for both analytic and clinical purposes is to figure out how to "carve this complexity" at the joints.[6]

In a sense, we began this process in our 1993 report, *The State of School Reform*.[7] We documented there how local reform efforts focused on a few major dimensions. First, principals were actively reaching out to parents and the local community to strengthen the social ties across historical divides.[8] Second, school leaders worked to expand the professional capabilities of their faculty. Third, these leaders began to direct increasing amounts of their discretionary resources toward enhancing the quality of instruction.

These ideas continued to evolve over the next several years through a combination of our analytic efforts to test and refine this framework and our direct engagement with numerous reform initiatives in Chicago. In its final and most encapsulated form, our framework begins with **leadership as the driver for change (essential support number 1)** and more specifically with principals as catalytic agents for systemic improvement. These school-based leaders build agency for change at the community level, nurture the leadership of others through a shared vision for local reform, and provide the necessary guidance over time to sustain a coherent program of schoolwide development. Their change efforts focus on

- Encouraging new relations with parents and local communities to repair the long-standing disconnect between urban schools and the children and families they are intended to serve. Through active outreach efforts, staff members seek to make the school a more hospitable and welcoming environment for parents and strengthen the connections to other local institutions concerned with the care and well-being of children and their families. (Essential support number 2: parent-community ties.)
- Enhancing the faculty's professional capabilities through deliberate focus on the quality of new staff, strengthening the processes supporting faculty learning and promoting a continuous improvement ethos across a school-based professional community. (Essential support number 3: professional capacity.)
- Nurturing an overall normative environment where students feel safe and are pressed and supported to engage (and succeed) in more ambitious intellectual activity. Such an environment is central to making school reform work for children. (Essential support number 4: a student-centered learning climate.)
- Cultivating the schoolwide supports concerning curriculum and instruction in order to promote more ambitious academic achievement for every child. (Essential support number 5: instructional guidance.)

An Alternative Perspective: "It's about instruction, stupid"

Our school improvement framework is rooted in a core set of ideas about how the organization and operation of schools could (and should) be restructured to enhance students' engagement with school and improve their learning outcomes. As noted earlier, the intellectual inspiration for much of this framework came from the organizational restructuring movements of the 1980s and early 1990s. These ideas, originating in corporate America, eventually migrated to numerous other sectors, including public education. In broad strokes, the reform literature criticized large bureaucratic organizations as failing to deliver the goods on the actual "job floor." Such organizations often did not respond well to local needs, had little capacity to learn, and stifled rather than nurtured innovation. "Downsizing the organization" was seen as key to systemic improvement.

Beginning in the mid- to late 1990s, a second and quite different orientation toward school improvement emerged. Adapting the phrase coined by Bill Clinton in his presidential bid—"It's the economy, stupid"—these reformers pointed out that too little attention had been focused directly on the core work of instruction in schools. As a counterbalance, this approach argued for a laserlike scrutiny of the most immediate causes of student learning—what happens within the "instructional triangle"—as teachers engage with students on subject matter. These reformers tend to be concerned with the academic content that students are exposed to, the intellectual demand with which students are expected to engage this content (as exemplified in the types of work products students are asked to produce), and the classroom pedagogies and instructional tools necessary to bring all of this about.

From this reform perspective, the primary responsibility of school principals is their continuous focus on improving instructional work in classrooms. "Principals as instructional leaders" are expected to be experts in teaching and learning, to spend the majority of their time in classrooms, and, more generally, to support improvements in instruction. As part of the instructional improvement process, they oversee ongoing programs of formative assessments and use these data to guide strategic follow-up actions.

Connecting School Organization to Classroom Instruction: Elaborating the Conceptual Foundation for Our Framework

Clearly, important and powerful ideas for guiding school reform are embedded in this direct emphasis on instructional improvement. In fact, it is inconceivable to us that major improvements in student learning can occur without fundamental changes in the way students interact with teachers around subject matter.[9] This realization forces us to confront a critical question: How then do we reconcile the two seemingly disparate visions of improvement summarized above?

Key here is to recognize that within the instructional perspective, the central focus is on what happens within classrooms. The rest of the school as an organization largely fades into the background. In contrast, our framework of essential supports focuses attention at the school level. This observation suggests that a creative yoking of these two perspectives might actually be quite beneficial. To the point, if restructuring school organization matters, its effects must largely accrue through influencing the conditions under which teachers work and engage with students around subject matter in the classroom.[10]

More specifically, an adequate framework for conceptualizing school improvement demands an explanation of how the *organization of a school* and its day-to-day operations, including its connections to parents and community, *interact with work inside its classrooms* to advance student learning. Thus, as we detail below in our conceptualization of the five organizational supports for student learning, we seek to articulate the systemic interconnections among these aspects of school organization and classroom life.

In order to accomplish this, we need first to unpack a bit further the psycho-socio-technical dynamics of classroom practice. Although classroom instruction is not the prime focus of the empirical work presented in this book, detailing our understandings of these processes is essential to the phenomena we are primarily interested in: how to better organize schools to support improvements in student engagement and learning.

Dynamics of Student Learning

We begin by focusing attention on the *technical core of instruction.* (See figure 2.1.) Of principal concern here are the classroom dynamics of a teacher (T) engaging students (S) in subject matter (SM). It is within this "instructional triangle" that learning principally occurs or fails to occur.[11] Such learning accrues as a product of the prior background and interests

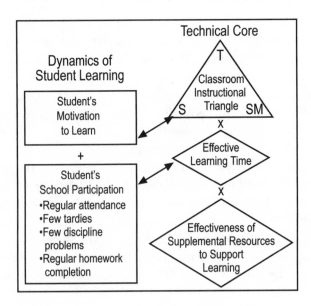

Figure 2.1. Inside the classroom black box.

of students in the classroom, the knowledge and skill that a teacher brings to bear, and how the teacher utilizes the resources and supports provided by the school to advance instruction in some particular subject. Each of these considerations is represented heuristically as a vertex within the instructional triangle.

The overall productivity of this classroom activity depends in turn on two additional factors that act to enhance or diminish its effectiveness. We conceptualize these factors as "multipliers" that may add to or detract from the value of a teacher's work. First is the amount of time available for student learning in any given subject. Increasing instructional time, especially in the core skill areas of reading and mathematics, is a major focus of many contemporary reform efforts. Such initiatives draw on the seminal theory of John Carroll, who posited that learning depends on the amount of time allocated for instruction and the quality of that instruction, while also taking into account students' aptitude and perseverance.[12] Of special significance for our work is evidence that the amount of instructional time varies substantially—not only among classrooms, depending on differences in teachers' management and organizational skills, but also among schools and districts, depending on a myriad of factors operating at each level.[13]

Second, the instructional productivity of a classroom also depends on the effectiveness of the supplemental academic and social supports for learning. Especially in highly disadvantaged urban schools, where many students have a wide range of academic, psychosocial, and health-related needs, a school's failure to respond adequately to these needs can have far-reaching instructional consequences. Not only will this undermine the learning of the specific students involved, but broader schoolwide problems can ensue that diminish effective instructional time for all students. While a school's primary mission is advancing students' academic learning, instructional productivity does depend on the effectiveness of a diverse array of student and family support services.

Operating in strong interaction with this technical core are the *psychosocial dynamics* of students' engagement with instruction. This consideration directs our attention to both students' basic motivation for learning and the regularity of their school participation.[14]

Motivating students to learn represents a daunting problem for many urban teachers. In the absence of strong organizational supports (see below), each teacher must learn to solve this problem on his or her own.[15] Similarly, the productivity of work within the instructional triangle also depends directly on students' regular school participation. To the extent that a classroom suffers from chronic absenteeism and tardiness, effective learning time may diminish.[16] When numerous students are frequently absent, teachers often feel a need to spend additional time on review before introducing new material.[17] Similarly, in response to widespread tardiness, teachers often delay the start of actual instruction in the school day.

Taken together, these psycho-socio-technical considerations are the main factors directly influencing student learning. Viewed through an organizational lens, each of these in turn becomes a direct target for school improvement efforts. How the five organizational subsystems, which we have dubbed the *essential supports,* interact to enhance or undermine the overall dynamics of student learning is our next consideration.

The School as an Organizational System

We delineate below the core elements that constitute each subsystem; the salience of each within our overall framework; how each influences the dynamics of student learning described above; and how these various subsystems interact with one another to create an overall organizational context conducive to improvement (or not).

A school's instructional guidance subsystem. This domain links directly to the subject matter vertex in the instructional triangle. (See figure 2.2.) It organizes the curriculum content that students are exposed to (often referred to as the "content map and sequence"), specifies the nature of the academic demand or challenge that is posed for students, and affords teachers a set of the tools to advance student learning (for example, instructional materials, assessments methods, and general pedagogies such as literature circles and cooperative grouping). Although substantial discretion may exist in how individual teachers draw on these resources, the efficacy of any individual teacher's instructional efforts remains dependent on the quality of the supports and direction provided here.

Unfortunately, in many disadvantaged urban schools this subsystem often lacks organization and coherence. Worthwhile elements may sit alongside others of highly dubious quality. Observed classroom practice may best be described as a hodgepodge of prior district mandates, new "silver bullet" initiatives, and personal preferences cobbled together by individual teachers over time. In some schools, no effective instructional guidance system may exist at all! In these cases, each teacher has the broad autonomy to do whatever he or she pleases within the confines of the classroom. The resultant lack of coordination and alignment of activity can

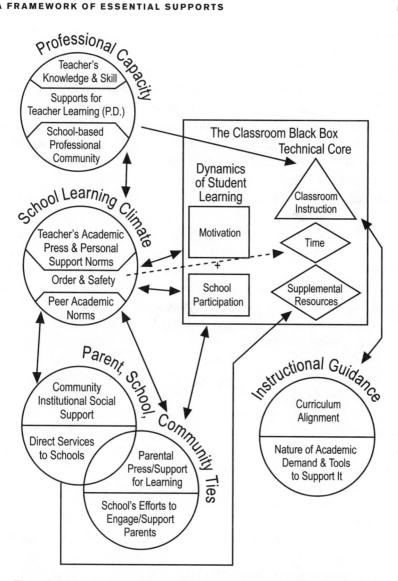

Figure 2.2. How four essential supports influence student learning.

have deleterious effects. Gaps in the curriculum, poor pacing of instruction and idiosyncratic expectations for student performance within and across grade levels, and incoherence between the regular and the supplemental instructional program can all weaken students' overall learning. Thus, strengthening this subsystem represents our first organizational support for improvement.

Conceptually, three elements constitute this subsystem. First is the arrangement of subject matter content and pacing over time and grades, and across classes. This element in a school's instructional system maps what students are expected to learn. The second element focuses on the intellectual depth expected of students as they engage this subject matter. The latter is reflected in the learning tasks assigned students. It is also reflected in the assessments used to inform instructional decision making and hold schools accountable. It is manifest in the types of work products that students are asked to produce and how these in turn are judged. Third are the pedagogical strategies, materials, and tools made available to teachers to support this activity and the general expectations about the teaching role enacted in the classroom.

In actual practice, the latter two elements tend to merge, as pedagogical methods and modes of assessment are logically connected through the core learning tasks to be advanced by instruction. For example, instruction aimed at students' acquisition of discrete facts and skills may rely heavily on didactic teaching with formal class question-and-answer recitation, substantial worksheet exercises to practice basic skills and demonstrate factual knowledge, and a reliance on multiple-choice tests for assessment purposes. In classroom activity aimed at higher-order intellectual tasks, by contrast, students may take on more open-ended projects, where work products might consist of longer essays, classroom presentations, and participation in group discussions. Teachers may embed direct, targeted "minilessons" while working within a classroom coaching role. Students may also have more choice about the work they engage in and be expected to take active responsibility for its completion.

This perspective eventually led us to frame our conceptualization of this subsystem around just two major ideas: the organization of the curriculum within a school, and the nature of the overall academic demand on students. In simple terms, we might describe this as the "what" and the "how" of instruction.

i. Curriculum organization. This is the "what" of instruction—the subject matter students are exposed to in any given grade, and how this is intended to build over the duration of schooling to form a coherent knowledge and skill base for each child. Educational policy initiatives focused on content standards directly aim to improve this aspect of the instructional guidance subsystem.

While states and districts now routinely generate such standards, these documents only come alive in the day-to-day life of schools as faculties study them and use what they learn there to guide discussions about the adequacy of their current instructional efforts and to organize subsequent improvement activities. In aiming for greater adherence to standards, faculty must critically examine their own teaching and be open to modifying their instruction in order to bring it into better alignment with an overall schoolwide plan. Without this, schools run the risk of weakening students' learning opportunities and achievement through delays, repetitions, and omissions in core knowledge and skill acquisition.[18]

ii. Advancing the academic goals of instruction. In elaborating our view of the "how" of the instructional guidance system, we need to digress a bit, to set this discussion in the context of the extraordinary global changes that now make unprecedented demands on schooling in the United States.[19]

Beginning with the 1983 report *Nation at Risk,* we have witnessed a sustained, widespread political movement to improve the quality of U.S. public education.[20] The goals of this movement, however, have dramatically shifted over the last quarter century. In the early 1980s, we would have triumphed as a success an increase in students' basic skill levels in reading and mathematics and a reduction in high school dropout rates. Now we seek "first in the world" academic attainment for every student.

Driving these developments are profound changes in the structure of the U.S. economy. In the 1970s, we saw large numbers of good blue-collar jobs begin to move offshore as second- and third-world nations rapidly industrialized. In the global knowledge-based economy of the 1990s, increasing numbers of white-collar jobs have been either replaced by technology or shipped offshore to exploit substantially lower labor costs.[21] Moreover, this movement is only beginning, and likely to accelerate in the years ahead.

The new "good jobs" in the knowledge economy make different educational demands on the labor force.[22] Traditional skills in reading, writing, and arithmetic for white-collar work remain important, but are no longer sufficient. As procedural tasks are being automated through technology, the new white-collar job involves problem solving that demands more complex intellectual skills of analysis, synthesis, and knowledge application.[23] Knowledge workers also need strong communication and interpersonal skills in public speaking, media-based presentations, and working in teams and with diverse groups. Interestingly, the educational desiderata for a knowledge economy now merge in significant respects with long-standing themes in progressive education: schools should form in every child the capacity to think and act well in an increasingly complex, pluralist, democratic society.[24]

Preparing a citizenry to undertake such activity means that schools must direct their efforts at both ensuring students' acquisition of a solid core of basic skills and cultural knowledge and developing students' abilities to apply these skills and knowledge to novel and challenging problems. Students need opportunities to engage in disciplined inquiry, drawing on relevant knowledge in a field (that is, the facts, the skills, and the ways these work together) as they seek to understand some problem, and effectively communicate their ideas about the problem and its possible solutions.[25] The latter is manifest in instructional tasks that require organization, planning, self-monitoring of progress; where authentic work products are used to chart student progress and assess learning; and where the social life of the classroom involves productive teamwork and critical conversations about academic ideas.[26] Not surprisingly, for teachers to carry out such instruction makes significant claims on the instructional guidance system in terms of the materials and pedagogic resources necessary to support such teaching, and on the tools and information available for evaluating student performance and guiding program improvements.

Professional capacity: the human resource subsystem. Our second support connects directly to the teacher vertex in the instructional triangle. All organizations depend on the quality of their people and their ability to work together. The human resource subsystem is especially critical for schools, however, because they operate within a rather modest technical core of instruction.[27] As a result, the effectiveness of schooling depends largely on the teachers' capacity to problem-solve regarding classroom concerns and to coordinate instructional work.

From an organizational perspective, this directs our attention to a school's ability to recruit and retain knowledgeable and skillful staff, the efficacy of its performance feedback and individual professional development programs, and a staff's capacity to form as a viable collective that shares responsibility for student learning and supports one another in continuous improvement.[28] We refer to this combination of skills, beliefs, dispositions, and work arrangements as *professional capacity.*

i. **Quality of human resources.** Teachers' knowledge of subject matter and effective pedagogies for teaching specific content and skills, along with particular knowledge about their students' backgrounds, interests, and learning styles, are central to effective teaching and learning.[29] Skillful teachers choose appropriate books and other materials, leverage technology, know how to convey ideas effectively, and motivate students to master basic skills and apply them in the context of complex problem-solving situations. Clearly, recruiting capable teachers is critical to creating the breadth and depth of expertise needed within a faculty to undertake significant school development. Equally significant is the capacity to reshape a faculty over time by removing chronically low-performing teachers. A school that tolerates manifest gross incompetence in a few teachers can be highly corrosive to the collective efforts toward improvement being made by others.[30]

ii. Quality of professional development. We must also attend to the continuing-education efforts a school provides to improve the effectiveness of its staff. Teachers must take part in ongoing professional development activity to keep abreast of new knowledge and to continue their individual growth. Recent research underscores the importance of teachers' continued engagement in professional development that directly relates to a school's instructional improvement priorities.[31] Such activity should build on (and on occasion challenge) teachers' prior beliefs and experience, provide sufficient time and follow-up for sustained inquiry and problem solving, and create opportunities for analysis and reflection.[32]

iii. Normative dispositions: An orientation toward continuous improvement. Undergirding any major school improvement effort is a distinct normative stance among the school faculty—a set of values and beliefs about teachers' responsibilities as active agents for change. These normative understandings manifest themselves in teachers' commitment to the school and its improvement. The faculty must bring a sense of agency to their work that embodies a belief that they have something important to contribute.[33] This stance also entails an orientation toward innovation, where teachers willingly examine new ideas and experiment with new approaches in their classroom. Such shared views among a school staff stand in sharp contrast to the "work to rules" mentality and externalization of responsibility for student failure that characterize practice in many urban schools.[34]

iv. Professional community. Institutionalizing a continuous improvement process within a school requires teachers to relinquish some of the privacy of their individual classrooms to engage in critical dialogue with one another as they identify common problems and consider possible solutions to these concerns. At base here is a relatively new idea of a school-based professional community.[35] This form of social organization sits between two polar extremes that have dominated past discussions about teachers' work in schools. At one end is the "teacher proof curriculum." Here, teachers are in essence replaceable actors expected to follow an instructional script organized around a detailed set of lesson plans. At the other extreme is a conception of teaching as a personal art form characterized as "each classroom a Leonardo."[36] In this view, practice is so complex and situation specific that formalized guidance can rarely be helpful. In contrast, the notion of a school-based professional community represents a creative middle ground that acknowledges the complex nature of teachers' moment-to-moment work in classrooms while still locating this activity within a common instructional system, where analysis of evidence from shared practice creates the common ground for disciplining and improving the practice.

In general, a school-based professional community entails new work arrangements for faculty that[37] (1) make teachers' classroom work public for examination by colleagues and external consultants; (2) institute processes of critical dialogue about classroom practices (for example, what is and is not happening in our classrooms? How do we know that something is actually working? Where is the evidence of student learning? Are there other practices that might work better, and how might we figure this out?); and (3) sustain collaboration among teachers that focuses on strengthening the school's instructional guidance system.

These three practices are in turn rooted in a system of normative control over teachers' work. At base here is a professional ethic of individual and collective responsibility to improve the learning of every child. In combination with the other teacher dispositions already detailed above, these beliefs, values, and associated work habits constitute a normative system that guides everyday behavior and thereby exercises effective social control over individual actions within the school community.[38]

We note that the concept of a school-based professional community has its origins in general organizational theory, which argues that organic forms of management are especially valuable when work tasks are ill-formed and ambiguous. This implies that normative control over teacher practice may come into greater play in some teaching domains, such as literacy learning, where instructional practice tends to be more variable than in others, like mathematics, which is typically guided by more specified instructional materials and procedures.[39] All of this has implications for interpreting the analyses presented in chapters 3 and 4, where we look at school improvement in both academic domains.

Taken together, the four elements of professional capacity discussed above are mutually reinforcing in promoting both individual and collective teacher growth. Thoughtful professional development that is aligned with the school's strategic goals creates occasions for enhancing professional community. In turn, a school-based professional community constitutes a significant social resource to individual teacher learning and improvement.[40] From another point of view, the collective capacity of a school-based professional community is contingent on the base quality of the staff recruited into the school; correspondingly, a school with a strong professional community is an attractive place for teachers to work, thereby enhancing the capacity of the school to recruit and retain such quality faculty.[41] Thus, it makes sense, even as we have carved the conceptual joints within this domain, to conceive of this ensemble of elements as a school's overall professional capacity.

Next we consider two additional organizational supports whose effect on classroom learning occurs primarily through their influence on the psychosocial interconnections among teachers and students.

The subsystem of parent-community-school ties. The elements that make up this subsystem have direct effects on students' motivation and school participation and can have a direct influence on the efficacy of work within the instructional triangle.[42]

Extensive research testifies to the importance of parent and community involvement in children's schooling.[43] Of key significance for a school *improvement* framework, prior research has shown that schools can enhance this involvement through deliberate action.[44] More specifically, research reviews identify three distinct dimensions meriting attention: (1) school efforts to reach out to parents, to engage them directly in the processes of strengthening student learning;[45] (2) teacher efforts to become knowledgeable about student culture and the local community and to draw on this awareness in their lessons; and (3) strengthening the network among community organizations, to expand services for students and their families. These three elements constitute the core components of the subsystem.

i. **Supporting parents to support learning.** A diverse array of parent education and involvement activities has been demonstrated to contribute to student learning. These include initiatives focused on strengthening parenting skills, communicating with parents to reinforce study habits and expectations, finding ways to engage learning activities between parents and students at home, inviting parents to volunteer at the school, and creating opportunities for a parent voice in school decision making.[46]

Among these diverse options, the most powerful effects are likely to accrue as teachers seek to involve parents more directly in their children's learning. This may take a variety of forms. Teachers may ask parents to read books with their children; they may send newsletters home previewing what the children will be doing in class and what parents can do at home to better support this learning; and they may offer suggestions for how to create routines at home to support homework. In addition to a direct influence on student learning, such activity can also have positive effects on parents. Good home-school collaboration can help parents better understand their children's development and consequently be more effective in carrying out their parenting role.

Enhancing parent-teacher trust is an important by-product of successful programmatic efforts in this area. Teachers depend on parents in a myriad of ways, including getting students to school on time, supporting schoolwork activities at home, and joint problem solving around student behavior concerns.[47] This dependency is expressed in the commonly heard sentiment from teachers that "parents are our essential partners."[48] Not surprisingly, the social ties between parents and school professionals represent a significant resource for diverse school improvement initiatives, from enhancing safety in and around schools, to addressing problems of absenteeism and tardiness, to assuring more consistent and effective homework sessions.

ii. Teachers' knowledge about their students' home culture and community. This element constitutes an extraordinarily valuable resource in teaching. As such, it represents a vital link between this subsystem and professional capacity.[49] Especially in inner-city schools, where they are often of a different race, ethnicity, or social class from their students, teachers need to develop a deep understanding of the life forces influencing "other people's children."[50] A fundamental premise in instructional design is that one builds on the basic background knowledge, interests, and skills that students bring to the classroom. At the psychosocial level, a deep understanding of students' background represents a powerful resource for teachers as they seek to establish the interpersonal connections necessary to teach. At an instrumental level, good teachers draw on such background knowledge as they attempt to connect seemingly abstract academic topics to student lives.[51] In this regard, knowing children well is essential to the effective design of classroom lessons that advance academic learning for all.

iii. School-community partnerships. A substantial proportion of students in inner-city schools require an array of supplemental services to address problems that interfere with learning. These may be as simple as a need for eyeglasses or tutoring, or more serious, such as assistance in coping with a chronic illness or mental health support in dealing with neglect and abuse. As we detail in chapter 6, the incidence of such needs is startlingly high in urban contexts like Chicago, where one-fourth or more of the elementary-school students might be living under an extraordinary set of circumstances, such as homelessness, foster care, domestic violence, abuse, or neglect.

As a result, a school's capacity to partner with community services has a direct impact on the effectiveness of the supplemental resources available to support learning. The African aphorism, "It takes a village to raise a child," applies just as well to inner-city neighborhoods. Partnerships with community health, recreation, and social service agencies, as well as with the police department, are vital to ensuring students' academic success.

It is important to recognize that many of the services that schools rely on in this regard are not provided directly by the school system itself, but rather arise through local arrangements with other public agencies and private institutions.[52] Thus, a coherent school community program for improving student learning requires managing a diverse array of academic and social support services and sustaining the relationships with the multiple institutions that provide them. To that end, school leaders must devote considerable time and attention to the details of program implementation; otherwise commitment ebbs, people lose interest, resources dwindle, or other problems crop up.[53] When school-community ties are strong, the development and maintenance of effective plans are easier to accomplish.

It is also important to recognize that strong connections to primary youth services, such as church groups, the Boy and Girl Scouts, and the YMCA, are a key resource in this regard. In general, urban children and youth are particularly vulnerable to mass-media images of the "gangsta" lifestyle and the enticements of gang and other illegal activity in their neighborhood.[54] Hence, whatever schools can do to enlist positive youth organizations as partners in the social and educational development of children, the greater the chance that students become and remain engaged in school.[55]

The subsystem of the student-centered learning climate. The social psychology of a school is an integrative product of the beliefs, values, and actual everyday behaviors among school professionals, parents, and students. This subsystem can have profound effects on student motivation and engagement with classroom instruction. In general, both teacher-student and student-student relations directly influence students' school participation and willingness to expend major effort on classroom learning.

i. **Order and safety.** A sense of safety and order is a basic human need. Its absence in school has a direct effect on student motivation for learning and school participation. In addition, a lack of safety and order directly affects learning time by disrupting school and classroom routines.

While assuring such order and safety is the prime responsibility of the school staff, it is important to recognize that many problems in this domain literally "walk in through the front doors" of urban schools. In this regard, strong community and parent ties, as detailed above, are a genuine asset to urban school leaders as they seek to establish and maintain order across a school community.[56] Similarly, a strong sense of shared professional responsibility is key here as well. In schools with weak social connections among the faculty, teachers often pull back and delimit their responsibilities to the confines of their classroom walls. The hallways, lunchrooms, bathrooms, and playgrounds in such contexts may become literally no-man's-land.

ii. Teachers' academic press and personalism. Assuming that a base of safety and order is established, one moves next to consider how school-developed norms can proactively support student learning. On one side, this directs our attention to the nature of student-teacher relations, more specifically the academic expectations that teachers hold for students.[57] Improving learning means pressing all students to engage in academic work with depth and rigor. This press for higher standards typically results in more homework, extended instructional time, more difficult tests, and more stringent requirements for grade promotion and graduation.

In tandem with this is how teachers extend the personal care and support that many students will need as they reach for these higher standards. With good reason, some reformers fear that when standards are raised, students with poor academic skills may become disheartened and disengaged, and drop out of school.[58] It is especially important then, as schools press disadvantaged students toward higher standards, that this be accompanied by ample social support to sustain students' efforts.[59] At base here is a complex interaction where a *press toward higher academic standards* must be coupled with *ample personal support* so that *disadvantaged students* have a realistic chance of responding successfully to these expectations.[60]

iii. Supportive peer norms. A similar set of issues emerges as we shift to consider student peer interactions. In effective schools, compliance with behavioral and academic norms is simply understood and supported by students as "this is what we do here." The presence of such student norms creates a powerful social control mechanism that informally guides much of the everyday student behavior in schools, freeing faculty to concentrate on teaching rather than policing the environment. The overall effectiveness of instructional time is thereby enhanced.

There is, however, an unfortunate tendency among educators today to assume that peer norms are "given" by the external environment and unalterable through school practice. Yet many counterexamples to this assumption now exist. In effective urban Catholic schools and a growing array of new charter schools, one finds sustained, deliberate efforts by adults to form school cultures for academically disadvantaged youngsters where "learning is cool" and where students exhort one another to "Work hard. Be nice."[61] To be sure, nurturing such supportive academic norms is difficult, but these cases demonstrate that it can be accomplished through careful thought and sustained action by a school's staff. When the professional community among the staff is weak, however, this is not likely to occur.

Leadership as the driving subsystem for improvement. Our fifth and final core support focuses on school leadership. It is remarkable how dramatically the education literature on this topic has changed over the last twenty years. In the mid-1980s, empirical studies and analytic treatises raised questions about the actual impact, if any, that principals had on school outcomes.[62] Today, it is an accepted fact among educational reformers that principals are the key levers for school-based change. But how school leadership actually matters in the processes of school improvement remains far less clear.

We were fortunate in this regard in that the broad changes sought by Chicago's decentralization reform provided an unusual window to observe up close the many distinct facets and consequences of leadership in action. Taken together, these observations led us to posit that three distinct elements—managerial, instructional, and inclusive-facilitative leadership—constitute this subsystem. Each has a somewhat different functional relationship to the other four core organizational supports. Taken overall, leadership has pervasive effects across the organization (see figure 2.3), with some aspects reaching directly into the technical core of classroom instruction.

i. **The managerial dimension.** This represents the most basic aspect of school leadership.[63] Its effects are most manifest in its absence—for example, a poorly run office, supply shortages, nothing starting or ending on time, poor communication with parents and staff, and little attention to administrative support for implementing new programs. Weaknesses in this domain can undermine teachers' classroom work by eating away at the amount of effective instructional time. It can also affect how teachers, parents, and community leaders come to "see" a school and influence their

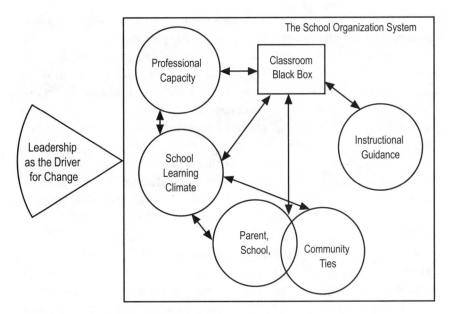

Figure 2.3. Leadership as the driving subsystem for improvement.

willingness to support new ideas and new programs that could potentially improve student learning. Building agency for change (a central objective under the inclusive-facilitative dimension, as described below) is made more difficult when little in the school seems to work properly.[64]

ii. The instructional dimension. This aspect of school leadership now stands at the core of many reform efforts. Its centrality is a function of the fact that instructional leadership directly impacts the dynamics of student engagement and learning. Deliberate actions by a school's principal can enhance instructional time and the effectiveness of supplemental programs. Principals can advance student learning through initiatives aimed at building the school's professional capacity and the quality of its instructional guidance subsystem.[65] These individuals can affect the collective knowledge and skill that teachers bring into classroom (in other words, the teacher vertex in the classroom learning triangle) and the technical resources that they have to advance student learning (that is, the subject-matter vertex).

Effective instructional leadership makes broad demands on principals' knowledge and skills with regard to both student and teacher learning. Principals must be knowledgeable, for example, about the tenets of learning theory and curriculum. They must be able to analyze instruction and provide effective, formative feedback to teachers.[66] Moreover, principals must be able to articulate high standards for student learning and support teachers' innovations to reach these standards. Their work should be guided routinely by a constant focus on evidence of student learning gleaned through both data reports and regular visits to classrooms. At base here they are constantly questioning: What is working and what is not (and why not)?

Successful leadership also entails a deliberate orchestration of people, programs, and extant resources. A strategic orientation must guide these efforts so that resources (both time and money) are effectively allocated to support the continuous improvement of classroom practice. Schools exist in a highly entropic external environment of reform ideas, products, and services. Thoughtfulness must guide the choice among potentially competing initiatives, to eliminate those that may take attention away from core improvement priorities. A host of questions demand ongoing consideration: How will some proposed initiative complement and add value to what the school is already doing? Where is this likely to lead over the long haul, and is this really where we want to go? How should initiatives be sequenced, and is the timing right for a particular activity? Absent this strategic orientation, school reform can resemble scattershot, uncoordinated projects that are likely to waste resources, be poorly implemented, and contribute to a staff's sense of resignation that "nothing really works here."[67]

Finally, instructional leaders are not reticent about using their role authority to "make things happen." They are willing to stake out significant positions for improving teaching and learning, challenge those who may be blocking these efforts, and use the full resources of their office to promote change.[68] In this regard, school leaders strive to achieve a subtle balance between aggressive efforts at advancing effective action and simultaneously seeking to nurture local followership and the emergence of a more distributed form of local leadership over time.

iii. The inclusive-facilitative dimension.[69] This aspect of leadership appears especially salient during times that call for fundamental organizational change. Broad-scale organizational transformation demands that leaders nurture individual agency and build collective capacity to support fundamental change. Key in this regard is a leader's ability to inspire teachers, parents, school community leaders, and students around a common vision of reform. A school community must come to believe that, regardless of what may have happened in the past, "together we can make this a better place." Inclusive-facilitative leaders exploit opportunities in both formal meetings and informal social encounters to advance a sense of quest: "Look at what we have already accomplished. We can do even more."[70] Likewise, they seek to catalyze an orientation, akin to a moral imperative, that "we can and must do this."

An inclusive-facilitative orientation is a key resource for school leaders in helping to manage the ambiguous processes of school change. When well executed, it functions as an effective lubricant for the many new activities occurring simultaneously within a reforming school.[71] If teachers feel a sense of influence on decisions affecting their work, the necessary "buy-in" for change is more readily established.[72] Also, teachers are more likely to remain in such schools and commit increased effort to carry out the long-term work of change.[73] Outreach to parents and community leaders has similar effects. As schools actively expand the base of parent and community involvement,[74] they deepen their pool of supportive human and social resources as well.[75]

Finally, over time, as school principals bring teachers, parents, and community members into new leadership roles, they enlarge the collective capacity to support a more productive and continuously improving school organization. While a principal holds substantial role authority to promote change, no one person can transform a school on his or her own. In the end, some form of more distributive leadership needs to emerge.[76]

The Systemic Character of Schools and the Dynamics of Change

In the previous section, we focused on "carving at the joints" the organizational life of a school. We now proceed to reintegrate these components, focusing attention on the systemic features that tie all of this together: the causal reciprocity of action across the separate subsystems, the organic and dynamic character of organizational change, and the institutional elements that undergird adult work in schools. In setting a context for this discussion, we begin with a brief recap on the core ideas introduced above.

Our framework of organizational supports for student learning starts with leadership as the driver for change. These school leaders focus their attention on four domains of work. They reach out to parents and communities to repair the long-standing disconnect between urban schools and the children and families they are intended to serve. Simultaneously, they work to enhance the professional capacity of their school through a deliberate focus on staff quality, strengthening the processes supporting faculty learning and a continuous improvement ethos. Likewise, they aim to expand teachers' capacity to work together to align curriculum and strengthen the overall instructional system. Central to making this work for children is an overall normative environment where students feel safe and are pressed and supported to engage (and succeed) with more ambitious intellectual activity. Key to achieving the latter are sustained efforts by all adults—the principal, teachers, parents, and school community leaders—to focus their improvement efforts on what works for "our children."

A Reciprocal Dynamic

On balance, it is important to recognize that while there is logic to reading figure 2.3 from left to right—leadership as the driver for changes in the four other organizational supports, culminating in enhanced student engagement and learning—the actual organizational life of a school is much more organic. The five organizational supports described above, as well as the dynamics of student learning, represent a set of interacting subsystems operating in strong reciprocal causation with one another. (Note that most of the "arrows" in figure 2.3 point in both directions.) For example, the efficacy of classroom instruction depends on student motivation for learning. However, high-quality instruction can also increase that motivation. Similarly, meaningful parent and community involvement can be a resource for solving problems with order and safety. The reverse is also true. When order and safety are strong, parent and community support for the school is likely to be greater. This reciprocity is true even as we conceptualize leadership as the driver for change. While a school principal has extraordinary formal authority as well as the symbolic position for driving change in the other four organizational subsystems, a school that is already strong in those four subsystems is easier to lead.

The presence of this reciprocal causality has important implications for the empirical work that lies ahead in subsequent chapters. Traditional analytic methods are best suited for sorting out the separate effects of one or more factors, holding everything else constant. The results from such linear additive models may not "add up," however, when inquiring into the workings of intrinsically interactive systems.[77] In response, we bring to bear in subsequent chapters a diverse array of analytic approaches as a way to systematically probe and come to understand better the organizational dynamics of improving schools.

"Baking a Cake": The Emergence of a Concept of Essentiality

During our early discussions with various local stakeholders, individuals opined at times that "what really matters is . . . " While it is tempting to argue about the significance of one individual support over another, we ul-timately came to view the five supports as an organized system of elements in dynamic interaction with one another. In a sense, school development is like baking a cake. So observed John Kotsakis, the former director of policy at the Chicago Teachers' Union and member of the CCSR's Steering Committee.[78] John argued by analogy that one needs an appropriate mix of flour, sugar, eggs, oil, baking powder, and flavoring to produce a light, delicious cake. Without the sugar, the cake will be tasteless. Without the eggs or the baking powder, it will be flat and chewy. Once one operates within the general confines of such a recipe, however, marginal changes in a single ingredient—a bit more flour, large versus extra-large eggs, and so on—may not have noticeable effects. But if one of the ingredients is absent, it is just not a cake.

Similarly, we argue that strong local leadership in tandem with the four other organizational elements constitute the essential ingredients for school development. Only if mutually supporting activity occurs across these various domains is student learning in classrooms likely to improve. Correspondingly, student outcomes are likely to stagnate if a material weakness persists in any of the supports. Thus, we argue that the ensemble of five supports is essential for improvement. Taken together, they consti-tute the core organizational ingredients for advancing student learning.

A Developmental Perspective: Reform Initiation Merging into Sustained Change

Looking back to our accounts in the prologue about the Hancock and Alexander schools, recall that their activities appeared to be reasonably similar during the first two years of reform. Both schools focused attention on strengthening order and safety, engaging parent and teacher leaders in local governance arrangements, connecting with outside resources to advance teachers' professional development in literacy and mathematics, and strengthening programs of social support for families and children. Yet by 1994, the two schools were in very different places organizationally. Most of the promising new activities had petered out at Alexander, and the initial enthusiasm for reform had largely subsided. In contrast, at Hancock there was a sense of synergy—productive reform activities were building on one another. The enhanced parent involvement was noticed and ap-preciated by teachers as an encouraging sign about the progress of their reform efforts. Similarly, teachers' success with curriculum alignment and new literacy assessments had nurtured an agency for even deeper instructional changes. The learning climate for students had changed dramatically as well. In essence, the diverse multiple strands of reform were merging into a fundamentally transformed organization, in terms of both the structure of its operations and the normative environment in which this work was carried out.

Two clear "take aways" are suggested here. First and as noted earlier, fundamental organizational change can be conceived as having two distinct periods: (1) an initiation phase and (2) a sustaining phase. *Democratic Localism* concluded that Chicago had been successful in catalyzing significant reform initiation in a large number of its school communities. Widespread school improvement at the elementary level was anticipated, assuming that schools stayed the course (that is, moved into the sustaining phase). It is clear now that some, such as Hancock, did, but others, such as Alexander, did not.

Second, the processes of systemic school improvement are multistranded—there is no single silver bullet that yields major improvements in student outcomes. Rather, sustained attention is required toward a system of concerns that we have termed the essential supports for school improvement.

To be clear, progress can begin along multiple alternative paths, and no one course is obviously best for all schools. How development starts and proceeds in any specific context will largely depend on the base capacity of that school, the characteristics of the community, and the particular interests and concerns of its leadership. Nonetheless, we posit that sustained work must eventually occur with regard to each of the essential supports. Stated somewhat differently, it is hard to envision improved student learning emerging in a school with poor leadership, weak parent-school ties, little professional commitment or adult learning, and/or undeveloped instructional resources. Similarly, it is hard to imagine a coherent program of local school development across these various areas without a process that engages a major portion of the adults in the school community in strategic action.

Links to Contingency Theory

Organizational theorists may quickly recognize that the theoretical framework detailed above has been strongly influenced by contingency theory.[79] Stated simply, this theoretical perspective argues that the most effective managerial form for an organization is contingent on the technical and environmental circumstances affecting the core work of the organization.[80]

Mechanistic forms of management (in other words, centralized decisions within a bureaucratic structure) are more likely to be effective in contexts where the core work on the job floor involves enacting standard routines and the organization operates within a relatively stable external environment. In contrast, organic forms of management are more likely to be deployed in dynamic environments where considerable uncertainty surrounds the execution of core tasks.[81]

The theory of essential supports developed in this chapter has roots in these ideas about organic management. For example, our perspective directs attention to the significance of inclusive leadership that nurtures opportunities for teacher influence in important school matters. Similarly, it places value on sustained efforts to nurture a strong, school-based professional community to support efforts in improving classroom instruction.[82] Finally, it accords value to strengthening the school's connections with parents and community, thereby sustaining the necessary political base to advance reform in what can often be a conflictual or unstable external environment. Thus, one can conceive of the analytic work that follows as an empirical test of the utility of contingency theory to inform improvement efforts in urban schools.

Placing the Development of the Essential Supports in a Larger Context

It is important to recognize that a school's capacity to actually develop the essential supports depends on an array of structural, institutional, and local community factors. Quite simply, the essential supports are more likely to emerge in schools where the base context is supportive of their development. Figure 2.4 illustrates this contextually embedded character of local school reform.

In brief, cultivating and maintaining the efforts necessary to secure long-term improvements requires a strong foundation of relational trust among teachers, between teachers and parents, between teachers and the principal, and between teachers and students.[83] As such, relational trust across a school community constitutes an overarching social resource for the growth of the essential supports.

Two structural features—small school size and a stable student population—also play a role in this regard. The smaller social networks inherent in a small school enable a friendly, more informal atmosphere, where teachers and students are more likely to know each other well. Assuming that positive exchanges actually occur here, small school size constitutes a

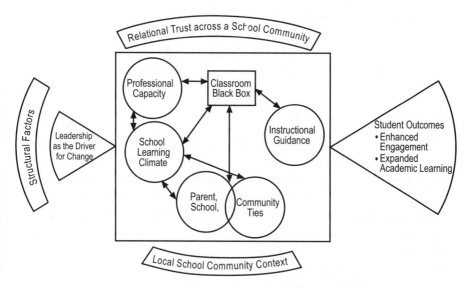

Figure 2.4. The larger school-community context for developing the essential supports for improvement.

facilitating factor, both for development of the essential supports and for promoting the relational trust on which the development depends.

Similarly, a stable student population can facilitate improvement efforts as well. It is not surprising that students who change schools frequently are academically disadvantaged.[84] Less well understood are the social consequences that sustained, high levels of student mobility can have on disrupting social networks, breaking down the natural flows of information, fomenting distrust, and weakening collective efficacy in disadvantaged school communities.[85] As a result, the necessary parent and community support for improvement efforts may not be forthcoming.

Last, we recognize in figure 2.4 the critical role played by the local community in a school's capacity to improve. In some neighborhoods, the stresses of poverty, crime, and other social problems simply make it more challenging to operate schools. When the density of these concerns is high and sustained, it can become very hard, in some cases nearly impossible, to maintain focus on the longer-term processes of school improvement. And the reverse is also true. Social resources in viable communities can contribute positively to school development. A dense network of vital institutions, such as churches and volunteer organizations, affords social capital between the school and community that can be appropriated for improvement purposes.

A more detailed theoretical account linking these contextual features to school improvement can be found in the opening sections of chapter 5 (trust, small school size, and enrollment stability) and chapter 6 (local school community context).

Measuring the Essential Supports

With its inception in 1990, the Consortium on Chicago School Research began building a comprehensive archive of survey items about schooling in Chicago. Through repeated use of these surveys, we have carefully honed items, analyzed their reliability and validity, and over time measured with increasing precision various aspects of the conceptual framework introduced above. In-depth field studies and firsthand experience with school change initiatives provided considerable insight and inspired many of the items and scales used here.[86] In addition, subsequent independent field studies created opportunities to validate further the survey measures, as observers compared our survey results to the events and conditions they were witnessing in schools.[87]

In evaluating this database, it is important to recognize that our framework was (and to some extent continues to be) a living document that evolved as new field evidence was brought to bear and attempts were made to capture emerging field-based concepts in a large-scale empirical system. As a result, by the time the natural experiment in school decentralization concluded, we had reliable measures for most, but not all, of the framework elements. In particular, no adequate measures were ever developed for either the managerial dimension of school leadership[88] or the school and community partnerships aspect of parent-community ties.[89]

Technical Details

Our statistical analyses draw primarily on surveys conducted in 1994, a point about halfway between the implementation of the decentralization reform in 1990–91 and the end of its first phase in the summer of 1996. Some aspects of the essential supports, however, were measured only in our 1991/1992 and 1997 surveys. In addition, some analyses in subsequent chapters examine changes over time from 1991 to 1994 and from 1994 to 1997 with linked survey data from two different years.[90] Since school organization tends to evolve slowly, we use the survey reports collected in 1997 as a proxy for the status of the essential supports in each school at the concluding time point in our analyses of changing academic productivity from 1990 to 1996.

We created a set of measures that sought to capture the degree to which the essential supports developed in Chicago elementary schools. Our analyses draw on 205 survey questions asked of teachers, 70 asked of students, and 8 asked of principals. From these 283 survey items, we created 36 different measures of the various elements within the essential supports framework. The teacher and student data were each averaged at the school level to create measures of some particular organizational element.

Finally, to achieve some parsimony in representing the empirical evidence collected in this study, we carried out a number of factor analyses that allowed us to combine some individual measures into factors. This process yielded ten composite indicators. We added to this four individual or "stand-alone" measures, arriving at a final set of fourteen overall indicators for charting organizational development in each school.

An Overview of Fourteen Indicators for the Five Organizational Subsystems

We offer below a brief description of each measure (highlighted in italics) and how we combined them to form the core indicators of school organization (highlighted in bold and italics). See appendix C for further details about the content of measures developed for each organizational subsystem. Details about the psychometric properties of these measures at both the individual and the school level can be found at the Web site in *Survey Measures, Factors, Composite Variables, and Items used in Organizing Schools for Improvement:* http://www.ccsr.uchicago.edu/publications/measures_in_ organizing_schools.pdf.

School leadership. We developed three measures apiece for the inclusive-facilitative and instructional leadership dimensions of this subsystem. One measure, *inclusive principal leadership,* focuses on principals' efforts in reaching out to faculty and encouraging parent and community involvement. A second measure directly assesses the extent of *teacher influence* across a range of local school decisions. Similarly, the third measure, *LSC contribution,* examines the degree of parent and community influence on improvement efforts through their Local School Council. As expected, these survey reports clustered strongly. This is consistent with our field observations that inclusive principal leaders nurtured meaningful engagement among teachers, parents, and community members in local school improvement.

The three measures for the instructional leadership dimension were anchored in teachers' assessments of their principal's initiatives in setting high academic standards, visiting classrooms, and other activities directly associated with instruction (*principal instructional leadership*). This measure is further supplement with a measure of *program coherence*, which focuses on the implementation of new school programs and the integration and coordination of instructional programs and services within the school. Finally, the third measure in this domain, *SIP implementation*, assesses whether the school improvement plan developed by the LSC was a living, guiding document for local reform or just "shelf ware."

For most of our analyses, we combined these six measures of inclusive and instructional leadership into an overall composite indicator that we simply termed **School Leadership.**

Parent-community-school ties. The first three measures in this domain focus on teachers' *knowledge of the community*, the depth of their *personal ties to the community*, and their *use of community resources* in their instruction. The survey items of which these measures are comprised focus on teacher reports as to how knowledgeable they are about issues in their local school community, how much time they actually spend out in the community, and whether they try to use various institutions, people, and concerns from the community in their instruction. We combined these three measures into a composite indicator of **Teachers' Ties to the Community.**

The second composite indicator in this domain, **Parent Involvement,** is composed of two measures: *teachers' outreach to parents* and *parent involvement in the school.* The first of these focuses on the proactive efforts of teachers to invite parents into their classroom, understand parental concerns, and embrace parents as partners in their children's education. The second measure focuses on the extent to which parents reciprocate by being involved in school activities and responding to specific concerns that teachers may raise about their child's schoolwork. Both of these are based on teacher survey reports aggregated to the school level.

Professional capacity. This was the most extensively measured subsystem within our framework. Some thirteen measures eventually formed six overall indicators for this domain. The composite indicator of **Teacher Background** was formed from two measures, teachers' *cosmopolitan experience* and the *quality of the undergraduate institution* that they attended. The latter, based on multiple sources of data about the selectivity of a teacher's undergraduate institution, is a proxy for the individual teacher's overall academic background. This was then averaged across teachers to form a school-level indicator. The cosmopolitan measure focuses on the extent to which teachers bring a diverse set of experiences into the classroom. Its formation was motivated by earlier research that described a troublesome phenomenon in Chicago, in which poorly educated CPS graduates attended weak undergraduate institutions in Chicago and then return to teach in the CPS.[91] Teachers who had experience in private schools or schools out-side Chicago were characterized as "cosmopolitan," and the proportion of those within a school became our organizational measure.

Our next two indicators in this domain, the *Frequency of Professional Development* and the *Quality of Professional Development,* were directly measured from teacher reports about the extensiveness of their partici-pation in such activities and the degree to which these activities formed coherent, sustained programs relevant to local improvement efforts. An-other indicator drew on principal reports about their capacity to hire quality teachers and remove problematic teachers, and the intensity with which they pursued both of these activities during the initiation of re-form in Chicago. In our earlier volume, we had identified such school-based *Changes in Human Resources* as a leading indicator of systemic school improvement.[92]

The normative dispositions element was operationalized in two mea-sures of teachers' orientation toward *innovation* and *school commitment.* These teacher survey responses capture critical aspects of teachers' will-ingness to try out new instructional practices in their classrooms, main-tain a "can-do" attitude, and internalize responsibility for improving their school. We combined these two measures into an overall indicator called *Work Orientation.*

Finally, the concept of school-based *Professional Community* was cap-tured in six separate measures that combined to form one overall compos-ite indicator by the same name. Four of the measures focus on specific prac-tices: *public classroom practice,* where teachers observe one another and offer suggestions for improvement; *reflective dialogue,* where teachers engage in critical conversations with one another about the improvement of instruc-tional practice; *peer collaboration,* where teachers work together on develop-ing curriculum and other school improvement activities; and *new teacher socialization,* where faculty are proactive in supporting new members and incorporating them into the school community. The final two measures in this domain consist of a set of teacher survey items that probe whether teachers embrace a *collective responsibility* for school improvement, with a specific focus on *student learning.* This combination of norms influences how teachers enact their daily instruction and engage with colleagues in the four work practices enumerated above.

Student-centered learning climate. The safety and order element in this domain was assessed with two measures: student reports about their perceived *safety* in and around school, and data from teachers on the incidence of *classroom disruptions* due to student misbehavior and other events. We combined these two measures into an overall indicator of *Safety and Order.*

The next two survey measures are based on student reports about the *press toward academic achievement in their classrooms* and whether this is coupled with the personal support from teachers that students need in order to succeed at this academic work (*classroom personalism*). Students were asked a variety of questions about whether teachers press them to work hard and do their homework, and whether teachers notice when they are having trouble and can be counted on to help. Together these items provide a window into the nature of teacher norms toward student instruction at the school. The next three measures—*classroom behavior, academic engagement,* and *peer support for academic work*—focus on the presence of supportive school norms among peers. Students were asked questions such as how often students make fun of their classmates, disrupt one another, and work hard at getting good grades. While teacher and peer norms are conceptually distinct elements within a student-centered learning climate, the five measures described above loaded together as one dimension in our factor analyses. For this reason, we combined these five measures into one overall indicator of *Academic Support and Press.*[93]

Instructional guidance. The nature of the school's curriculum content map—the subject matter that students are exposed to as they move across grades—constitutes the first element in this subsystem. We were able to develop a school indicator based on teacher reports about the content emphases in their mathematics instruction. At each grade level, we asked teachers how much time they spent teaching some fifty-four possible topics in mathematics during the school year, ranging from simple arithmetic to algebraic equations involving two unknowns. By combining this information across teachers at various grade levels within a school, we could assess the pacing with which new topics were introduced into the curriculum at that school. We then compared this to a content analysis of the subject matter demand (and how this varied by grade level) in the standardized mathematics tests used by the CPS. Taken together, these data provided us with an overall indicator that we called *Curriculum Alignment.*

The last elements in our indicator system focus on the instructional emphases in a school's curriculum and the related pedagogical methods used to advance this. While each teacher regularly makes decisions about these within his or her classroom, the decisions are structured by the set of available school resources and accountability press (if present).[94] To operationalize this combination of resources and pressure, we chose to aggregate information from teachers' reports about their instruction in both reading and mathematics and the extent to which they emphasized basic skills and/or applications work in their classroom. We developed four measures—two each in math and language arts—based on teachers' reports about the nature of their assignments (such as completing worksheets versus longer-term projects), classroom pedagogies employed (such as extensive teacher lectures versus facilitated classroom discussions), and the types of student assessments used (such as reliance on standardized tests versus analysis of students' written work products from project-based activities). Two of the measures combined survey reports to assess the degree of didactic teaching with a basic skills emphasis in the school, and the other two focused on students' active engagement in tasks that required applications of knowledge. We eventually combined these four measures from language arts and mathematics into two overall indicators of the school's *didactic teaching focus on basic skills* and *active student applications emphasis.* In subsequent chapters we refer to these simply as a *Basic Skills* and *Applications Emphasis.*

Hancock and Alexander: Substantial Differences on the Organizational Indicators

Recall from the prologue that the Hancock and Alexander schools followed different change trajectories and accumulated different trends in reading and mathematics achievement, with Hancock students substantially outperforming their counterparts at Alexander by the end of our study. Figure 2.5 compares these two schools on our fourteen organizational indicators. These statistical data are consistent with field accounts that document substantial differences in school leadership and in the depth and scope of organizational improvements.

On school leadership, Hancock was at the 99th percentile among the elementary schools surveyed in 1994; Alexander stood at the 20th. On parent

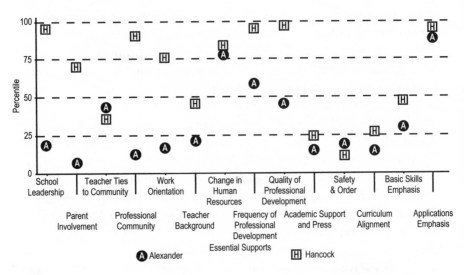

Figure 2.5. Percentile rank of essential support variables for Hancock and Alexander Elementary Schools. Note: Most essential support indicators are based on 1994 data, but Change in Human Resources is from 1992, and Teacher Ties to Community, Teacher Background, and Quality of Professional Development are from 1997.

involvement, Hancock scored at about the 65th percentile, while Alexander was at the 6th. Teachers' ratings put Hancock at about the 85th percentile on professional community, while Alexander was only at the 12th. Hancock also significantly outscored Alexander on teacher work orientation, teacher background, and the frequency and quality of professional development. Although Hancock was a bit stronger with respect to academic support and press for students, both schools struggled with their school learning climates. This is not surprising, given the relatively high crime rates and other community problems in their respective neighborhoods.

Regarding instruction, Hancock appeared somewhat stronger on the alignment of its mathematics curriculum. Interestingly, both schools reported an emphasis on instructional applications in enacting their curriculum. Hancock, however, coupled this press toward engaging instruction with sustained attention to basic skills development. In contrast, the reports from Alexander were relatively weak on the basic skills indicator. These results provide our first glimpse at a relatively complex pattern of relationships, which unfold over the next two chapters, regarding these two pedagogic indicators.

Taken overall, these organizational data suggest large, broad-based differences between these two schools halfway through reform. (We find similar reports on only four of the fourteen indicators—teacher ties to the community, academic support and press, safety and order, and applications emphasis.) Even without knowledge of corroborating field accounts from these two schools, the statistical data alone suggest very different organizational developments.

TABLE 2.1. Interrelationships among the Essential Supports

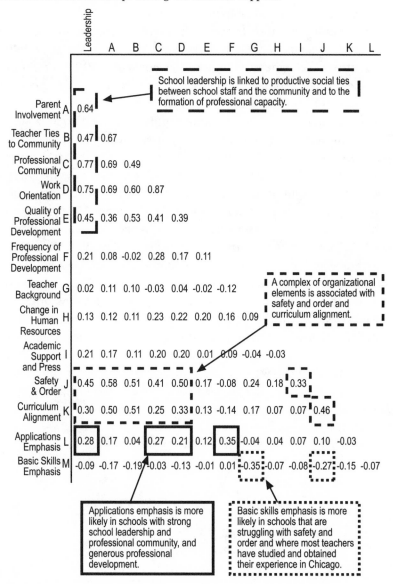

School leadership is linked to productive social ties between school staff and the community and to the formation of professional capacity.

A complex of organizational elements is associated with safety and order and curriculum alignment.

Applications emphasis is more likely in schools with strong school leadership and professional community, and generous professional development.

Basic skills emphasis is more likely in schools that are struggling with safety and order and where most teachers have studied and obtained their experience in Chicago.

	Leadership	A	B	C	D	E	F	G	H	I	J	K	L
Parent Involvement A		0.64											
Teacher Ties to Community B		0.47	0.67										
Professional Community C		0.77	0.69	0.49									
Work Orientation D		0.75	0.69	0.60	0.87								
Quality of Professional Development E		0.45	0.36	0.53	0.41	0.39							
Frequency of Professional Development F		0.21	0.08	-0.02	0.28	0.17	0.11						
Teacher Background G		0.02	0.11	0.10	-0.03	0.04	-0.02	-0.12					
Change in Human Resources H		0.13	0.12	0.11	0.23	0.22	0.20	0.16	0.09				
Academic Support and Press I		0.21	0.17	0.11	0.20	0.20	0.01	0.09	-0.04	-0.03			
Safety & Order J		0.45	0.58	0.51	0.41	0.50	0.17	-0.08	0.24	0.18	0.33		
Curriculum Alignment K		0.30	0.50	0.51	0.25	0.33	0.13	-0.14	0.17	0.07	0.07	0.46	
Applications Emphasis L		0.28	0.17	0.04	0.27	0.21	0.12	0.35	-0.04	0.04	0.07	0.10	-0.03
Basic Skills Emphasis M		-0.09	-0.17	-0.19	-0.03	-0.13	-0.01	0.01	-0.35	-0.07	-0.08	-0.27	-0.15	-0.07

The Essential Supports as Mutually Reinforcing:
Our First Statistical Evidence

Our comparison of the school improvement indicators from Hancock and Alexander is also consistent with a key theoretical claim that the organizational subsystems of a school are mutually reinforcing and operate in tandem to improve student learning. These systemic interconnections are also documented in the simple correlations among the fourteen organizational indicators in the full analytic school sample.

Table 2.1 draws attention to the most salient interrelationships among our fourteen organizational indicators. Local leadership is clearly linked to productive developments among the school staff and the community and to the formation of professional capacity. (Notice the strong correlations of school leadership with the next four indicators outlined in the box at the top of the table.) Similarly, a complex of several organizational elements—local leadership, parent involvement, teacher ties to community, professional community, work orientation, and academic support and press—is associated with safety and order and curriculum alignment (see the boxes to the right of rows J and K). Moreover, different instructional emphases are associated with distinct school conditions, although the relationships observed here are somewhat weaker. An active applications focus is more likely in schools with strong local leadership and professional community, and generous professional development (correlations highlighted in three boxes in row L). On the other hand, a didactic basic skills emphasis is more common in schools that are struggling with safety and order and where most teachers neither attended college nor had teaching experience outside Chicago (the negative relationship to the teacher background indicators highlighted in two boxes in row M). It is useful to bear these interrelationships in mind as we move on in subsequent chapters to investigate the linkages between the essential supports and improvements in student engagement and learning.

CHAPTER 3 TESTING THE FRAMEWORK OF THE ESSENTIAL SUPPORTS

We argued in the previous chapter that a *system* of five organizational elements combine to *support* improvements in student learning. *School leadership* functions as the driver, directing attention to strengthening the *ties among school professionals, parents, and the local community* and to expanding the *professional capacity* of the school's faculty to advance student learning. All adults within the school community share responsibility for fostering a *student-centered learning climate* that promotes pupils' engagement with more challenging academic work in the classroom, with these studies being scaffolded by a coherent schoolwide *instructional guidance system*.

We first described each of these organizational elements as *supports* to signify that, while all these elements may not directly cause student outcomes, their presence makes the attainment of valued student outcomes much more likely.[1] Taken together, these five organizational elements create conditions that substantially influence the dynamics of teaching and learning in classrooms, and ultimately student achievement. Thus, we would expect to find that contexts rich in one or more of these resources demonstrate an enhanced likelihood of improvements in student engagement and learning.

Second, in characterizing each of these supports as *essential*, we imposed a considerably stiffer criterion than simply being helpful to or facilitating improvement in a school. Specifically, if strength in each of these organizational elements is truly essential, as we have claimed, then the presence of a sustained material weakness in any one of them implies that meaningful school improvement would be extremely unlikely. This chapter presents our initial look at the evidence warranting this claim.

Third, the argument that these five organizational elements form a *system* of supports has direct analytic implications. A systems perspective implies that the five essential elements interact strongly with one another (we presented our first evidence of this in the closing section of the previous chapter). As a result, a material weakness in any one element should greatly reduce the likelihood of strengths in the other four supports. We will examine this claim as well in the pages ahead.

As a whole, this theoretical perspective of multiple, interacting, and mutually reinforcing (or, sometimes, mutually undermining) organizational elements posed novel questions about methods of analysis. Quite simply, what constitutes appropriate empirical evidence for examining a claim that *system of essential supports* undergirds school improvement? The standard "additive" statistical models that estimate the net effects of each element, controlling for all the others, seemed not especially helpful. It makes little sense, for example, to ask, "What is the effect of professional capacity, holding leadership constant?" since improving professional capacity is a key aim of leadership. Similarly, as professional capacity improves, the effectiveness of efforts to enhance parental engagement should also improve. And, the reverse is true as well. It is easier to assemble and maintain a quality staff in a context where professionals' work is supported by parents and the local community. Moreover, even the capacity of leadership can increase over time as a result of improvements in the other four essential supports. Successful initial efforts at school change not only expand the agency of individual leaders on subsequent initiatives—these leaders may also now access more human and social resources across the school community.

The organization of this chapter and the one that follows form a kind of analytic spiral. Using a large longitudinal database, we probe progressively deeper into the logic of a system of essential supports for school improvement. Both the nature of the theoretical framework and the expansiveness of our evidence base made for an extraordinarily complex undertaking. In the end, this work proved quite different from most applied quantitative social science inquiry in which we have previously engaged. Typically, the research question has been straightforward, such as "What is the relative effectiveness of public versus private schools?" but the methods of analysis might be quite complex. In contrast, our theoretical framework poses a complex, interrelated set of propositions for which we could discern no single best analytic model. Instead, we sought a myriad of smaller interrelated tests of the nomological web formed by our conceptual framework. Although the methods that we use below are often quite simple, considerable complexity resides in assessing the adequacy of the resultant body of evidence as a test for the theoretical arguments that we have offered.[2]

A Simple First Question: What Is the Evidence That Each Organizational Element Actually Supports Improvements in Student Outcomes?

As detailed in chapter 2, we developed 36 separate organizational measures on each school, which we subsequently combined into 14 overall indicators of the five essential supports. We now seek to examine the relationships between these indicators and (1) observed improvements in students' engagement with school and (2) changes in student learning in reading and mathematics. Even at this level of summarizing a school's organizational capacity (that is, the 14 indicators), the pattern of evidence quickly becomes complex and can easily feel overwhelming. In working our way into this evidence base, we have chosen first to consider in this chapter a core set of five of these indicators, one for each essential support. (We expand our inquiry in chapter 4 to consider in more detail the full set of 14.) Our selection of these five core indicators was based on the following criteria: each indicator was measured in both 1994 and 1997; each had high measurement reliability; and each reflected a general pattern of relationships with student outcomes that exists within the fuller set of fourteen indicators.[3] Table 3.1 provides summary information about the composition of the five core indicators. Further details can be found in chapter 2 and appendix C. In the analyses presented below, we use the organizational data only from 1994.[4]

Recall from chapter 1 that we categorized schools as "improving" or "stagnant" based on their membership in the top or bottom quartile on their adjusted seven-year attendance trend and on their productivity trends in reading and mathematics over the same period. Given this simple descriptive classification, each school has an expected probability of improvement (and of stagnation) of 0.25 just by chance alone. That is, if we simply selected a school at random, absent any real knowledge about it, the likelihood that this school would show substantial improvements (or stagnation) between 1990 and 1996 was 1 in 4.

We use this fact as a core consideration in most of the analyses described below. Specifically, if an organizational element truly supports improvement, we would expect to find that a strength or weakness on an indicator for this element differentiates between schools in the observed rates of improvement and stagnation on our three student outcome trends.

TABLE 3.1. Core indicators for the five essential supports

Essential Support	Core indicators
School Leadership	**Leadership composite:**
	Inclusive leadership—degree to which teachers viewed their principal as an inclusive, facilitative leader, focused on parent and community involvement and creating a sense of community in the school.
	Instructional leadership—degree to which teachers viewed their principal as setting high standards and exercising leadership for instructional reform.
	Teacher influence—a measure of the extent of teachers' involvement in school decision making.
	LSC contribution—teachers' ratings of the effectiveness of the Local School Council.
	Program coherence—teachers' reports about the quality of implementation and coordination of programs within the school.
	SIP implementation—teachers' evaluations of the school improvement plan and its centrality to the school's efforts to improve student learning.
Parent-Community Ties	**Parent Involvement composite:**
	Teacher outreach to parents—teachers' assessments of their efforts to develop common goals and understandings with parents and work together to strengthen student learning.
	Parent involvement in the school—teachers' reports about how regularly parents pick up report cards, attend parent-teacher conferences, attend school events, and other activities.
Professional Capacity	**Work Orientation composite:**
	Teacher orientation toward innovation—teachers' assessments about whether their colleagues are continually learning, seeking new ideas, and have a can-do attitude.
	School commitment—teachers' reports of how loyal and committed they are to the school.
Student-Centered Learning Climate	**Safety and Order composite:**
	Safety—students' perceptions of personal safety inside and outside the school and traveling to and from the school.
	Classroom disruptions—teachers' reports of disruptions due to students' behavior and administrative interruptions.
Instructional Guidance	**Curriculum Alignment measure:**
	Assesses the pace with which new math content is introduced into the school's curriculum across the elementary grades and how well this aligns with established grade-level skills and knowledge.

Predicting Improvement

Our first look at the evidence of the supportive role played by each organizational element in advancing school improvement is displayed in figure 3.1. We categorized schools as strong on an essential support if they placed among the top quartile of Chicago elementary schools based on the 1994 survey data for that core indicator. Similarly, schools ranked in the bottom quartile on a core indicator in 1994 were classified as weak on that essential support.[5] Key here is the extent to which a reported strength or weakness in an organizational support alters our predictions about the likelihood of improvement in attendance, reading, and math from the chance level of 1 in 4, or 25 percent. The black bars in figure 3.1 illustrate the results for schools strong on an essential support; the white bars, those that are weak.

Notice that all the white bars fall well below the 25-percent reference line. This means that a reported weakness in any of the five core organizational indicators substantially reduces the probability of improvement to below the chance level. The likelihood of improvement in both reading and mathematics was especially low among schools that were weak in school leadership, parent involvement, teacher work orientation, or curriculum alignment. Only 11 percent of schools weak on the school leadership indicator improved substantially in reading, only 10 percent weak on the parent involvement indicator improved, and the same was true for just 9 percent of the schools weak on teacher work orientation. The comparable results for mathematics—6, 4, and 9 percent, respectively—were even more pronounced.

A similar pattern of effects, although weaker in magnitude, occurs for the attendance trend outcome. The most distinct differentiation among schools on this outcome is associated with the safety and order indicator. Only 11 percent of the schools weak on this indicator (in other words, 1 in 9) showed improvement in attendance over the seven-year period of our study.

Correspondingly, the black bars in figure 3.1 indicate the probability of improvement in student outcomes among schools having a strong report on each of the organization indicators measured in 1994. All these bars exceed the 25-percent reference line for both the reading and the mathematics outcomes. A reported strength on any single core indicator substantially elevates the probability of improvement.[6] For example, 40 percent of the schools with strong parent involvement improved substantially in reading, and 42 percent improved in math. Comparable results

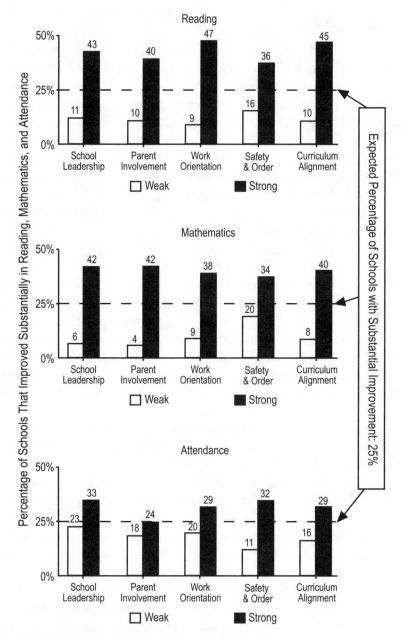

Figure 3.1. Likelihood of substantial improvements in reading, mathematics, and attendance, given weak or strong essential supports.

occurred for the school leadership, work orientation, safety, and curriculum alignment indicators. A similar although weaker pattern of associations appears for the attendance outcome trend. The only exception is the parent involvement indicator, where a reported strength does not appear to enhance the likelihood of substantial improvement in attendance.

A comparison of the relative lengths of the white and black bars is especially informative. The differences seen here reflect each indicator's capacity to differentiate a school's likelihood of improvement based on the school's score on that single indicator. In general, a school having a strong report on any one of the five core indicators is typically four to five times more likely to demonstrate substantial improvement in reading and mathematics than a school whose survey report locates it among the bottom quartile of schools on that same indicator. These differences are especially striking in several cases. For example, the probability of substantial improvement in math is seven times higher among schools with strong school leadership than among those with weak leadership (42 percent, compared with 6 percent). Similarly, schools strong on parent involvement are ten times more likely to improve in mathematics.

Although the differentiation capacity of the core indicators for the attendance trend outcome is not as strong, the likelihood of attendance improvement was still typically 50- to 100-percent higher among schools having strong reports as compared with schools having weak indicator data. We suspect that these weaker results are associated with the fact that the attendance trend is subject to a "ceiling effect."[7] As noted earlier, it is difficult for any school to maintain an attendance level much higher than about 95 percent. Since a significant portion of our schools began relatively near this threshold, their capacity to demonstrate improvement was constrained, which in turn limits the differentiating capacity of the core indicators considered here.[8]

Even so, we observe a noteworthy difference as we compare results across the three outcome measures. The safety and order indicator shows the weakest differentiating effect for reading and mathematics improvement; however, it demonstrates the strongest relationship for improving attendance. Only 1 in 9 schools having a weak safety and order report improved attendance; in contrast, schools having a strong report were three times more likely to improve.

Embedded here is our first evidence that the essential supports for improving students' engagement with schooling (as indicated by the attendance trend outcome) might function somewhat differently from the way they do for improvements in academic productivity. Institutional safety and order is the most basic prerequisite for students' academic participation. Unfortunately, this sense of safety is not characteristic of all urban schools. Its absence provides a good reason for students not to attend school. In contrast, while a safe and orderly environment is also a basic requirement for student learning, advancing gains in learning makes more expansive demands on a school's organization. We return to this consideration in chapter 4, where we probe further into possible differences in the organizational mechanisms yielding improvements across our three outcomes.

Exploring Stagnation

Complementing our examination of the likelihood of school improvement, we now shift to consider whether a weakness in the organizational supports predicts stagnation. That is, to what extent does a weakness on one of our core indicators differentiate between the stagnant and non-stagnant schools identified in chapter 1? In principle, the indicator patterns for predicting stagnation may be somewhat different from those for predicting improvement. It is quite possible that a material weakness in an organizational support could foster stagnation, while great strength in that support might not contribute much to the actual improvements recorded by our top quartile of schools.

In general, we find corroboration here for the significant role played by all five of the organizational supports. Schools having a weak report on any one of the five indicators are at least two times more likely to stagnate in reading and mathematics than schools having strong indicator reports. (Figure 3.2 displays this evidence.) The probability of stagnation is substantially elevated in schools having a weak report on school leadership; these were four times more likely to stagnate in both reading and mathematics. Similarly, weak reports on work orientation were four times more likely in schools with stagnant reading trends and three and a half times more likely in schools stagnant on the mathematics outcome.

In considering the attendance trend outcomes, we find that the organizational indicators differentiate more sharply in predicting stagnation than we saw previously in predicting improvement. A weakness in a school report on work orientation, parent involvement, or curriculum alignment, for example, more than doubles the probability of stagnation. Especially noteworthy is the association of safety and order problems with attendance stagnation. One out of every two schools having a weak report on safety and order in 1994 stagnated on attendance. In contrast, only one out

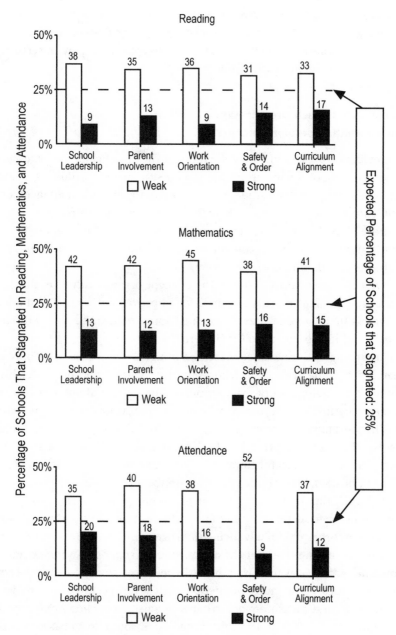

Figure 3.2. Likelihood of stagnation in reading, mathematics, and attendance, given weak or strong essential supports.

of eleven schools having a strong safety and order report remained in this category. These results provide further corroboration of the significant role that a safe, orderly, student-centered climate appears to play in securing student engagement in schooling.

Question 2: Is Each Organizational Element Truly Essential for Improvement?

The evidence presented so far documents the significant role that core aspects of school organization can play in supporting (and/or impeding) improvements in valued student outcomes. Gains in student engagement and learning are much more likely in schools displaying strengths in one or more of the five organizational supports. Moreover, the corollary is also true: a significant weakness on one or more of the indicators substantially increases the likelihood of stagnation.

We now move on to examine the concept of *essentiality*. If each organizational element is truly essential for improvement, then a sustained weakness in any one of these elements should reduce the probability of substantial improvement to nearly zero.

Returning to the evidence presented in figure 3.1, we see that approximately 5 to 10 percent of the schools having a weak report on leadership, parent involvement, work orientation, or curriculum alignment still recorded a significant improvement in either reading or math productivity. This improvement rate rises to almost 1 in 5 for the safety and order indicator. For the attendance trend, only 1 in 9 schools with a weakness on the safety and order indicator improved. The improvement rates for the four other indicators, however, ranged from 16 to 23 percent.

This raises an interesting question about how strong the statistical evidence must be to sustain a claim that an organizational support is essential versus merely helpful for advancing improvement. Because of imprecision in both the measurement of the organizational supports and the student outcome indices, it is unreasonable to expect perfect agreement between these statistics. Some faulty predictions will surely occur in our analyses by virtue of these measurement artifacts. That is, some schools may appear to improve that we would not have predicted would do so based on our extant organizational evidence. Exactly how many such misclassification we might reasonably expect becomes critical for judging the statistical evidence assembled so far.

In general, three major sources of error are present in our measurement system. First, there is measurement unreliability associated with both the organizational indicators and the student outcome trends. Although considerable care was taken in developing each measure, they are nonetheless fallible statistics. Second, the analyses presented above are based on five core indicators rather than comprehensive measures of each essential support. Even if each organizational indicator were perfectly reliable, we would still expect some misclassification error due to underrepresentation of the organizational construct by a single indicator. To be precise, our hypothesis of essentiality is posed for the organizational constructs (for example, the role of the instructional guidance system in affecting reading improvement), and not for the observed indicators of these constructs (for example, how the curriculum alignment measure relates to the reading productivity trend index). Third, the dynamic nature of school development introduces still another source of error. The results presented above are from a single survey administered partway through a seven-year change process. As such, this evidence provides a single, narrow window onto a long-term local school reform initiative that may have spurts, plateaus, and even reversals. Temporal instability in underlying change processes may contribute some additional faulty predictions. Taken together, these factors provide multiple, independent reasons why a small proportion of schools might appear to improve where our theory would not predict them to do so.

To assess the likely effects of the first factor, indicator unreliability, we used information that we had developed about our measures' psychometric properties to estimate the likely misclassification rates in the data system due to this source of error.[9] For the purpose of this analysis we were conservative and used a relatively high overall estimate of reliability of 0.90 on a scale of 0 (no reliability) to 1.0 (perfect reliability) for both the organizational and the school improvement indicators. If we make some reasonable assumptions about the random nature of the measurement errors, we can construct a probability distribution around the underlying true score on each organizational and student outcome indicator, thereby deriving an estimate of the likelihood of a false negative occurring for that case. When aggregated, these error analyses suggest a plausible underlying misclassification rate of 4.2 percent due to errors of measurement in our school organization and productivity indicators.[10] As for possible misclassifications from construct underrepresentation by the indicator system, these are harder to assess empirically. It is reasonable to posit, however, that these validity errors might be at least as large as those associated with indicator unreliability. If this were the case, an overall estimated misclassification rate in the range of 8 to 9 percent would occur. Viewed against this standard, many of the observed results in figure 3.1 seem reasonably consistent with a claim of essentiality. Notice in this regard that the schools reporting weak leadership, work orientation, parent involvement, or curriculum alignment yet showing improvement in reading or mathematics all cluster closely around our estimated misclassification rate of 8 to 9 percent. One notable exception here is the safety and order indicator. In contrast, when we focus on the trend results for improving student attendance, it is this indicator where the most compelling results occurred. Only 11 percent of the schools weak on this core indicator improved, which is reasonably consistent with our estimated misclassification rate. However, the case for the other four core indicators predicting attendance improvement is less convincing. Even in schools where these other indicator reports are weak, about 20 percent still managed to improve.

Next, we considered the possible effects associated with the underlying temporal dynamics of school improvement. In principle, we would expect that this phenomenon would just add to the observed misclassification rates. As noted earlier, a school that appeared weak organizationally in 1994 could subsequently take off if, for example, a new principal was appointed. Similarly, another school may have started strong change efforts but then languished in subsequent years, when, for example, a leadership change undermined promising initial developments. In different ways, each of these scenarios would produce a misclassification in our prediction analyses. The organizational indicators could be perfectly accurate at the time gathered; they just do not stand in these cases as a good indicator for a long-term change process.

A full examination of the dynamics of school change would require even more fine-grained longitudinal data than those available to us. The best test that we could muster with the data at hand was to focus on the subset of schools having consistently weak reports on an essential support across the two separate survey administrations of 1994 and 1997. It is reasonable to assume that schools scoring in the bottom quartile on a core indicator at both occasions were likely to have been consistently weak on this support over the entire period from the fall of 1993 through the spring of 1997. If the support is truly essential, we should find a very low probability of improved student outcomes in this subsample of schools. Although the overall sample size for this analysis is relatively small, since schools had to participate in both the 1994 and the 1997 survey and score low on both occasions,[11] it is still instructive to consider what actually happened in the 20 or so schools where such survey data reports were recorded.

Figure 3.3 displays the results for this subset of schools.[12] Of 18 schools

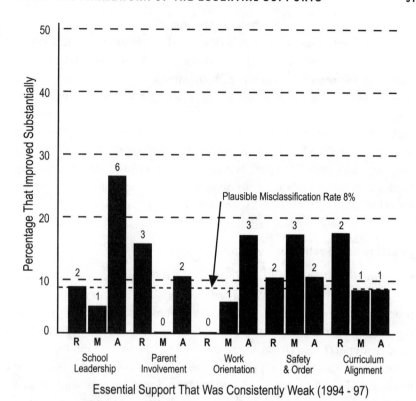

Figure 3.3. Percentage of schools consistently weak on an essential support indicator that demonstrated substantial improvement on a productivity indicator. Note: The number of schools is shown above each bar. R denotes reading; M, mathematics; A, attendance.

having chronically weak reports about teachers' work orientation, not one improved in reading. Of 19 schools where parent involvement reports were weak on both occasions, not a single school improved in math. In addition, only one school where reports about leadership or work orientation remained consistently weak showed improvement in mathematics.

For a more global summary of these results, we compared the overall improvement rates in figure 3.3 with those previously reported in figure 3.1. Of the 15 separate comparisons (5 indicators by 3 outcomes), 10 rates in figure 3.3 dropped relative to the comparable rate in figure 3.1, 3 increased, and 2 remained about the same. Although this is not an especially strong finding taken alone, it is another piece of evidence consistent with the essentiality argument. As one last test, we undertook a probability experiment to evaluate the overall pattern of results presented in figure 3.3. We again took a conservative stance and assumed in this experiment that the underlying misclassification rate due to all three sources (indicator unreliability, construct underrepresentation, and temporal instability) was 8 percent. We then calculated the probability distribution for the number of misclassifications that would be expected to occur under these conditions. The actual results presented in figure 3.3 are highly consistent with such a phenomenon. That is, the observed results, where a small number of schools appeared to improve under circumstances of a chronic weakness on an essential support indicator, could easily have occurred as a consequence of fallible measurement. (See appendix D for a complete description of this probability experiment and the statistical results.)

Question 3: A System of Supports?

We argued in chapter 2 that the five essential supports operate as a dynamic, interactive system. While initial efforts at school development may proceed along varied paths depending on base-state circumstances and resources, organizational strength must eventually emerge on all the essential supports for reform to culminate in improved student outcomes. From this perspective, a high-performing school should evidence at least a modicum of strength across all five organizational supports and certainly not demonstrate a material weakness in any one of them. In contrast, schools left behind by reform will likely display significant weaknesses across multiple elements. While organizational irregularity (such as genuine organization strength coexisting with a manifest weakness) may well characterize schools in transition, this is not a stable organizational state. The persistence of a clear weakness in any organizational element will eventually undermine whatever strengths might have been assembled elsewhere. For example, a school may do a terrific job at the outset of reform in strengthening its ties to parents and the local community. However, if the teachers' capacity to engage a more ambitious and coherent instructional program does not eventually emerge, this parental engagement will likely atrophy.

This line of reasoning suggests that we should not expect to find stable patterns of gross inconsistency across the five essential supports, where schools are very strong in some supports and very weak in others, and in fact we do not. Only 31 percent of the schools in the bottom quartile on at least one core indicator in 1994 were simultaneously in the top quartile on at least one other indicator. If the five organizational supports functioned independently, we would expect 68 percent of the schools weak on one indicator to show strength on some other indicator.[13] In short, the co-occurrence of strong and weak indicator reports represents a fraction of what we might otherwise have expected.[14] Moreover, it is important to remember that these data capture only a single snapshot from a seven-year developmental process. At any single point in time, significant reform may only be starting in some schools, which may well produce an organizational indicator report where both strengths and weaknesses coexist.

More significant than whether the indicator results simply cluster together is whether this clustering in turn predicts actual improvements in student outcomes. Up to this point, we have focused on the relationships between each separate organizational support and measured trends in student outcomes. Our framework, however, suggests that a school's capacity to improve derives from its *overall* organizational strength across all the essential supports. Therefore, we now look at cumulative effects associated with all five supports simultaneously.

For purposes of this analysis, we created an overall school organizational capacity score based on aggregating each school's data from the five core indicators of the essential supports.[15] Schools were credited with a +1 if they ranked in the top quartile on each indicator and a −1 if they ranked among the bottom 25 percent of the schools. An indicator report between the 25th and 75th percentiles was scored as 0 (neutral). We then aggregated these five indicator scores into an overall school organizational capacity measure. These overall scores ranged from −5 (weak on all five essential supports) to +5 (strong on all five supports). For the purpose of displaying these results, we have categorized schools as weak in most of the supports (scores of −5 to −3), weak in a few supports (−2 to −1), neutral (0), strong in a few supports (1 to 2), and strong in most supports (3 to 5).

The solid lines in figure 3.4 chart the percentage of schools that improved substantially in reading, mathematics, and attendance based on their overall strength across all supports as measured in 1994.[16] These data demonstrate the critical connection of the system of essential supports to improved student outcomes. Schools strong in most supports were at least ten times more likely than schools weak in most supports to show substantial gains in both reading and mathematics. Half the schools strong in most supports improved substantially in reading. Not a single school weak in most of the supports (that is, with organizational capacity scores of −5 to −3) showed substantial improvements in mathematics. As before, the essential supports demonstrate a weaker relationship with improvement in attendance, likely due to the ceiling effect on the attendance trend measure.

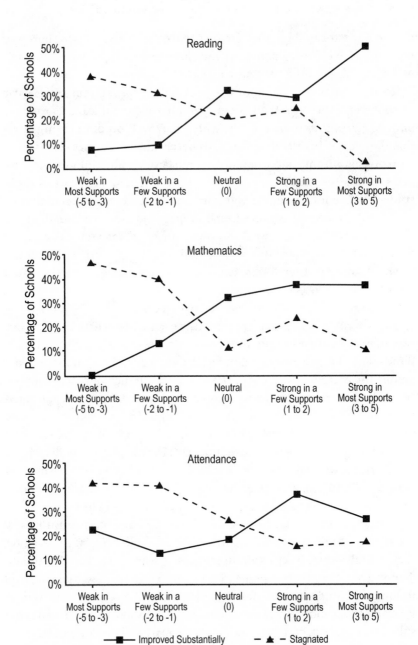

Figure 3.4. Percentage of schools that improved substantially or stagnated in reading, mathematics, and attendance by strength in the five essential supports.

Correspondingly, the dashed lines in figure 3.4 track the percentage of schools that were stagnant on each student outcome based on schools' overall organizational capacity score. The results for predicting stagnation in reading and mathematics mirror those for predicting substantial improvements. Schools weak in some or most supports were much more likely to stagnate than schools having neutral reports across the five supports. In contrast, schools with strengths across most of the supports were very unlikely to stagnate. Comparable results also occur for the attendance trend outcome. Paralleling what we found in examining the effects of individual indicators on stagnation in attendance, schools demonstrating weakness on most of the core indicators were three times more likely to stagnate than schools with strong overall organizational capacity scores.

The impact of strong organizational capacity appears particularly important for reading improvement. Half the schools strong on three or more essential supports improved substantially in reading; not a single school in this group stagnated over the seven-year period during which we conducted this research. In contrast, extensive weaknesses on the organizational supports seem more differentiating for mathematics. No school weak on three or more supports showed substantial gains in mathematics, and almost half these schools were stagnant. (Notice that the big differences in figure 3.4 are on the left-hand side for the mathematics panel and on the right-hand side for reading.)

Summing Up the Evidence and What It Means for Practice

In this chapter we have examined a broad array of statistical evidence on how a set of organizational elements combine to form a system of essential supports for improvements in student learning. Our analyses have relied on a small number of core indicators of the capacity of five distinct subsystems that constitute a school's organization. We found that schools having strong indicator reports were up to ten times more likely to improve students' reading and mathematics learning than those where one or more of these indicators were weak. Moreover, a low score on even just one indicator can reduce the likelihood of improvement to less than 10 percent. While the results linking our indicators of the essential supports to improvement in student engagement with schooling were somewhat weaker, the most powerful single finding present was the association of student attendance with school safety and order. Over half the schools reporting problems with safety and order on our surveys remained stagnant on student attendance from 1990 to 1996. This pattern of results suggests that school improvement may make somewhat different claims on organizational resources, depending on the particular outcome of concern. A more in-depth probing of this theme constitutes the central focus of the next chapter.

Taken together, the results presented here provide a strong warrant that all five of the organizational elements detailed in chapter 2 are critical for school improvement. We found that a sustained, material weakness in any one of these subsystems undermined virtually all attempts at improving student learning.

The inquiries presented in this chapter forced us to think explicitly about whether our empirical evidence supports the claim that the five organizational supports are truly essential. From the point of view of pure logic, statistical evidence can never warrant a claim of absolute certainty. Only a single contrary case—for example, one school with weak professional capacity that somehow managed to improve student learning— would falsify the proposition. Clearly, we have not offered such proof.

Even so, we would argue that the assembled evidence does warrant a claim of practical essentiality. As school districts think about the task of strategic planning for school improvement at scale and redesigning their central offices to support such work, our evidence does suggest that districts are highly unlikely to succeed absent sustained attention to all five of these organizational subsystems. We make a similar claim about the efforts of leaders at the school building level as they engage in the day-to-day work of promoting meaningful local change. School community leaders must direct attention to strengthening the ties among school professionals, parents, and the local community and to expanding the professional capacity of the school's faculty. Adults within the school community must join together to foster a student-centered learning climate that promotes pupils' engagement with more challenging academic work in classrooms. Finally and most important, a coherent schoolwide instructional guidance system must scaffold and integrate this collective academic activity. Strong evidence has been presented here that a sustained material weakness in any one of these domains is likely to doom efforts at improving student outcomes. In this sense, each element is an essential ingredient in the overall recipe for school improvement.

CHAPTER 4

**PROBING DEEPER:
ORGANIZATIONAL MECHANISMS**

In chapter 3 we presented an array of statistical results in examining our claim that five organizational supports are essential for school improvement. We also introduced a first round of evidence concerning the systemic nature of such improvements. These findings are consistent with the basic conceptual framework detailed in chapter 2, where we argued that an interrelated set of social subsystems influences students' participation in schooling and their academic learning. As a consequence of this systemic character of schools as organizations, efforts directed at improving productivity will typically entail coordinated progress on multiple fronts.

In this chapter, we probe more deeply into the nature of these systemic interconnections. To explore this phenomenon further, we move beyond the five core indicators used in chapter 3 to now consider the full set of 14 indicators previously introduced in chapter 2. Specifically, we expand our indicators of parent-community ties to include *teacher ties to the community,* which includes reports about teachers' knowledge of student culture and their use of community resources. In terms of a student-centered learning climate, we add an indicator of *academic support and press for achievement,* which combines survey data from students and teachers about both peer and teacher-student relations. With regard to the instructional guidance system, we include two additional indicators that focus on the *basic skills emphasis* and *applications emphasis* in classroom pedagogy and methods. The greatest expansion of indicators is for the professional capacity subsystem. Here we add two indicators that focus on the quality of human resources at the school. The first of these, *teacher background,* combines data on the quality of teachers' undergraduate experiences and the degree to which they bring a cosmopolitan orientation (that is, some experience outside the

Chicago public education sector) to their work. This is complemented by an index of the local *change in human resources* during the first three years of reform.[1] Two additional indicators focus on the *quality of professional development* and its *frequency* to support continuous adult learning at the school, and a final composite indicator, *professional community,* assesses the faculty's capacity to work together on improvement initiatives. (For further details on each of these indicators, see chapter 2 and appendix C.)

We begin this chapter by examining the interconnections among the four primary subsystems—parent and community involvement, professional capacity, student-centered learning climate, and instructional guidance—as they affect improvements in attendance and reading and mathematics learning. We then proceed to consider how school leadership, our fifth subsystem, functions as the catalyst for change in nurturing, guiding, and coordinating efforts to improve the other four core subsystems. As part of these latter analyses, we examine how both instructional and inclusive-facilitative leadership play significant, albeit somewhat different, roles in school improvement.

As in chapter 3, we focus on the likelihood of schools improving or stagnating and consider whether subsystem interactions operate somewhat differently in this regard.[2] We describe below a number of distinctive patterns of association among subsets of the organizational indicators that link strongly with improvement (or stagnation) in reading, mathematics, and attendance. Each of these indicator combinations provides a window into the actual functional relationships at work in school improvement—identifying core organizational mechanisms that shape both success and failure.

Our Approach to This Inquiry

Before proceeding to our substantive findings, we offer a few words about the overall analytic strategy that drove this inquiry. The results presented below emerged from an intensive data investigation. During the initial stages of this inquiry, we scrutinized an extensive array of possible combinatorial effects across the 14 indicators discussed above. We employed a number of exploratory analytic strategies at this point, most notably data mining through CHAID,[3] in an attempt to discern what our data suggested about the possible organizational interrelationships entailed in school improvement. Counterbalancing this initial broad-based exploration, we deliberately imposed a much more conservative stance during the second stage of our investigation as a safeguard against overinterpreting our preliminary findings. Specifically, we narrowed our attention to those effects that were large in size, where we had at least some evidence that they replicated in both the 1994 and the 1997 data[4] and for which we could offer a meaningful explanation about the likely mechanisms actually at work. This chapter summarizes what we have learned as a result.

The Organizational Mechanisms Influencing Attendance

For each of the 14 organizational indicators, figure 4.1 displays the percentage of schools that substantially improved in attendance, and the percentage that were stagnant in attendance. As in chapter 3, the expected percentage improvement or stagnation by chance alone is 25 percent.[5] To the extent that an organizational indicator predicts improvement or stagnation, the black bars (strong on the indicator) and white bars (weak on the indicator) deviate from the 25-percent chance reference line.

In general, the relationships documented in chapter 3 for the five core indicators extend to the full set of 14 presented here. Attendance trends are related to many of the separate, individual indicators, including safety and order, parent involvement, and measured aspects of the faculty's professional capacity and of the nature of the instructional guidance system. As in the results previously presented in chapter 3, our organizational indicators are more predictive of schools stagnating on attendance than those improving.[6] This is reflected in the fact that the bars in figure 4.2 are considerably longer than those in figure 4.1.

The two strongest individual indicators of attendance trends remain those previously introduced in chapter 3: safety and order and parent involvement. Over half the schools having poor reports on safety and order stagnated on attendance, while only one in nine improved.[7] Similarly, over 40 percent of the schools reporting weak parent-school ties stagnated on attendance. Such schools were twice as likely to stagnate as to improve. Of special note, the two organizational subsystems signified here, parent-community ties and a student-centered learning climate, appear strongly interconnected. As we saw previously in chapter 2 (see table 2.1), the strongest correlate of school safety and order is parent involvement. The magnitude of this association even exceeded that of school leadership with safety and order (0.58 versus 0.45). Manifest in this evidence is the importance of strong social ties among adults in a school community as basis for creating a supportive social order among students. We return to this theme in chapter 6, where we examine how the social context of the school's external community also comes into play in this regard.

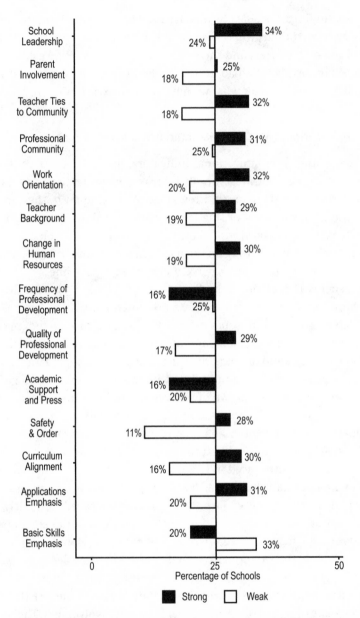

Figure 4.1. Percentage of schools that improved substantially in attendance by strength in the essential supports. Note: Most essential support indicators are based on 1994 data, but Change in Human Resources is from 1992, and Teacher Ties to Community, Teacher Background, and Quality of Professional Development are from 1997.

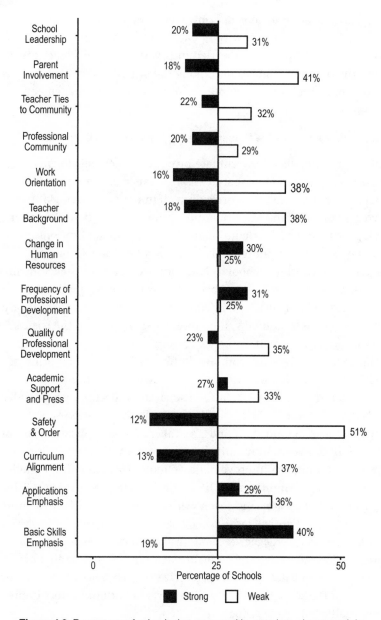

Figure 4.2. Percentage of schools that stagnated in attendance by strength in the essential supports. Note: Most essential support indicators are based on 1994 data, but Change in Human Resources is from 1992, and Teacher Ties to Community, Teacher Background, and Quality of Professional Development are from 1997.

We now move on to consider how trends in attendance improvement or stagnation may associate with strengths and/or weaknesses on *combinations* of the 14 indicators. Embedded in this statistical evidence are clues about how the interconnections among the organizational subsystems of a school may function to promote (or inhibit) student engagement.

Engaging Instruction: Active Student Roles in a Well-Paced Curriculum

While an unsafe, disorderly climate promotes absenteeism, engaging instruction encourages regular student attendance. All three of the instructional guidance indicators—curriculum alignment and basic skills and applications emphases in the curriculum—come into play here. Schools using a well-paced, aligned curriculum and deploying an applications-oriented pedagogy were much more likely to show significant improvements in attendance. In contrast, schools relying heavily on didactic teaching methods with constant repetition of basic skills worksheets, practice drills, and teacher-directed instruction tended to stagnate. Most significantly, these aspects of the instructional system interact strongly with the basic social order in the environment.

Figure 4.3 displays the combined effects of applications-oriented instruction and curriculum alignment on attendance improvement. For comparison, the relationship of each separate indicator with attendance trends is shown first, in the hashed bars. (The latter are the same data previously presented in figures 4.1 and 4.2.) Taken alone, applications-oriented instruction and curriculum alignment demonstrate only weak relationships with attendance improvement. Schools strong on either single indicator were only slightly more likely than average to improve. Schools strong on both indicators, however, were six times more likely to improve than to stagnate. *Over half the schools (55 percent) that reported extensive use of applications-oriented pedagogy combined with good curriculum alignment demonstrated substantial improvements in attendance.* A parallel finding emerged when we examined data patterns predictive of attendance stagnation. Only 8 percent of the schools having weak reports in both indicators improved substantially; half these schools stagnated.

Taken together, these results suggest that attendance is strongly affected by classroom practice. At base here lies an unproductive dynamic of instructional decision-making and chronic attendance problems. Poor attendance leads teachers to review material previously taught and to drill on basic skills rather than attempting more ambitious, and potentially more interesting, project work.[8] But this penchant for "getting the basics

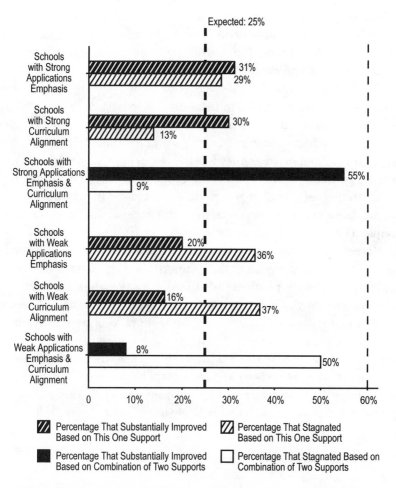

Figure 4.3. Improvement in attendance is supported by well-paced, applications-oriented instruction. Note: All indicators are from 1994, and cross-validated with data from 1997.

under control" often only exacerbates the problems of student disengagement and absenteeism.

From the students' perspective, when instruction becomes interesting and has personal meaning, they are motivated to attend. Students are more likely to be engaged in schools using an interesting curriculum, where they can take an active role in instructional activities and exercise some choice in their work as well as be regularly exposed to new problems and ideas through a well-paced set of courses. In contrast, didactic instruction, which typically places students in a passive role, can create a deadening experience, especially when combined with a "drill and kill" repetition of the same basic skills, over and over. Students' choice to exit is not irrational in the face of the extreme version of this instruction found in some urban classrooms.[9]

The strong relationships between instructional methods and attendance improvement revealed in these data are consistent with both basic research in the learning sciences and recent applied studies of student motivation and schooling. In general, we know that children are more engaged in schooling when they feel in control of their own learning, are actively participating in the learning process, are interested in the topic being studied, and are able to respond to the challenge before them. They are much less motivated by classes where they are cast in the role of passive recipients of knowledge to be delivered by the teacher.[10]

Moreover, didactic instruction places a heavy burden on teachers, as fostering student engagement falls primarily on their shoulders. Since all students are typically required to do the same work at the same time, there is less opportunity to build on students' individual interests and their intrinsic motivation associated with working on tasks of personal value. In contrast, applications-oriented instruction encourages engagement by providing some space where students can work actively with others and where each can guide at least some aspects of his or her own learning. Not surprisingly, then, in schools where such instruction is being advanced, improving attendance is also more likely to be found.

A Reinforcing Cycle When Safety and Order
Concerns Combine with Deadening Instruction

The consequences of deadening instruction are amplified when they co-occur in schools where safety and order issues prevail. We found virtually no chance of improving student attendance in schools that lacked safety and order *and* where instruction alignment was weak or predominantly basic-skills oriented (see figure 4.4). *Not a single school weak in both curriculum alignment and safety and order improved its attendance. Similarly, not a single school improved when weak on applications-oriented instruction and order. Parallel findings emerged when we examined schools emphasizing basic skills instruction and weak in safety and order.* Such schools were ten times more likely to stagnate than to improve. Overall, two-thirds of these schools failed to improve student attendance.

At base here is a complex organizational syndrome that occurs frequently in urban schools. Given the larger community context, concerns

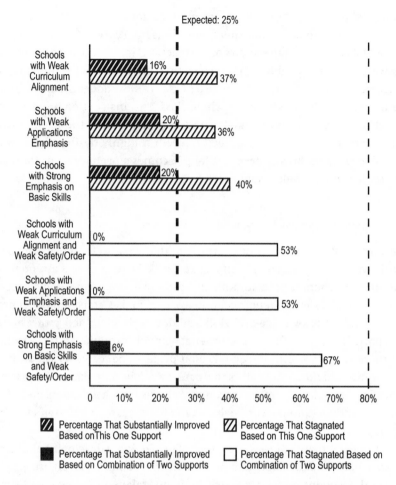

Figure 4.4. Attendance stagnation: An unsafe, disorderly climate coupled with repetitive basic-skills emphasis in instruction. Note: All indicators are from 1994.

about safety are never too far removed, even in schools which on the surface may seem quite orderly. Staff knows well from their experiences that their work environment can quickly spin out of control if constant vigilance is not maintained. A natural response, then, is to tightly control instruction: keep students quiet and working individually at their seats under firm teacher direction. From this perspective, individual project activity and group work only increase opportunities for the kinds of misbehavior about which teachers are deeply worried. On numerous occasions, we have heard this concern expressed as "My kids cannot do that kind of work." Unfortunately, such statements often have much more to do with teachers' concerns about classroom management than students' intellectual capability to undertake more ambitious instruction.[11]

Efforts to "tighten the screws on instruction" in the face of absenteeism, however understandable, can have negative consequences for students' engagement. A natural response by teachers is to slow down the curriculum and to reteach lessons with the whole class. This instructional repetition, however, only contributes further to the problem, and the whole social and instructional system can feed itself in a highly dysfunctional way. Helping teachers break out of this loop becomes a primary focus for quality professional development.

Developing Professional Capacity as a Key Antidote

Given this argument, it is not surprising that we also found that schools with weak professional capacity were unlikely to improve attendance. As noted in chapter 2, sustaining engaging instruction in disadvantaged school contexts is challenging adult work. It makes considerable claims on individual knowledge and skill and demands sustained professional support. Not surprisingly, student engagement atrophies in the absence of these resources. This dependence on professional capacity is manifest in several individual indicators in figure 4.2, including teachers' work orientation and educational background. Schools with a weakness on either indicator, for example, were twice as likely to stagnate on attendance as to improve.

Of special significance is the power of professional development in contexts where student safety and order concerns abound. (See figure 4.5.) In general, frequent professional development, taken on its own, had little predictive value with regard to attendance trends. Our second indicator, the quality of professional development, did demonstrate some modest individual association with attendance trends. Schools with poor-quality professional development were twice as likely to stagnate on attendance as schools with strong professional development. However, large, interocular effects (so big they hit you right between the eyes) became manifest when reports about safety and order problems occurred simultaneously with a lack of quality opportunities for professional improvement. *Attendance stagnated in two-thirds of the schools where serious safety and order issues combined with minimal access to professional development. To the point, not a single school with reports about poor-quality professional development and serious safety and order problems improved student attendance.*

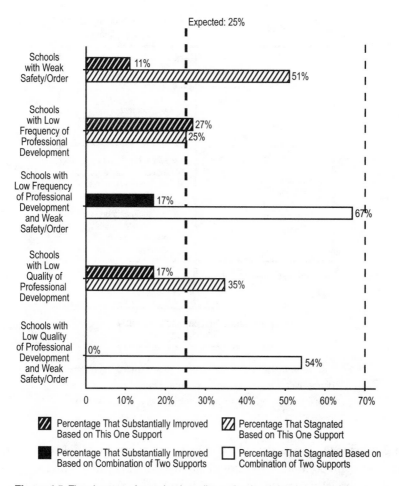

Figure 4.5. The absence of sustained, quality professional development: A key impediment to attendance improvement in schools with safety and order problems. Note: Combinations of supports are based on 1994 data, except for combinations involving Quality of Professional Development, which was only measured in 1997. Safety and Order was from 1997 when combined with Quality of Professional Development.

Pulling It All Together: How the Organization of Schools Influences
Efforts to Improve Student Engagement with Schooling

We summarize in figure 4.6 the basic functional relationships that influence student attendance. Strong parent-school ties create a core resource for maintaining safety and order within the school community. Combin-

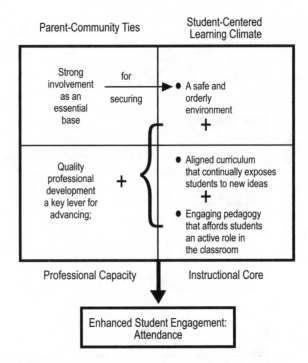

Figure 4.6. The organizational dynamics of improving attendance. Note: Horizontal arrow denotes implied causal connection; plus sign indicates implied subsystem interconnections.

ing this sense of security with an engaging curriculum yields an overall
environment conducive to student participation. Key to making all of this
work at the school level is high-quality professional development aimed at
enhancing teachers' capacity to orchestrate more engaging instructional
pedagogy under the very trying circumstances that most confront daily.
When this combination of organizational elements co-occurs, the basic
recipe for improving student engagement with schooling is activated.[12]

The Organizational Mechanisms Affecting Student Learning

Figures 4.7 through 4.10 display the percentage of schools that substantially improved and those that stagnated in their reading and math productivity trends across all 14 indicators of the essential supports. As seen
previously in figures 4.1 and 4.2, the chance association between an organizational indicator and improvement or stagnation is represented by the
25-percent reference line. Deviations from this line capture the degree to

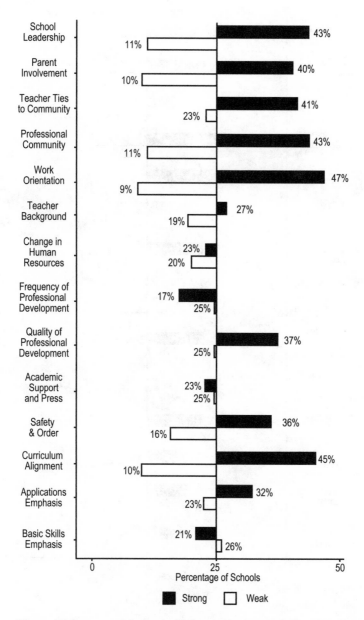

Figure 4.7. Percentage of schools that improved substantially in reading by strength in the essential supports. Note: Most essential support indicators are based on 1994 data, but Change in Human Resources is from 1992, and Teacher Ties to Community, Teacher Background, and Quality of Professional Development are from 1997.

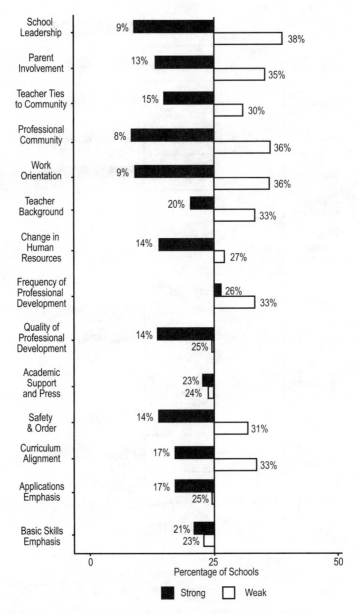

Figure 4.8. Percentage of schools that stagnated in reading by strength in the essential supports. Note: Most essential support indicators are based on 1994 data, but Change in Human Resources is from 1992, and Teacher Ties to Community, Teacher Background, and Quality of Professional Development are from 1997.

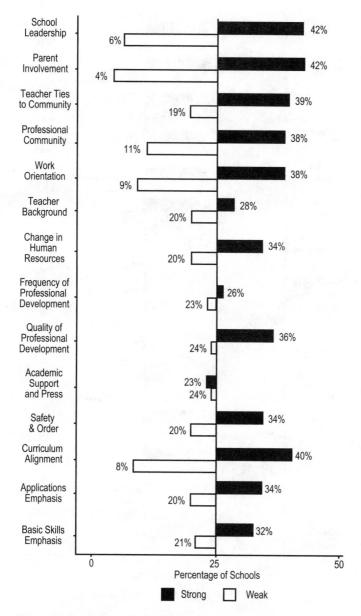

Figure 4.9. Percentage of schools that improved substantially in mathematics by strength in the essential supports. Note: Most essential support indicators are based on 1994 data, but Change in Human Resources is from 1992, and Teacher Ties to Community, Teacher Background, and Quality of Professional Development are from 1997.

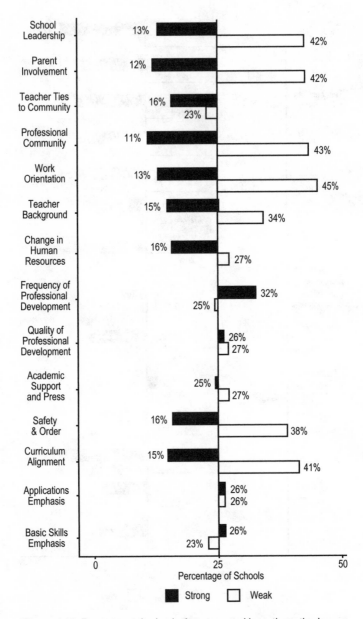

Figure 4.10. Percentage of schools that stagnated in mathematics by strength in the essential supports. Note: Most essential support indicators are based on 1994 data, but Change in Human Resources is from 1992, and Teacher Ties to Community, Teacher Background, and Quality of Professional Development are from 1997.

which a strength or weakness on an individual indicator predicts a particular organizational consequence (improvement or stagnation).

Scanning across the 14 indicators, we observe considerable commonality of relationships for improvement and stagnation in both reading and mathematics. Reiterating the basic findings from chapter 3, learning gains were more prevalent in schools where professionals were committed to that community and oriented toward innovation. Schools with substantial parent involvement were four times more likely to improve in reading and ten times more likely to improve in math than schools with poor parent involvement. Similarly, schools whose faculties demonstrate strong work orientation and professional community were about four times more likely to improve in reading and math than those demonstrating a weakness on one of these indicators. Correspondingly, stagnating schools were marked by distinct weaknesses on these indicators. Schools were three to four times more likely to stagnate in both reading and mathematics when an organizational indicator pointed to a weakness in either parent-community ties or a school's professional capacity. Complementing these social resources was a safe and orderly environment with sustained attention to curriculum alignment. We found substantially elevated improvement rates in both reading and math when these two indicators were strong. Both indicators also discriminated among schools with stagnating productivity.

We now shift to examine how combinations of these indicators of organizational strengths and weaknesses amplify their influence on our reading and mathematics productivity indicators. Probing this statistical evidence provides clues about how the organizational subsystems of a school interconnect to advance (or impede) improvements in student learning.

A Key to Improvement: Quality Professional Development in the
Context of a Supportive School-Based Professional Community

Taken alone, reports about poor-quality professional development were not especially predictive of differences in academic productivity rates. All four of the white bars associated with weaknesses on this indicator in figures 4.7 and 4.10 cluster closely around the 25-percent reference line. However, *high-quality professional development in the context of a supportive professional community and where teachers were oriented toward improvement appears powerfully related to gains in academic productivity.* Figure 4.11 illustrates this. Over half of all schools improved in reading and math when a strong faculty work orientation combined with quality professional development. A similar, although slightly smaller proportion of schools also improved

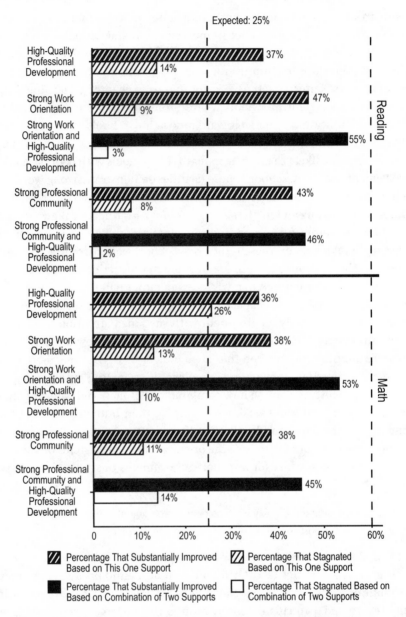

Figure 4.11. A key to improving academic productivity: Quality professional development in the context of a strong professional work environment. Note: Data are from 1997, the first year for which we have records on the quality of professional development.

when quality professional development combined with a strong report on school-based professional community. These findings are consistent with extant smaller-scale field research which documents that teachers are more likely to take up and use professional development opportunities well when these occur within a supportive collegial context.[13]

In addition, we note that this indicator discrimination is especially strong with regard to reading improvement. The presence versus absence of this combination of organizational resources differentiated reading improvement rates by a factor of 20. Moreover, virtually no schools stagnated in reading when this combination of organizational resources was present. While substantial differentiation also occurred in mathematics, these effects are somewhat weaker.

This pattern of results is consistent with the basic elements of contingency theory introduced in chapter 2. The demands that instructional improvement place on an organization depend in part on the particular subject matter being addressed. This contingency occurs because the nature of the core instructional tasks is somewhat different in each subject.[14] The work of improving students' literacy learning is viewed as more ambiguous and uncertain and less routinized than mathematics.[15] Typically, literacy instruction is not guided by a structured text, such as a mathematics curriculum series, and extensive local adaptation and ongoing problem solving characterizes the work. Improvement in such activity presumably makes stronger demands on the social resources among local school professionals. In accord with contingency theory, a school-based professional community should be a more productive organizational form to support this work. To be sure, our evidence indicates that substantial improvements in mathematics also occur under these same organizational conditions; the dependency is just not as strong.

Another Key to Improvement: Focusing Collective Teacher Effort on Aligning Curriculum

On its own, curriculum alignment was a good predictor of changes in reading and mathematics productivity. Some 45 percent of the schools with strong curriculum alignment showed substantial improvement in reading, and 40 percent did in math. Here, too, we found evidence of the contextual effects of a supportive professional community where teachers are oriented toward innovation. Under these supportive social circumstances, gains in academic productivity were even more likely to result. Notice in figure 4.12 that *half to two-thirds of the schools substantially improved in*

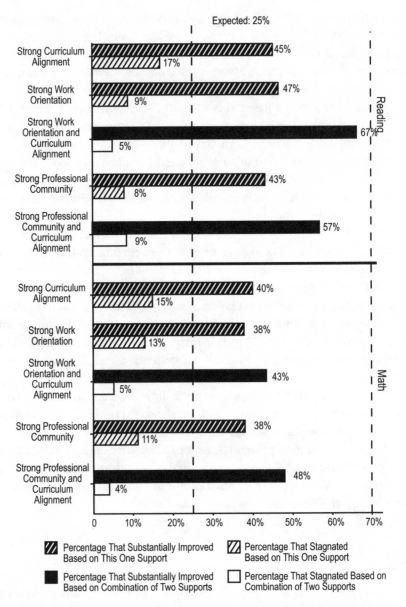

Figure 4.12. Schools with a strong professional work environment focused on curriculum alignment were much more likely to improve student learning. Note: All indicators are from 1994.

reading when strong curriculum alignment occurred in the context of a supportive professional community where teachers shared a positive work orientation. Under these same conditions, over 40 percent of the schools showed substantial improvement in mathematics.

The salience of these organizational interconnections is especially clear when we examine stagnation rates. Very few schools with reported strengths on this combination of organizational indicators stagnated. *Most powerful of all, not a single school that reported a combined weakness in these areas improved in either subject.* (See figure 4.13.)

The results presented here document an important fact: curriculum alignment is a social activity as well as a technical act. Its development entails sustained work among teachers within and across grades. Its quality implementation is contingent on teacher buy-in and cooperative problem solving among the school staff. When engaged with some enthusiasm, such a curriculum provides a strong frame for organizing the work of the many individuals who make up the school community.

Moreover, a productive reciprocity exists here between the basic activity of creating and enacting such an aligned curriculum and the social resources of a school community. Undertaking this activity places considerable demands on a school's social resources. Successful engagement with this task and subsequent enactment of such a curriculum, however, can potentially create new social resources. This occurs because good curriculum alignment reduces some of the uncertainty that teachers experience in their day-to-day work and as a result increases the likelihood of their feeling efficacious. Such palpable consequences for individual teachers from working productively together expand individual predispositions toward future collaboration, thereby enhancing the social resources of the community for its next round of improvement efforts.

In the remainder of this section, we shift from an improvement focus to consider organizational stagnation as a distinct phenomenon meriting its own inquiry. Some compelling evidence about stagnation has already been introduced in figure 4.13. We now build on this in the pages that follow.

A Disabling Combination of Weak Human
and Social Resources across a Faculty

Arguably, the single most important element in good schools is faculty quality. Gathering good data on this, however, has proved elusive for both educational research and educational practice more generally. Absent di-

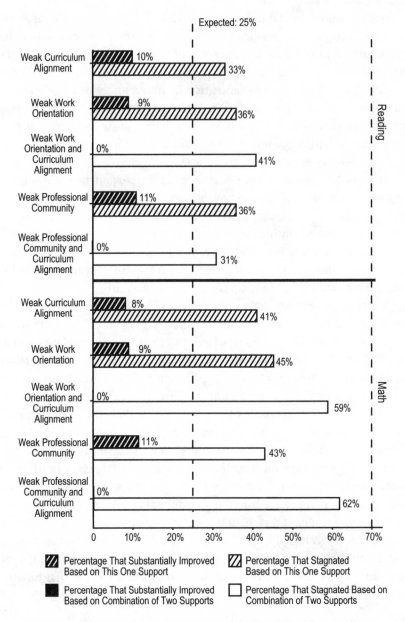

Expected: 25%

Reading

Weak Curriculum Alignment 10% 33%

Weak Work Orientation 9% 36%

Weak Work Orientation and Curriculum Alignment 0% 41%

Weak Professional Community 11% 36%

Weak Professional Community and Curriculum Alignment 0% 31%

Math

Weak Curriculum Alignment 8% 41%

Weak Work Orientation 9% 45%

Weak Work Orientation and Curriculum Alignment 0% 59%

Weak Professional Community 11% 43%

Weak Professional Community and Curriculum Alignment 0% 62%

0   10%   20%   30%   40%   50%   60%   70%

Percentage That Substantially Improved Based on This One Support

Percentage That Stagnated Based on This One Support

Percentage That Substantially Improved Based on Combination of Two Supports

Percentage That Stagnated Based on Combination of Two Supports

Figure 4.13. Not a single school with a weak professional environment and weak curriculum alignment improved in either reading or math. Note: All indicators are from 1994.

rect testing of teachers and extensive observations of their actual class-room practice, objective judgments about quality remain tenuous. No large-scale data of this sort existed in Chicago during the course of this natural experiment in school reform, nor did it exist anywhere else for that matter.[16]

As a proxy, we developed an indicator for teacher background that combines information about the selectivity of the educational institutions from which teachers received their degrees, and the extent to which teach-ers have had schooling experiences outside Chicago. (See chapter 2 and appendix C for further details on the rationale for this indicator and its construction.) The indicator provides evidence about the basic academic preparation of teachers and the extent to which their perspectives on schooling and their expectations for students have been shaped by some larger set of experiences. A quality faculty should demonstrate strength in both of these areas; in fact we view these data as a gross measure of the base quality of a school's faculty. While strength on the indicator may not assure high-quality teaching, manifest weaknesses should be a point of concern.

On its own, teacher background was only weakly related to changes in academic productivity, especially when compared with the strong rela-tionships found for professional community and work orientation. *A par-ticularly disabling combination was detected, however, when teachers with weak educational backgrounds clustered in schools with weak work orientation and pro-fessional community.* As shown in figure 4.14, *approximately half the schools with these indicator combinations stagnated in both subjects.* Less than 5 percent of these schools improved in either math or reading.

Stepping back a bit, these statistical findings direct our attention to two interacting organizational mechanisms. First, schools with negative pro-fessional climates and weak faculty community are not attractive places for new teachers. Given a choice, individual teachers tend to eschew ap-pointments in such schools. Similarly, teachers who have other options, by virtue of their individual abilities and initiative, tend to exit rapidly from these schools, even if appointed there.[17] Thus, labor-market selection forces drive the faculty composition in such contexts toward a low com-mon denominator.

Second, teachers' capacity to engage more ambitious instruction in their classroom depends in part on collegial resources in their larger school environment. Quite simply, teachers learn a great deal about instructional practice from their local colleagues. Absent supportive environmental

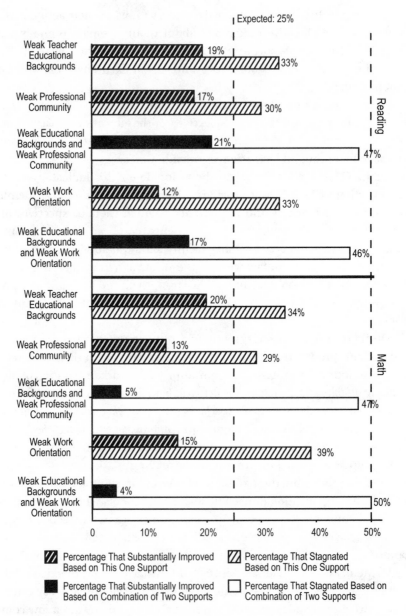

Expected: 25%

Weak Teacher Educational Backgrounds — 19% / 33%
Weak Professional Community — 17% / 30%
Weak Educational Backgrounds and Weak Professional Community — 21% / 47%
Weak Work Orientation — 12% / 33%
Weak Educational Backgrounds and Weak Work Orientation — 17% / 46%

Reading

Weak Teacher Educational Backgrounds — 20% / 34%
Weak Professional Community — 13% / 29%
Weak Educational Backgrounds and Weak Professional Community — 5% / 47%
Weak Work Orientation — 15% / 39%
Weak Educational Backgrounds and Weak Work Orientation — 4% / 50%

Math

0 10% 20% 30% 40% 50%

▨ Percentage That Substantially Improved Based on This One Support

▨ Percentage That Stagnated Based on This One Support

■ Percentage That Substantially Improved Based on Combination of Two Supports

☐ Percentage That Stagnated Based on Combination of Two Supports

Figure 4.14. Schools with weak human capital in the context of a weak professional environment were likely to stagnate. Note: Data are from 1997, the first year for which we have records on teachers' educational backgrounds.

conditions for trying out new ideas and learning from one another, weak teachers have fewer resources for improvement and less incentive to do so. The faculty who do not choose to exit such contexts tend to solidify further the base school culture. In the end, then, the absence of resources supporting job-embedded learning combines with labor-market forces to sustain school dysfunction.

Adding Further to Instructional Stagnation: Poor Curriculum Alignment Coupled with a Weak Applications Focus

We saw in our analysis of school attendance trends that well-paced, applications-oriented instruction supported improvement. The results presented in figure 4.15 mirror these findings as we consider this same combination of indicators with regard to reading and mathematics productivity. *When reports of poor curriculum alignment coupled with a weak applications focus in instruction, we found that the likelihood of improved student learning dropped to zero. Literally, not a single school improved in either reading or math with this combination of indicators.* Likewise, the stagnation rate in reading was 39 percent for schools with weak reports on these two indicators, and for mathematics the corresponding rate was 46 percent. These results further strengthen the conclusion offered earlier in this chapter. Engaging instructional tasks within a well-organized curriculum is an essential base for improving student learning.

On balance, we also need to emphasize that we found little evidence that a strong applications focus in instruction, taken by itself, made a major contribution to improving student learning. We found, for example, only a weak association for applications focus with reading improvement in the 1994 data. (See results previously reported in figure 4.7.) Moreover, this finding did not replicate in 1997, nor did we find any evidence of such an effect in our examination of the mathematics productivity data. In addition, no strong effect patterns emerged when a reported strength in applications-oriented instruction combined with strong reports on other indicators.[18] While there are good educational arguments about why such pedagogies can be efficacious, this lack of strong, consistent results across our two waves of indicators for both reading and mathematics does offer reason to pause.

Taken together, these results suggest that introducing constructivist pedagogies that involve more active student learning in project-based work can act as a productive resource for engaging students in school

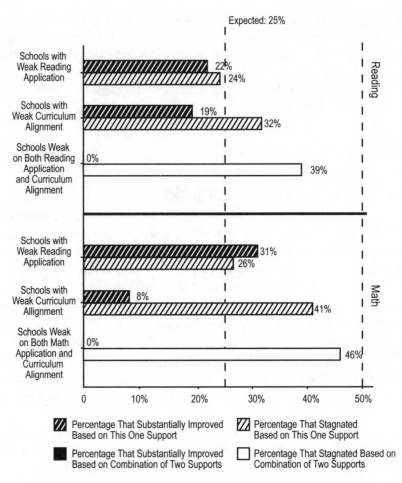

Figure 4.15. Not a single school with weak curriculum alignment and a weak applications emphasis improved in either reading or math. Note: All indicators from 1994.

more generally. In this regard, such instruction provides a significant base on which schools can build to improve student learning. Having acknowledged this, however, we also need to recognize that the recipe for strengthening student learning is actually more complex and subtle than just doing lots of applications-oriented work in classrooms.[19] Again, specifically on this point, we found no evidence that such activity per se adds substantially to improved student learning gains, especially in comparison with the other organizational factors considered here.

The Final Organizational Impediment to Enhancing Student Learning:
A Negative Student-Centered Learning Climate in the Context
of Poor Adult Relations

So far, we have documented how interactions among a school's professional capacity and its instructional guidance system strongly influence academic improvements in both reading and mathematics. This is basically a story about the "technical core"—how the organization of instruction and a school's professional resources, both human and social, interact to promote (or impede) academic improvement. The evidence on these points appears quite compelling.

We have said little, up to this point, about the other two subsystems constituting a school's organization: the activity structure that ties parents and community leaders to the school staff and the nature of the learning environment for students. Although we found no evidence that parent involvement interacts significantly with the technical core (that is, we detected no strong indicator combination effects here), it is important not to lose sight of the strength of the separate relationship of parent involvement with academic improvement. Recall from figures 4.7 and 4.9 that schools were four times more likely to improve in reading and ten times more likely to improve in mathematics when parent involvement was strong. Similarly, we noted earlier that the safety and order indicator played a major role in securing student engagement with schooling and had moderate predictive power with regard to academic productivity. In short, both factors represent core elements in the social resource base for school improvement.

As for our other indicator of a student-centered learning climate, academic support and press, taken alone it displayed mixed and inconsistent results with regard to all three outcomes. However, when we combined these student climate reports with data on the nature of the activity structure among adult members of the school community, a notable pattern of effects appeared. Figure 4.16 documents stagnation rates that were typically 40 percent or higher when weak academic support and press for students combined with weak professional community, work orientation, or parent involvement. Most dramatically, *not a single school improved in either reading or mathematics when reports from students of weak academic support and press co-occurred with accounts from teachers attesting to weak social relations among the faculty and with parents.*

This finding, taken together with some of the other results presented in this chapter, points toward a much more general consideration about how

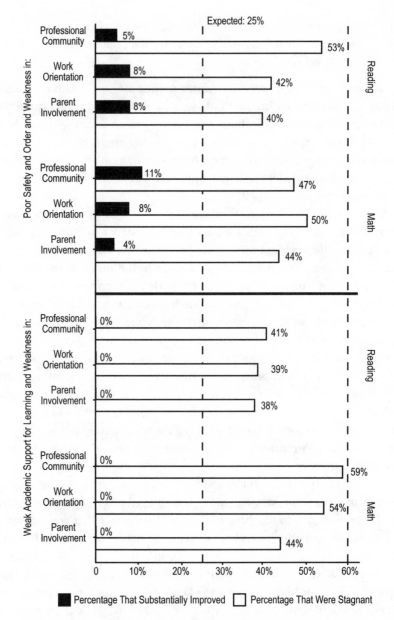

Figure 4.16. Schools with poor student learning climates and weak adult relations were likely to stagnate. Note: All indicators from 1994.

the quality of the social relationships within a school is a core resource for improvement. We return to consider this in more detail in the next chapter.

Finally, one caveat is in order about the results presented in figure 4.16. We wish to emphasize that we found no evidence that would support the idea that narrowly targeted efforts around strengthening teacher-student and/or student-peer relations contribute significantly to improvements in student learning. Our results indicate that adults and students may well report positive social ties, but this does not mean that significant improvements in student learning are also likely. However, the complement appears not to be the case. The press of a negative student environment coupled with weak social ties among the adult members of the school (including here both professionals and parents) clearly signify a troubled context. While increased learning may not follow directly from strength in this domain, manifest weaknesses represent a clear impediment to such improvements.

Pulling It All Together: The Organizational Mechanisms for Improving Academic Productivity

We have developed two stories here: one describes a syndrome of sustained stagnation and the second details an interacting set of mechanisms for promoting effective change. Figures 4.17 and 4.18 present a heuristic summary of these results. On the first account, schools with sustained dysfunction are characterized by clear weaknesses in their instructional guidance system. Specifically, they have poor curriculum alignment that couples with a weak applications focus for engaging students in schooling. These instructional system weaknesses combine in turn with limited faculty resources working within a feeble professional community. Finally, undergirding all of this is an anemic activity structure interconnecting students, parents, and teachers.

In contrast, improving student achievement uses quality professional development as a key instrument for change. Maximum leverage is achieved when these opportunities for teacher learning occur within a supportive professional work environment where teaching is grounded within a common, coherent, and aligned instructional system. Finally, undergirding all of this is a solid base of parent and community ties with the school and its professional staff.

While in retrospect this may all seem rather straightforward and easy

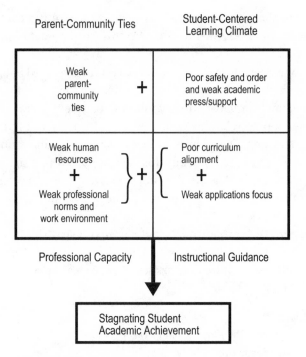

Figure 4.17. The organizational dynamics of academic stagnation. Note: The plus sign denotes subsystem interconnections.

to summarize, establishing the empirical warrant for these conclusions has been far from simple. Even more significantly, we know from the diverse and multiple strands of our work in Chicago that such activity is certainly not easy to initiate and sustain in school communities, especially those in highly disadvantaged contexts. We will have more to say about this in chapter 6.

Leadership as the Driver for Change

As detailed in chapter 2, we conceptualize school leadership as the catalyst for local change. School principals cultivate a local followership and over time nurture the emergence of multiple local leaders who support and take responsibility for an expanding base of improvement efforts. At the heart of this work is a sustained focus on instructional improvement and how various aspects of the school community must be transformed to support this. Specifically, leadership attention focuses on strengthening the professional capacity of the faculty, the coherence and academic

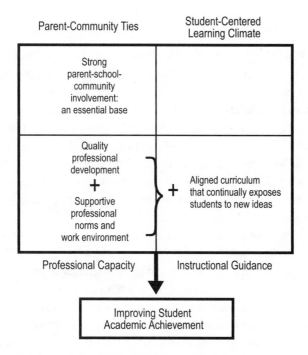

Figure 4.18. The organizational dynamics of improving academic productivity. Note: The plus sign denotes subsystem interconnections.

demand of the school's instructional programs, and the overall normative environment that surrounds and infiltrates the daily work of adults and students. Finally, at a much more basic level, effective operations management is critical. Especially in times of change, when innovations are being attempted and multiple new activities put into motion, an inability to support effective daily school operations can quickly grind these change processes to a halt.

The correlations previously presented in table 2.1 document the strong interconnections of leadership with parent involvement (0.64) and community ties (0.47), and with multiple indicators of a school's professional capacity (0.77 with professional community, 0.75 with work orientation, and 0.45 with quality professional development). Somewhat weaker, although still highly significant, associations were found for school safety and order (0.45) and curriculum alignment (0.30). Taken together, these statistical findings are consistent with current professional wisdom that developing local school leaders is essential in school reforms seeking change at scale.

A Stronger Causal Test

On balance, it is important to recognize that the data reported in table 2.1 are cross-sectional in nature. Most of the indicators presented there came from the same set of teacher and student surveys, primarily from 1994. It is possible that these strong correlations of leadership with other indicators simply reflect an overall teacher and student satisfaction with the school, which carries over into the survey reports about local leadership. Moreover, as we explicitly noted in chapter 2, there are good reasons to believe that some causal reciprocity may be at work here. As school leaders advance some productive organizational changes, these in turn can facilitate subsequent leadership activity.

To test more rigorously the idea that leadership is the driver (rather than simply a correlate) for development of the other essential supports, we undertook a set of longitudinal analyses. Specifically, we examined the linkage of the base level of leadership in a school community in 1991, and then again in 1994, with subsequent changes in the other four organizational subsystems from 1991 to 1994 and 1994 to 1997, respectively. The key question here is, Does the base level of leadership in a school community enhance the likelihood of significant organizational improvements over the next three years? In conducting these analyses, we controlled for the base level on each organizational indicator (1991 and 1994, respectively) and school size, enrollment stability, and racial composition; and neighborhood social status, concentration of poverty, and crime rate.[20] We also included change in the leadership indicator (1991 to 1994 and 1994 to 1997, respectively) to assure that we were estimating the base-level effects of leadership.[21]

In general, we found very strong statistical relationships between the base level of school leadership and subsequent changes in our core organizational indicators. Moreover, this pattern of effects, first seen for the 1991 to 1994 period, also replicated in the second period, from 1994 to 1997. To illustrate the magnitude of these effects, we developed a simple organizational change prediction model based on the results from these analyses. The basic idea represented in the prediction model is as follows. Suppose that we compared two schools that were alike in composition, enrollment stability, size, base level of the essential support indicators, and even the amount of leadership change reported over the next three-year period. The only measured difference between the two schools was in the base level of reported school leadership.

Figure 4.19 illustrates the comparative organizational development in

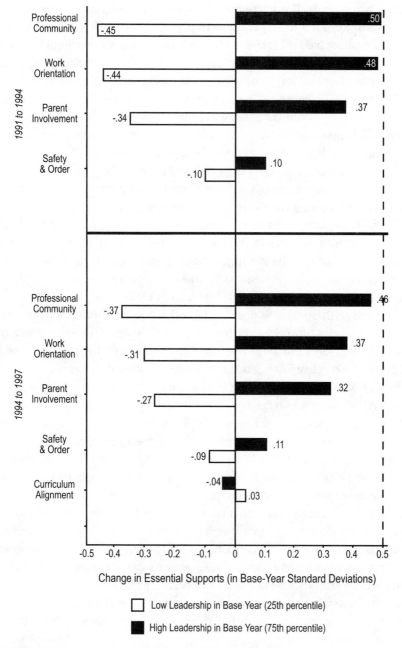

Figure 4.19. Leadership promotes development of the essential supports.

these two schools. The white bars show the change in each essential support indicator for a school at the 25th percentile on leadership in the base year. The black bars show the predictions for a comparable school but with strong leadership in the base year, at the 75th percentile. A school that had a high level of leadership in 1991 could be expected to increase its level of professional community between 1991 and 1994 by about 0.5 standard deviations (SD). A similar effect was found for work orientation (0.48 SD), and a slightly smaller estimate for parent involvement (0.38 SD). In contrast, significant declines on these same three indicators (-0.44 SD, -0.43 SD, and -0.33 SD, respectively) were predicted for schools weak on leadership in 1991. A smaller although still consistent effect occurred for safety and order. (The actual regression results can be found in appendix F, table 1.)

A similar pattern of results, albeit slightly weaker in magnitude, occurred for the 1994 to 1997 change analyses. This is not surprising, given the nature of our analyses and the phenomena under study here. In contexts where strong school leaders advanced major organizational improvement in the 1991 to 1994 period, it is reasonable to expect smaller indicator jumps in these schools over the next three-year period. Since the 1994 to 1997 analyses control for the base level on each organizational indicator (and thereby any prior improvement effects attributable to local leaders), we would expect reports about major organizational changes in the second period to accrue primarily in the subset of schools where new local leadership had just emerged.[22]

In addition, the relative magnitude of the effects displayed in figure 4.19 is consistent with the basic organizational theory set out in chapter 2. Specifically, the strongest leadership effects accrue for the two subsystems most directly under the influence of school principals: strengthening parent-community ties and improving the professional capacity of the faculty (that is, the professional community and work orientation indicators). Correspondingly, the weaker relationships with safety and order and curriculum alignment are consistent with the idea that both are intrinsically social phenomena where improvements make significant demands on schools' larger social context. As a result, principal leadership effects operate somewhat more indirectly here, working at least in part through strengthening the organizational subsystems that connect adults across the school community.

Even so, the absence of a stronger statistical association between our indicators of school leadership and curriculum alignment is a bit surprising and merits comment. We suspect that this simply reflects the rather conservative nature of the analysis models that we employed. Specifically, by controlling for the base level of curriculum alignment in 1994, we parceled out of these estimates any leadership effects that may have influenced developments in this domain before 1994. That is, the 1994–97 analyses only estimate the incremental effects over the last three years of the study. If most of the improvement in curriculum alignment occurred in many schools before 1994, we would have no way to assess the causal contributors to these effects. All we know for sure is that the leadership composite indicator measured in 1994 does have a moderate association with curriculum alignment measured in the same year.

To place the overall pattern of statistical evidence in a somewhat more substantive context, we note that an upward movement of 0.5 SD on an organizational indicator for an average school would take that school from the 50th percentile on that indicator during the base year to about the 70th percentile three years later. Similarly, a decline of 0.5 SD would drop an otherwise comparable school to about the 30th percentile.[23] Thus, our analyses predict that an average school community with a strong leadership base would have a set of organizational indicators three years later that approached the top quartile of schools in this study; in contrast, the comparable school community with weak leadership would be heading toward the bottom quartile. Given the documented outcome differences for students associated with such strengths and weaknesses on our organizational indicators, the consequences of strong local leadership appear quite large indeed.

The Interplay of Inclusive-Facilitative and Instructional Components of Leadership

We also argued in chapter 2 that leadership for school reform entailed a dynamic interplay of an inclusive-facilitative orientation coupled with sustained attention to instructional improvement. Our composite indicator of school leadership consists of six separate measures, three apiece for the inclusive-facilitative and instructional dimensions. In order to examine the tenability of our claim about this dynamic interplay, we took our composite indicator apart and examined how each separate component predicted organizational consequences in the other four supports. Specifically, for five core organizational indicators, measured in 1997, we conducted a series of regression analyses that controlled for the base level of the support indicator in 1994, school size, and a series of school com-

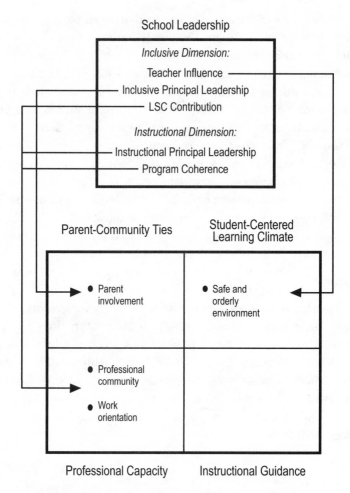

Figure 4.20. The complex interplay of school community leadership.

munity demographic variables (neighborhood social status, neighborhood crime rate, and concentration of poverty in the surrounding community). At the last stage, a stepwise algorithm was employed that allowed each of the separate leadership measures to enter the model depending on its relative predictive power. The leadership measures that were most strongly and stably related to change in each support from 1994 to 1997 are indicated by the arrows in figure 4.20. (The actual regression results can be found in appendix F, table 2.)

First and foremost, we found strong effects involving measures from both dimensions of leadership. This is highly significant in that contemporary reform arguments tend to emphasize the significance of instructional leadership (which clearly is important) while extending much less consideration to the inclusive-facilitative dimension. Our results indicate that both are important.

Second, the observed pattern of differential effects among the leadership measures is consistent with the basic arguments set out in chapter 2. The measures for the instructional dimension (principal instructional leadership and program coherence) had the strongest connections to professional community and teachers' work orientation. In contrast, the inclusive-facilitative measures focusing on the principal's interpersonal style and the degree of teacher influence over selected school matters had the strongest relationships with parent involvement and safety and order indicators.

Taken together with results from the previous section, we conclude that it is essential for school leaders to build supportive relationships with and among the other adults who form the school community. Inclusive, facilitative leaders connect parents more fully to the school, and also actively engage teachers, creating space for them to lead as well. These findings are consistent with other research on the importance of principal leadership in building teamwork among adults.[24] By working together, teachers, parents, and principals can improve the learning climate in the school and build a base of social resources to support efforts directed at the technical core. It is here where the complement of the instructional leadership is activated. Strong instructional leaders promote the growth of a professional community around a shared system of teaching and learning and also stay the course, guided by a coherent, strategic plan that aims to advance the entire enterprise over time.

Summing Up the Evidence and What It Means for Practice

Over the previous two chapters, we have presented an increasingly detailed and complex array of evidence on how core elements in the organization of schools affect their capacity to improve student engagement and learning. Recall that these findings are based on an investigation of student outcomes from several hundred Chicago public elementary schools over a period of seven years. This extensive database has provided an extraordinary window to examine the complex interplay among the core organizational supports for school improvement, to detect interconnections that we might otherwise have missed, and to offer a solid empirical warrant for the findings set out here. Before moving on to other considerations, a brief recap of what we have learned across these two chapters seems in order.

Following this, we return to the accounts of reform in the Alexander and Hancock schools. We use these to illustrate how critical differences in the core aspects of school organization that we have examined in these two previous chapters actually played out over time to impede progress in one school and advance change productively in another.

A Quick Recap

The basic social order of school life transcends the narrow boundaries of its public school property. A social dynamic with important organizational consequences operates through the network of relations among school professionals, community leaders, parents, and students. Not surprisingly, then, we found that schools with robust ties to parents and the local community benefited greatly from this resource as they sought to create a safer and more orderly environment that would enhance students' participation in schooling. In turn, this combination of social resources among adults along with a more supportive overall environment for students constitute an essential resource for the needed improvements in teaching and learning to occur. The data presented in this chapter provide ample testimony to these social facts. Taken together, this subset of results substantiates a long-standing observation about urban school improvement (and one central to Chicago's 1988 reform legislation): reconnecting local schools to the parents and community that they are intended to serve is central to urban school reform.

In shifting our focus to measured improvements over time in students' academic learning, we also found strong evidence attesting to the importance of the organizational subsystems most directly tied to the technical core of instruction. Our results affirm that quality professional development is a key instrument for school change. Most significantly, maximum leverage is achieved from reform efforts when this professional development occurs within a supportive professional work environment where teaching is grounded in a common, coherent, and aligned instructional system.

Finally, our empirical results also attest that school leadership is the catalyst for change. Efforts to strengthen school-community ties and the professional capabilities within a school's faculty are much more likely to succeed in a context where leaders encourage broad involvement while also working to guide and coordinate activity around a coherent vision for instructional improvement. In short, a dynamic blend of both instructional and inclusive-facilitative leadership is needed.

Putting a Human Face on These Results:
Revisiting Alexander and Hancock Schools

The disabling combination of weak human and social resources was abun-
dantly clear at Alexander Elementary School. The school fell in the bottom
quartile on our measure of teacher background (see figure 2.5 in chapter 2).
Many teachers at Alexander had attended Chicago public schools as students, received their bachelor's degree at a local, nonselective university,
and had little or no experience teaching outside the CPS. Though some
individual teachers were surely effective, when a faculty is primarily made
up of weaker human resources, there is less opportunity for new ideas and
expectations to percolate into the staff's professional psyche.

Most troubling, Alexander scored in the lowest quartile on professional
community, with most teachers working in the isolation of their private
classrooms. Although there had been a few attempts to engage teachers
in schoolwide reform efforts, none of these projects had taken hold. Many
of the faculty had taught at Alexander for more than twenty years and
had witnessed the gradual deterioration of the neighborhood, which they
found frightening and demoralizing. They often expressed a deep sense of
discouragement. While some teachers took individual steps to help students and parents, there was no collective sense of purpose or responsibility and no conviction that the school could be fundamentally different.
The malaise was so strong that many among the faculty even resisted offers of professional development.

Ultimately, Betty Green, the school principal, was simply unable to cultivate leadership among the other adults within her school community.
She believed that she alone had to hold the school together. Not surprisingly, the school fell into the bottom quartile on the school leadership indicator. Without inclusive, facilitative leadership to nurture a professional
community and without instructional leadership to establish a clear direction, there was limited organizational capacity to support change and
little strategic thinking to guide its evolution.

In contrast, at Hancock Elementary School the combination of human
and social resources was impressive and empowering. While Hancock
scored only at about the 45th percentile on teacher background, the blend
of a vibrant professional community (around the 90th percentile) and very
high-quality professional development (around the 99th percentile) created a solid foundation for the school to launch a sustained campaign to
upgrade the curriculum and transform instruction. The faculty worked

together over several years to examine closely the results of standardized tests, their own internal assessments, and students' classroom work in order to determine the areas of strength and weakness in academic performance. These detailed analyses led to significant changes, including the adoption of a common framework for literacy instruction that included regular formative assessments of student progress that were used across all classrooms and grades.

Bonnie Whitmore combined an inclusive and a facilitative approach to leadership, with a sustained, strategic focus on instructional improvement. Whenever an individual teacher left, Principal Whitmore took care to recruit smart, committed individuals who cared about the Oak Meadows community and would augment the school's instructional improvement efforts. She also invested heavily in professional development, while simultaneously using this as an opportunity to nurture a collegial spirit among the faculty. Not surprisingly, teacher survey reports placed Hancock school at the 99th percentile on our overall school leadership indicator.

Over time, Whitmore sought to nurture a more distributed form of local school community leadership as individual teachers stepped forward to take responsibility for various projects, and parent and community members did so as well. This pluralized leadership greatly enhanced the overall human and social resources across the school community to support improvement—whatever the next task might be. As Whitmore explained, "I can't be the leader of everything, and there are leaders within the school, people with strengths and talents. As the overall leader, part of my job is to help these other leaders emerge."

CHAPTER 5 TRUST, SIZE, AND STABILITY: KEY ENABLERS

We found in chapters 3 and 4 that strong local school leaders working in tandem with parents and faculty can advance systemic changes in the organizational life of their school, resulting in improvements in student learning. Although specific details may vary greatly from school to school, such organizational improvement will likely entail a combination of activities aimed at strengthening ties to parents and local communities, enabling the professional capabilities of a school's faculty, nurturing a more student-centered learning environment, and enhancing the technical core of instruction with new tools, materials, and instructional routines.

In this chapter we probe more deeply into the nature of the relational dynamics that make all of this possible. We begin by summarizing the key elements, identified in previous research, that form relational trust within a school community; then we discuss how the presence of this trust in turn enables fundamental change. Subsequently, we consider how certain structural features in the organization of schools act to facilitate such change. Specifically, we consider how school size and enrollment stability may operate both to enhance trust and to influence directly the development of essential supports for school improvement.

Relational Trust as a Social Resource for School Improvement

Relationships are the lifeblood of activity in a school community.[1] The patterns of exchanges established here and the meanings that individuals draw from these interactions can have profound consequences on the operation of schools, especially in times that call for change.

The Microdynamics of Trust

Embedded within all the social exchanges in school communities is an interrelated set of interdependencies. This observation is key to understanding the significant function served by relational trust in school improvement. Regardless of how much formal power attaches to any given role in a school community, all participants remain dependent on others to achieve desired outcomes and feel efficacious about their efforts. These structural dependencies create a sense of vulnerability for all involved. This dynamic plays out within each of the major sets of adult roles within a school community—the school principal with teachers, teachers with one another, and school professionals with parents. All parties in these role sets maintain an understanding of their personal obligations and hold some expectations about the obligations of the "other." These understandings and expectations form the basis for judging the actual social exchanges that occur within each role set.

As individuals go about their everyday lives in schools, they are constantly engaged in a process of discerning the intentions embedded in the actions of others. These discernments take into account the history of interactions that have previously occurred between the parties. In the absence of prior interpersonal contact, participants may initially rely on the general reputation of the other party and also on ascriptive similarities—for example, commonalities in terms of race, gender, age, religion, or upbringing. The actual process of making trust discernments fuses several considerations, including the likelihood of achieving instrumental outcomes and the ability to influence the processes that directly affect these outcomes; psychic concerns about advancing one's sense of status, self-esteem, and efficacy; and ethical considerations about "doing right by children."

At the most basic level, relational trust is grounded in social respect. Key in this regard are the conversations that occur within a school community. Respectful exchanges are marked by a genuine sense of listening to what each person has to say, and in some fashion taking this into account in subsequent actions. Even when people disagree, individuals feel that the value of their opinions has been recognized. Such social exchanges foster a sense of connectedness among participants and promote affiliation with the larger institutional context.

Personal regard represents a second important criterion operating in trust discernments. Social encounters in the realm of schooling are more intimate and sustained than those typically found in most other modern institutions. Powerful interpersonal bonds can form when members of the school community sense that others really care about them. A key practice in this regard is participants' willingness to extend themselves beyond what is formally required by a job definition or a union contract. "Going the extra mile" for another person may take many different forms, such as a teacher's staying after school to work with a colleague or parent, or a principal's taking a personal interest in a staff member's career development or family situation. Actions such as these can be deeply meaningful for the parties involved and forge strong social ties between them.

Third, discernments about role competence also constitute a critical concern. Each participant in a school community assesses the likelihood of attaining desired outcomes when interacting with others. Quite simply, do colleagues have the knowledge, skill, and/or technical capacity to deliver on their intentions and promises?

Finally, perceptions about personal integrity shape trust discernments as well. At a basic level, we ask whether others can be trusted to keep their word. Judgments about reliability—aligning "the walk" with "the talk"—are essential to trusting another. At a more fundamental level, we seek to discern whether a moral-ethical perspective guides the activity of others: Do I see their behavior as really being about the children, their education and welfare?

In short, relational trust is forged in day-to-day social exchanges. Through their actions, school participants articulate their sense of obligation toward others, and others in turn come to discern the intentionality enacted here. Trust grows over time through exchanges in which the expectations held for others are validated by actions. Even simple interactions, if successful, can enhance capacities for more complex subsequent actions. In this regard, increasing trust and productive organizational changes reciprocate each other.

Macro-Organizational Consequences: How Trust Supports School Improvement

Relational trust within a school community affords resources for improvement in three distinct ways. First and most generally, broad teacher and parent buy-in on reform efforts occurs more readily in schools with strong relational trust. Regardless of which of the essential supports that local leaders might emphasize (enhancing parent outreach, professional capacity building, improving the quality of the student learning environment, or the instructional guidance system), trust facilitates the initiation of these improvement efforts. This feature is especially significant in times that call for major structural change, as was the case in the Chicago Public Schools throughout the 1990s.

Second, relational trust creates a motivating force for taking up the difficult work of school reform. Most teachers work hard, doing the best they can for as many students as they can. Reform, however, typically asks teachers to take on extra work as they engage with colleagues in planning, implementing, and evaluating school improvement initiatives. Similarly, it asks teachers to confront conflict, as this commonly occurs in organizational change processes. From a purely self-interested point of view, it would seem quite reasonable for teachers to ask, Why should we do this? A context characterized by high relational trust provides an answer. In the end, trusting that colleagues share a belief that "reform is the right thing to do" can provide a powerful moral catalyst for action.

Third, reform initiatives are more likely to be deeply engaged by individual teachers and to diffuse broadly across the school when relational trust is strong. At the individual level, relational trust reduces the risk associated with change. When school professionals trust one another and feel supported by parents, they feel safe to experiment with new practices in the classroom and to launch initiatives for reaching out to parents. Similarly, relational trust facilitates the social exchanges among school professionals as they seek to learn from one another in the trial-and-error phase of implementing new practices. To be able to talk honestly with colleagues about "what's working, what's not" means exposing one's ignorance and making oneself vulnerable. Absent trust, genuine conversations of this sort remain unlikely.

We note that this concept of social learning, along with efforts to enhance collective responsibility among a school's faculty for improving student learning, forms the core functional and normative elements that constitute a school-based professional community, as introduced in chapter 2.[2] In essence, trust functions as the social glue necessary for this work of school reform to coalesce and be maintained.

In pulling this all together, it is important to recognize that relational trust among the adults in a school community does not directly affect student learning. Rather, it creates the basic social fabric within which school professionals, parents, and community leaders can initiate and sustain efforts at building the essential supports for school improvement. In short, trust facilitates core organizational change processes that instrumentally contribute to improving academic productivity.

Measuring Relational Trust

The conceptualization of relational trust, summarized above, evolved during our longitudinal research. The instrumentation for measuring trust evolved in tandem with this theory development. Our measure-development effort was also informed by direct school observations and the analysis of results from earlier attempts at measuring this concept. Were we launching this research anew today, we would ask each key participant (the school principal, teachers, and/or parents) about the judgments that they make regarding one another. In the context of this study, however, we are limited to teachers' reports about their discernments of other teachers in the school, their principal, and parents. Specifically, teachers were asked a series of survey questions as to whether respect, personal regard, integrity, and competence in execution of basic role responsibilities characterized each role set of which they were a part. In 1991, we had a simple omnibus measure consisting of 10 relatively general items about role relations within the school community. By 1997, this had expanded to three distinct and highly reliable measures, based on a total of 27 survey items that focused separately on teacher-teacher trust, teacher-principal trust, and teacher-parent trust. (For further details on the 1991, 1994, and 1997 measures, see appendix C.) Subsequently, these measures were cross-validated against direct field observations.[3] Based on relatively brief visits to schools, independent observers have described palpable differences in the quality of day-to-day social exchanges occurring in schools classified in the top versus the bottom quartile on these measures.

Evidence Linking Relational Trust to Improvements
in the Essential Supports

In theory, the base level of trust at any given time point conditions a school's capacity to undertake new reform initiatives. In addition, we have argued that a reciprocal dynamic operates between relational trust and the processes of school change. "Small wins" at school improvement help expand relational trust, thereby creating an enlarged capacity to undertake more complex changes in the future. Assuming that subsequent efforts are also successful, this should further enlarge the social resources of the school community for the next round of work. In short, the processes of school improvement and relational trust development occur together over extended time periods and in a real sense fuel each other.

Analytic approach. Consonant with this theoretical perspective, we would expect to find improvements over time in our indicators of the essential supports in school communities where the base level of relational trust is reported as relatively high. Conversely, improvements in the essential supports should be very unlikely in contexts that begin reform with a weak trust among the adult members of the school community. This observation directs us toward examining the linkages, if any, between the reported *base level of relational trust* at any given point and *subsequent changes in the essential support indicators* during the next period. Similarly, if a reciprocal dynamic operates between relational trust and school improvement, as suggested above, we would also expect to find that changes in these two domains occur in tandem with each other. This observation directs us then to examine possible linkages between *changes in relational trust* measures and *changes in the essential supports* indicators over time.

Specifically, we posed an array of analytic models similar to those used in chapter 4, where we examined the effects of school leadership. These models allowed us to assess the effects of the base level of trust in 1991 on changes from 1991 to 1994 in teachers' work orientation, outreach to parents, and reports about school safety and order. They also allowed us to examine the link between *changes in relational trust* over time (1991 to 1994) and changes over this same period in these three core organizational indicators. To extend and cross-validate these findings, we then replicated these analyses using changes in the organizational indicators from 1994 and 1997 as the outcomes to be explained. In addition, we were able to analyze changes in the curriculum alignment indicator during this period.[4]

As in chapter 4, we controlled for various aspects of school context, including school racial composition and the social class of the local neighborhood.[5] We also controlled for school size and enrollment stability. As detailed in the next section, these two structural features may both facilitate the development of trust and directly affect the development of the essential supports. By including both variables in these analyses, we were able to estimate trust effects net of these structural conditions.

Effects of the base level of trust on school improvement. Figure 5.1 documents substantial differences in school improvement associated with relational trust. Essential supports were more likely to improve between 1991 and 1994 and again between 1994 and 1997 in schools that began each period with a strong base of relational trust. In contrast, schools lacking such social resources found the task of improvement much more difficult.

Specifically, we found strong effects for the base level of relational

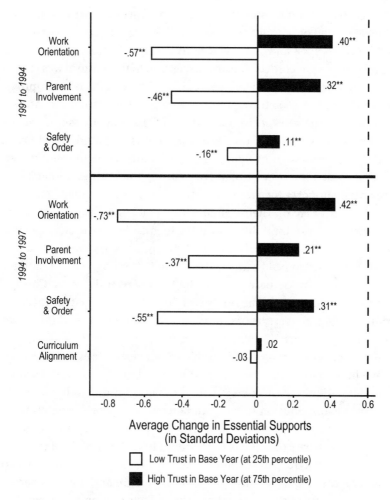

Figure 5.1. Net effect of the base level of relational trust on improvements in the essential supports. Note: Asterisks denote relationships significant at $p < .01$.

trust on subsequent improvements in work orientation from 1991 to 1994. Those schools that were at the 75th percentile on relational trust in 1991 improved their measure of work orientation (teachers' embrace of innovation and commitment to the school) by 0.40 standard deviations (SD) in 1994 (black bar on the graph). At the same time, schools that were at the 25th percentile on relational trust in 1991 declined in work orientation by 0.57 SD (white bar) by 1994. This means that there was a difference of 0.97 SD in the measure of work orientation three years later between schools beginning reform with high versus low trust.

The comparable effect on changes in parent involvement was 0.78 SD, and for safety and order it was 0.27 SD. Similar large effects appear for the period between 1994 and 1997, where respective SD differences of 1.15, 0.58, and 0.86 were recorded. The only exception to this pattern was for the curriculum alignment indicator, where the estimated effects for improvements in the period 1994 through 1997 were small and insignificant.

To illustrate the substantive magnitude of these relationships, we developed several examples of the organizational changes predicted based on the results presented in figure 5.1. Specifically, we computed the effects of the base level of relational trust on subsequent developments in the essential supports for two different schools. We assumed that both schools were average on their school compositional measures, the same with regard to size and stability, and at the median level of each respective essential support indicator in the base year (1991 or 1994). We allowed just one significant difference between them: the first school had a relatively low level of trust in the base year (at the 25th percentile of the Chicago school distribution), while the other was fairly high on trust (at the 75th percentile). Given the results of our analyses, how much would these two schools diverge on each essential support three years later?

Figure 5.2 documents quite large effects. Consider, for example, the effects on changes in work orientation. Our model predicts that the school with high relational trust in 1991 would move from the 50th percentile in the Chicago distribution to the 70th percentile on work orientation by 1994. In contrast, the first school, which was comparable in all regards except for a weak base of trust in 1991, would have dropped from the 50th percentile to the 33rd percentile over the same period. For the 1994 to 1997 period, the projected differences were even greater, the 75th versus the 27th percentile. Although the projected effects are somewhat smaller for changes in parent involvement and safety and order, they are still striking, with differences exceeding 25 percentile points in three of the four cases.

Evidence of a reciprocal dynamic between trust development and school improvement. Figure 5.3 summarizes our results concerning concurrent changes over time in trust and in the essential support indicators.[6] Each bar in the figure displays the degree to which changes in trust levels align with changes in the core organizational indicators, even after controlling for the base state of trust in the school, the base state of the respective organizational indicator, and other school-level background characteristics. For example, consider the changes in parent involvement from 1991 to 1994.

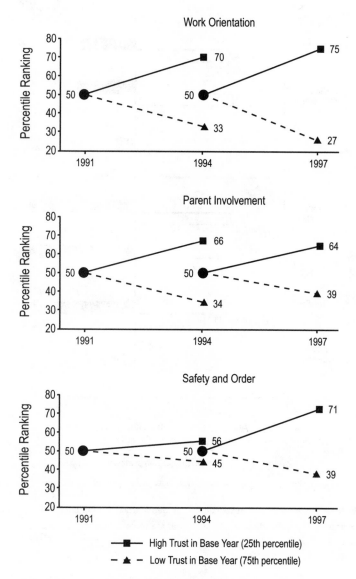

Figure 5.2. Projected effects of the base level of relational trust on improvements in the essential supports.

The difference between schools with strengthening trust over this period (at the 75th percentile in terms of observed change in trust) and those where trust is atrophying (at the 25th percentile in the change distribution) aligns with a corresponding change in parent involvement of 0.84 SD. The comparable effects on changes in work orientation and safety and

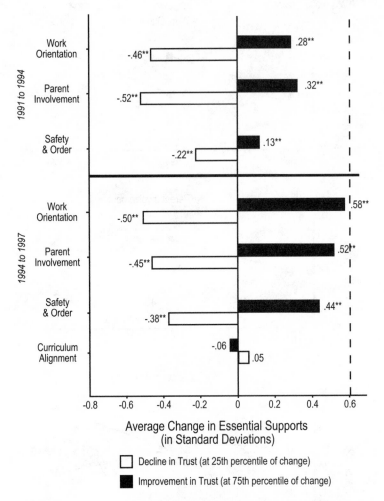

Figure 5.3. A reciprocal association: changes in trust and the essential supports over time. Note: Solid black and white bars represent relationships significant at $p < .01$.

order over the same period are 0.74 and 0.35 SD, respectively. Moreover, all three of these associations are substantially greater for the 1994 to 1997 period (1.08, 0.97, and 0.82 SDs, respectively).

In general, we see that as trust grew in schools so did improvements in teachers' work orientation, the school's engagement with parents, and the sense of safety and order experienced by students. And the opposite was also true. Schools with deteriorating trust experienced significant declines in these three core indicators of organizational functioning. The only exception to this overall pattern occurred with the curriculum alignment indicator, where no change relationship was found.

Pulling It All Together: The Influences of Trust on School Improvement

These results build on and extend the overall pattern of evidence that we have been developing over the previous several chapters. They further advance the empirical warrant for our overall account of the influence of school and community on student engagement and academic learning. We have seen that strengthening the core organizational subsystems of a school is key to improving its academic productivity. We now also know that the state of relational trust in the school community conditions the school's capacity to enhance the functioning of these core organizational subsystems. Presumably, then, schools that initiate reform with weak relational trust and weak organizational subsystems are doubly challenged. Much change is needed in these contexts in order to effect desired improvement in student engagement and learning, but few social resources exist to fuel this. We will return to this theme in chapter 6, where we extend our examination to consider the social capital in the community surrounding each school and the influence that this has on the processes of school improvement. Before proceeding there, however, we first consider how two key structural features of school communities may differentiate the dynamics of school improvement as well.

Structural Factors Affecting Organizational Improvements

We theorized in chapter 2 that school size and the stability of the student-parent group also affect a school's capacity to improve. Previous research suggests that both of these factors influence the formation and maintenance of relational trust, and that both may also have a direct influence on the development of some essential supports.[7] Figure 5.4 illustrates these hypothesized relationships.

Benefits of Small School Size

Early studies by the Consortium on Chicago School Research (CCSR) suggested that school size acts as a facilitating factor for improvement.[8] These CCSR findings are consistent with a larger body of evidence about the positive impact of small school size on teachers' work satisfaction, student engagement in learning, and the efficacy of school change efforts.[9] More

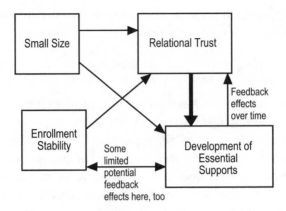

Figure 5.4. Conceptual model illustrating how size, stability, and trust may interact to enable improvements in the essential supports. Note: The width of the arrows reflects the hypothesis about the relative strengths of each effect.

generally, we know from basic sociological theory and research that as organizations expand in size, subgroup structures form in order to coordinate work. Concomitantly, informal social networks also arise, frequently based on common work group assignments and/or ascriptive characteristics (such as commonalities by age, gender, or race/ethnicity). The overall result is that personal interactions across the organization become more delimited and relations more bureaucratic.

This structural fact about organizational size is especially salient for efforts aimed at fundamental school change, as many of these activities demand broad-based collective action among the adult and student members. For example, improving curriculum alignment requires extensive, coordinated activity among a school faculty. Similarly, improving order and discipline requires sustained efforts across both the adult and the student social networks that constitute a school community. However, the large size of many urban schools can act as a significant impediment to these improvement efforts. To be sure, a dysfunctional small school can be just as anomic a social environment as a large one. Changing the latter, though, poses more difficult organizational problems.

In addition, prior research suggests that small school size may also contribute indirectly to the development of the essential supports by facilitating the formation and maintenance of relational trust across a school community. The social network of a small school is typically less complex, allowing personal communications to flow more readily than in a larger school. As a result, relational trust should be more likely to form and be sustained here. In contrast in larger schools, social misunderstandings can more readily occur, and once such misunderstandings do arise, they may be harder to correct. In the end, the persistence of such miscommunication acts to undermine trust.

Benefits of a Stable School Community

We have already demonstrated the important role that strong school, parent, and community ties play in students' engagement in school and how much they ultimately learn. Part of these effects accrue directly through efforts to improve parents' capacity to support the education of their own children. In addition, significant effects can accrue through enhancing the social capital across a school community. When parent-school relationships are strong, for example, school professionals are more likely to experience the personal support that sustains their motivation for the hard work of advancing school improvement. Active parent and community leaders are also key resources for solving problems at the school-community interface, such as issues of safety and order. Similarly, these local leaders can help to engage and nurture a broader, communitywide institutional network aimed at supporting the education and welfare of children.

We posit, however, that such social capital formation is harder to achieve in the contexts of high enrollment instability. First, social capital is predicated on dense, sustained social interactions across a school community. When parents and students are frequently on the move, this network density is weakened. Moreover, case study evidence suggests that in highly disadvantaged school communities it is the parents in leadership roles who may be more likely to move.[10] Consequently, this diminishes both the human and social resources available to support local action in these communities.

Second, social capital formation assumes that relational trust characterizes the quality of the social exchanges occurring within a social network. This is easier to achieve in school communities with more stable student populations, assuming that the repeated social exchanges occurring here have positive valence. In contrast, building trust with a mobile parent community is more difficult and demands constant individual attention. Moreover, even in contexts where positive reputations have been built up over time as a consequence of previous social exchanges among parents and staff, this reputation is less likely to be known to new families, as the community-based social networks that would normally share such information are weaker here.[11] Absent this information, it is not unreasonable for parents new to a school to fall back on a predisposition to distrust, especially if many of their past school encounters tend to reinforce this worldview. Unfortunately, this is often the case in highly disadvantaged communities.[12]

Similarly, the presence of student instability can heighten the salience of both teacher-teacher and teacher-principal trust in the functioning of disadvantaged urban schools. Absent sustained strong support from the larger community, a higher premium is placed on the relationships among school professionals in carrying the burden of reform. Random acts of disrespect and disregard toward teachers may frequently occur in schools with high mobility, since many parents and some students may never get to know the staff well and have reasons to trust them. While school staff may understand the social forces that contribute to this negative parent behavior, it is also quite reasonable for them to feel dispirited. A high level of trust among school staff acts as a leavening agent in this regard.

Taken together, these arguments suggest that efforts to reduce student mobility can lead to improvements in achievement for *all* students, not just those who frequently move. Such efforts can both enhance the likelihood of trust formation, and enlarge the base of human and community resources that directly support school improvement. The collective presence of these resources, as well as any "small wins" subsequently effected in school operations, in turn creates good reasons for parents to go to some length to keep their children enrolled in such a school. In short, a reciprocating process initiates. Subsequent reductions in enrollment instability lead to a further expansion of resources within the school community, which in turn positions the school for even more ambitious reform efforts. Over time, this dynamic eventually dampens as the school establishes new-enrollment equilibrium, but now with a significantly lower student mobility rate.

Evidence Linking Size and Stability to Organizational Improvements

We first examine the overall impact of size and enrollment stability on the development of the essential supports. Second, we assess how much school size and enrollment stability directly affect the essential supports and how much influence accrues indirectly through facilitating trust formation, which we have already shown has a powerful influence on essential supports development.

Analytic approach. We conducted a set of analyses that examine how school size and enrollment stability link to subsequent changes in teachers' work orientation, outreach to parents, school safety and order, and curriculum alignment. We undertook these analyses for the period of 1991 through 1994 to examine whether these structural characteristics facilitated reform initiation.[13] We also conducted parallel analyses for the second phase of 1994 through 1997 to examine whether these same features added further value over the next three years. That is, any estimated effects during the second time period on improvements in the essential supports are above and beyond those that may have already accrued during the first. We controlled for the same school composition characteristics as in the earlier analyses reported in this chapter.[14] During the first set of analyses, we focused on estimating the overall or total effects that might be associated with size and enrollment stability.

Next, we sought to partition these total effects into their "direct versus indirect" components. For this purpose, we ran a second set of analyses, which included the base state of trust (1991 and 1994, respectively) in predicting the changes in the essential supports over the periods of 1991–94 and 1994–97. This allowed us to separate out the direct effect of size and enrollment stability on the essential supports from those operating indirectly through trust formation.

Overall effects of school size and enrollment stability. Figure 5.5 documents that the essential supports were more likely to improve in small elementary schools with enrollments of 350 students or less. During the period of 1991 to 1994, small schools showed greater improvements in work orientation, parent involvement, and safety and order (SD effects of 0.40, 0.61, and 0.44, respectively) than did their larger school counterparts. During the second period (1994–97), substantial effects of small school size appear on both safety and order (SD effect = 0.63) and curriculum alignment (SD effect = 0.46). We found no evidence, however, of further improvements in either work orientation or parent involvement during the second period.[15]

We note that the benefits of small school size on teachers' work orientation and parent involvement appear to have been especially helpful during the chaotic early years (1991 through 1994) of initiating local school improvement under Chicago's decentralization reform.[16] These findings are certainly consistent with the idea that the smaller size of adult networks formed in small school communities can facilitate the processes of adults uniting to improve opportunities for children. Whatever benefits

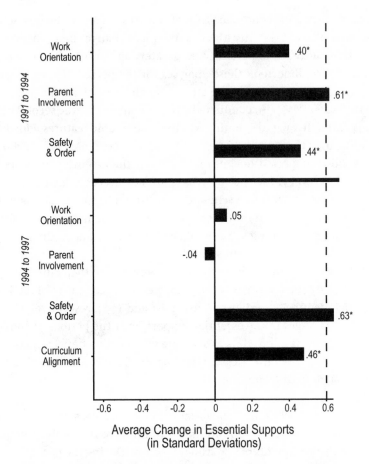

Figure 5.5. Overall effects of small school size on development of the essential supports. Note: Small schools have 350 students or fewer. Asterisk denotes relationships significant at $p < .05$.

may have accrued as a result of small school size were manifest by 1994, and no incremental effects over and above these were recorded as reform headed into its sustaining phase in 1994 through 1997.

We also found smaller but still significant effects for enrollment stability. (See figure 5.6.) Schools with more stable enrollments in 1991 showed significantly greater improvement in parent involvement and in safety and order by 1994 than did schools with low stability. The differences between schools at the 25th versus the 75th percentile on enrollment stability in 1991, holding all other factors constant, amounted to an SD effect of 0.20 on improvement in parent involvement between 1991 and 1994. The comparable effect on safety and order was 0.18. Likewise, schools with more stable enrollments in 1994 were likely to post additional improvements over the next three years in work orientation, parent involvement, and safety and order (SD effects of 0.17, 0.31, and 0.25, respectively). Again, no effect was observed on changes in curriculum alignment. We note that the greater effects of enrollment stability on changes in parent involvement and safety are consistent with the ideas introduced in chapter 2, that the subsystems of parent, school, and community ties and student-centered learning climate connect directly back to greater forces at work in the

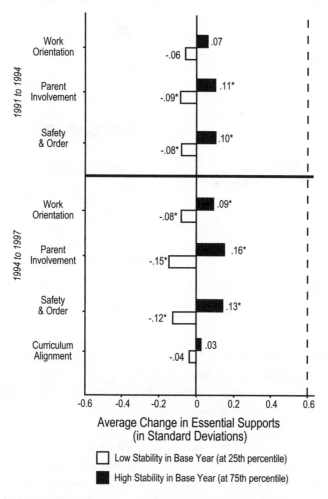

Figure 5.6. Overall effects of enrollment stability on development of the essential supports. Note: Asterisk denotes relationships significant at $p < .05$.

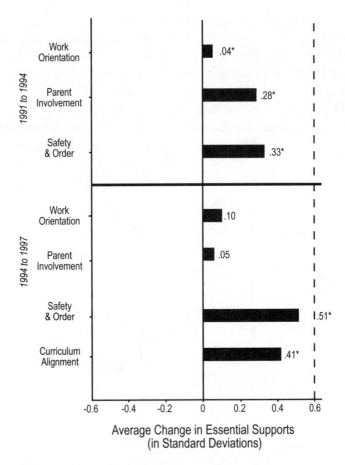

Figure 5.7. Net effects of school size on development of the essential supports. Note: Small schools have 350 students or fewer. Asterisk denotes relationships significant at $p < .05$.

external community. In contrast, teachers' work orientation and curriculum alignment are more dependent on intraschool adult activity, which is consistent with the weaker findings recorded for enrollment stability on these organizational indicators.

Size and enrollment stability effects operating through trust formation. So far we have been considering the total effects of school size and enrollment stability on changes in the essential supports. We now partition these total effects into those that may operate directly on the essential supports and those that influence these supports indirectly through school community trust formation. Figures 5.7 and 5.8 represent the direct effect of school size and enrollment stability on development of the essential supports, net of any effects operating through relational trust. The differences between these direct effects and the total effects previously presented in figures 5.5 and 5.6 represent the magnitude of the indirect effects that are mediated through trust.

In comparing the results across these two sets of analyses, it appears that some of the small-school-size effect operates indirectly through enhancing relational trust formation across a school community. Notice in

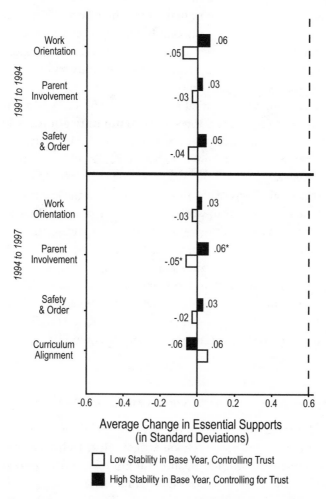

Figure 5.8. Net effects of enrollment stability on development of the essential supports. Note: Asterisk denotes relationships significant at $p < .05$.

figure 5.7, for example, that the estimated direct effect of school size on work orientation in the first period is only 0.04 SD as compared with a total effect of 0.40 SD previously seen in figure 5.5. This means that virtually all the benefit of a small school on the development of teacher work orientation accrues through relational trust that more readily forms in small schools. Similarly, about half the overall relationship between small school size and parent involvement also appears to come about through trust formation. Notice in this regard that the total effect size of 0.61 for parent involvement in figure 5.5 drops to a direct effect of 0.28 in figure 5.7.

In contrast, small size maintains a substantial direct effect on safety and order and on curriculum alignment. (The direct effect estimates in figure 5.7 are 0.51 and 0.41, respectively, for the second period, compared with the total effects displayed in figure 5.5 of 0.63 and 0.45, respectively.) This implies that the structural feature of size directly facilitates a school's capacity to organize and sustain this subset of school improvement activities. Not surprisingly, the smaller adult network of staff within the school and parents and staff across the school community affords a structural resource for attacking safety and order problems. Similarly, the smaller size of the teacher network makes redressing curriculum alignment problems a bit easier.

As for the total effects of enrollment stability on the essential supports, almost all of these appear to work indirectly through the development of relational trust. We see in this regard that almost all the effects of enrollment stability, previously reported in figure 5.6, have dropped close to zero in figure 5.8. The only significant direct effect of enrollment stability was on parent involvement, and this was quite small (0.06 SD). To be clear, enrollment stability does matter for school improvement. These effects, however, operate primarily through how enrollment stability conditions the development and maintenance of more trusting relationships across a school community.

Summing Up the Evidence and What It Means for Practice

In concluding this chapter, we return to a central theme of this book: improving disadvantaged urban schools is a complex, multifaceted endeavor. Even under good conditions, meaningful improvements can take several years to unfold, and entail concurrent changes in the multiple subsystems that form the social organization of a school.[17] We have documented in this chapter how a core social phenomenon—the base of relational trust in a school community—and two key structural facilitators—small school size and a stable student enrollment—assist in advancing organizational change in these multiple areas and thereby contribute to enhanced student learning. In essence, we have another layer of detail to our school improvement recipe.

One fact clearly stands out as we look at the pattern of results presented here. The impact of the effects of trust on subsequent developments in the essential supports is quite large in both relative and absolute terms. These results offer strong testimony that trust formation in a school community is a key mechanism in advancing meaningful improvement initiatives. Returning to our "baking a cake" metaphor introduced in chapter 2, if the five essential supports are the core ingredients for school improvement, then trust represents the social energy, or the "oven's heat," necessary for transforming these basic ingredients into comprehensive school change. Absent the social energy provided by trust, improvement initiatives are unlikely to culminate in meaningful change, regardless of their intrinsic merit.

Finally, although the overall effects associated with school size and enrollment stability are lesser in magnitude, these two structural factors still play a significant role. Much of this works through their facilitating trust formation. In addition, we found some direct influence of school size on selected aspects of the essential supports. Taken together, these findings offer a glimpse into the complex interplay of factors at work in realizing good schools.

THE INFLUENCES OF COMMUNITY CONTEXT

Up to this point, we have focused primarily on how the internal social organization of schools supports (or impedes) improvement. We now turn our attention to the broader social context in which schools exist and the role that such contexts may play in developing the essential supports and ultimately in shaping student outcomes.

As noted in the introduction, the Chicago School Reform Act of 1988 shifted primary responsibility for school improvement from the school system central office out into local communities. Decentralization reformers argued that, with sufficient resources and authority, parents and community leaders could become effective advocates for school improvement and could help mobilize community resources behind local problem solving. The key to using democratic localism as a lever for change was parents' shared interest in securing a quality education for their children. Consistent with democratic political theory, this common interest would motivate the necessary voluntary associations among parents and community residents to improve their local schools.[1]

Implicit in this argument was the idea that all school communities have a base of resources that can be drawn on to leverage school change. But the types of resources needed and how they might be best deployed were left largely unspecified by reformers. Critics of decentralized reform worried that, while schools located in neighborhoods with strong human and financial resources might well improve on their own, other schools located in more-disadvantaged, low-resource neighborhoods would be left behind. They questioned whether sufficient capacity existed in all communities to get this job accomplished.[2] We now know that some schools in some highly disadvantaged contexts, like Herbie Hancock Elementary

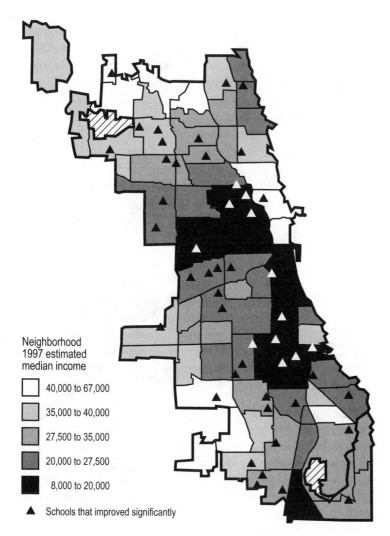

Figure 6.1. Substantially improving schools, by median family income.

School, achieved substantial improvements in student learning. However, others, like Alexander Elementary, did not.

From the outset, we anticipated that the decentralization reform in Chicago would produce diverse outcomes.[3] Moreover, the possibility that these consequences might be inequitably distributed among school communities was a regular part of the Consortium on Chicago School Research's (CCSR's) research agenda, beginning with our very first study in 1991. During the first two years of reform, we found no evidence of such inequities by race/ethnicity, income, or any other demographic feature.

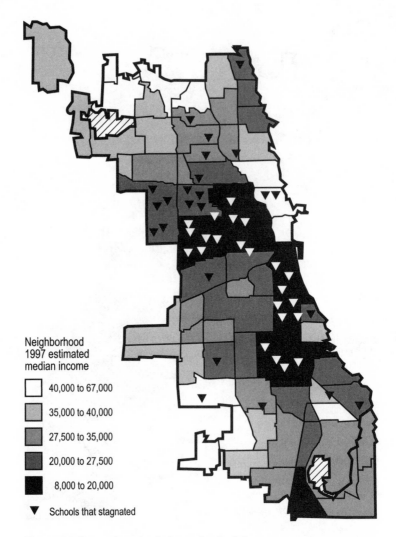

Figure 6.2. Stagnating schools, by median family income.

By 1994, however, a somewhat different picture began to form. As reform moved from the early mobilizing/initiation phase into making demands for sustained adult efforts at improvement, evidence of social inequities began to appear. The overall pattern, however, was quite complex. The glass was literally both half full and half empty.

Proponents of the decentralization reform were correct. Schools with improving academic productivity were broadly dispersed across the city's neighborhoods (see figure 6.1). The critics, however, were also correct. When we shift our consideration to nonimproving schools, these were

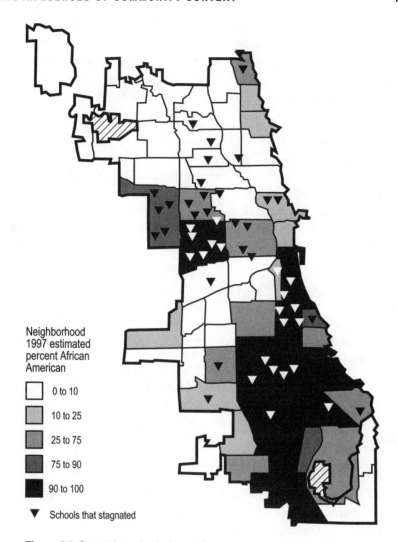

Figure 6.3. Stagnating schools, by racial composition.

disproportionately located on the South and West sides of the city, in the lowest-income communities (see figure 6.2) that have traditionally housed Chicago's large African-American population (see figure 6.3). So yes, schools in all parts of the city did improve, but these improvements were more likely to occur in neighborhoods where the base levels of socioeconomic resources were higher.

It would have been easy to stop at this point with a simple descriptive fact—decentralization did not work as well in low-income African-American communities—and leave it to the readers' interpretation as to why

this might be so. We felt a need, however, to push beyond just document-
ing variation in performance by the standard markers of social class and
race/ethnicity. Simply knowing that these differences exist does not tell us
much about the possible underlying causes and affords little insight as to
how such inequities might be better addressed in the future.

This led us to explore three interrelated questions:

- What more could we learn about the distribution of reading and mathematics improvements across different types of school communities in the city?
- What underlying school community factors, if any, might be linked to these
  patterns of school improvement? And,
- To the extent that schools in disadvantaged communities were less likely to
  improve, was this primarily a result of difficulties in sustaining development
  on the essential supports, or might the model of essential supports simply
  not apply in these contexts?[4]

This chapter reports on what we have learned in this regard.

A Closer Look at Improvement by School
Race/Ethnicity and Social Class

We noted in the introduction that the standard school demographic
marker of percentage of low-income students enrolled (that is, the proportion of students who meet the federal eligibility standard to receive a free
or reduced-price lunch) was not a very useful statistic for distinguishing
among disadvantaged schools in a major urban context like Chicago. As
we brought additional information to form a better indicator of the school
community's socioeconomic status, clearer distinctions emerged. These
patterns became highly salient when combined with information on the
racial and ethnic composition of schools.

In figure 6.4, we display the distribution of schools on the expanded
SES indicator, broken out by basic categories of school racial/ethnic composition.[5] These data demonstrate a clear link between a school's socioeconomic composition and its racial and ethnic makeup. With only one exception, all the integrated and racially mixed schools were above average
in terms of the SES of their students.[6] The predominantly Latino and predominantly minority schools (a mixture of Latino and African-American
students) tended to cluster around the middle of the socioeconomic range.
In contrast, predominantly African-American schools were found across
the entire social-class spectrum in the city of Chicago. While a significant
number of predominantly African-American school communities were

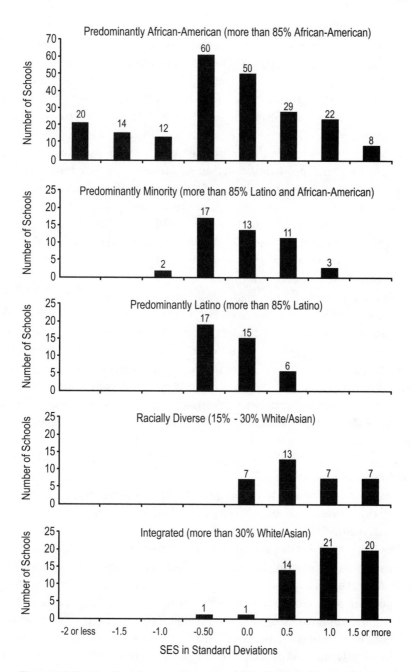

Figure 6.4. Variation in socioeconomic status among schools of different student racial and ethnic composition.

relatively advantaged, all the most impoverished schools were predominantly African American. These are the truly disadvantaged schools identified in the introduction.[7] In Chicago, extreme poverty combines with racial isolation.

Given the strong interconnections between race/ethnicity and social class in Chicago's schools, it made little sense to attempt to investigate the independent effects of these two factors. Instead, we decided to classify schools into seven distinct groups based jointly on their racial/ethnic composition and social class data.[8] In addition to the four relatively discrete groups previously identified in figure 6.4 (integrated, racially diverse, predominantly Latino, and predominantly minority schools), we further subdivide the large pool of predominantly African-American schools along social class lines into a "truly disadvantaged," a low-SES, and a moderate-SES African-American group. Table 6.1 provides additional descriptive statistics on these school communities.

Marked differences are manifest among the seven groups of schools. Seventy percent of families lived below the poverty line in truly disadvantaged school communities, compared with only 7 percent in the communities served by integrated schools.[9] Similarly, the median family income (1990 Census) in integrated school communities was about $37,000; in truly disadvantaged communities, it was only one-fourth of that. Moderate-SES African-American schools and racially diverse schools looked relatively similar on a range of SES markers. Predominantly minority and predominantly Latino schools looked comparable as well. In contrast, low-SES African-American schools appeared more disadvantaged than all four of these other groups.

As expected, we also found large and significant differences across the seven categories of schools with respect to trends in academic productivity in both reading and mathematics. (See figures 6.5 and 6.6.) Almost half the schools in truly disadvantaged, racially isolated communities remained stagnant with regard to students' reading, with only 15 percent of the schools in this group showing significant improvement. In contrast, over 40 percent of the integrated schools improved in reading and less than 20 percent remained stagnant. The mathematics improvements in integrated schools were especially noteworthy. Almost 60 percent of these schools substantially improved, while only 5 percent stagnated. In this regard, integrated schools far outpaced every other school community subgroup.

It is important to recognize that we are employing in these analyses a relative classification of school communities within a school district that is predominantly low income overall. While it is easy to slip into language de-

TABLE 6.1. Summary statistics on the racial-SES classification of school communities

	Truly disadvantaged	African American low-SES	African-American moderate-SES	Predominantly minority	Predominantly Latino	Racially diverse	Racially integrated
Number of schools	46	95	74	45	39	34	57
% African-American	100%	99%	99%	34%	3%	21%	14%
% Latino	0%	1%	1%	61%	93%	56%	35%
% White	0%	0%	0%	4%	4%	17%	40%
SES*	−1.9	−0.6	0.4	−0.3	−0.3	0.5	0.8
% Low-income students in school	96%	90%	83%	93%	94%	86%	70%
Male unemployment rate in block group	64%	46%	32%	29%	24%	24%	22%
Median family income in block group	$9,480	$19,385	$33,413	$23,293	$23,381	$33,156	$37,350
Percentage of families below the poverty line in block group	70%	38%	14%	30%	25%	17%	7%

*The socioeconomic status (SES) indicator was standardized on a sample of 460 schools.

SOURCES: Data on students' race, ethnicity, and percentage eligible for free or reduced-price lunch were supplied by CPS. Using school and students' addresses, we located schools and students' neighborhoods in census block groups, and from these we obtained estimates of the proportion of male residents not employed, median family income, and percentage of families below the poverty line.

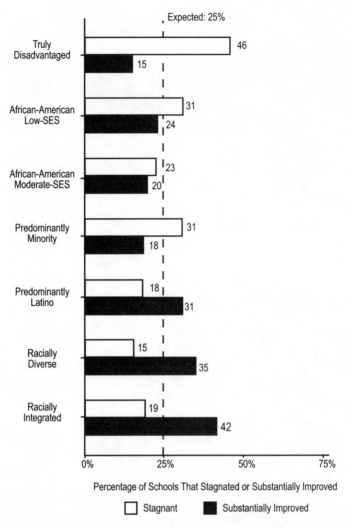

Figure 6.5. Stagnation or substantial improvement in reading, by race/ethnicity and socioeconomic status of students and their communities.

scribing integrated schools as "advantaged," many schools in this category were actually quite disadvantaged in absolute terms. The average school in this group, for example, had a 60-percent minority enrollment, with 70 percent of their students qualifying for free and or reduced-price lunch. From this perspective, the improvement rates observed in this subgroup of schools strikes us as quite remarkable.

Even so, the overall message still remains clear. Increasing inequities marked the period of school decentralization in Chicago. Integrated, Latino, and racially diverse schools were much more likely to progress than schools that were predominantly minority (a combination of Latino and African-American students) or predominantly African-American, including the moderate-SES subgroup. Most significantly, even though moderate-SES African-American schools looked similar to racially diverse schools on basic socioeconomic factors and appeared more advantaged than predominantly Latino schools, their stagnation rates were substantially worse. Es-

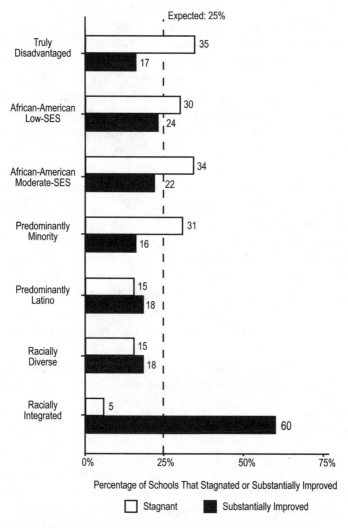

Figure 6.6. Stagnation or substantial improvement in mathematics, by race/ethnicity and socioeconomic status of students and their communities.

pecially troubling, truly disadvantaged schools faired least well of all, with only 15 percent of these schools improving in reading and 17 percent in mathematics. So while some schools like Herbie Hancock "beat the odds," many of their demographically similar counterparts did not.

Probing Deeper: School Community Factors
Affecting the Capacity to Improve

As we sought to bring our work to a close on *Organizing Schools for Improvement*, we remained haunted by this question: What made reform so difficult to advance in these school communities? Faced with this puzzle, we first considered possible insights that might be gleaned from other related research on urban communities. Contemporary inquiries on the nature and functioning of community-level social capital seemed especially relevant. A number of such studies have documented a significant link between the quality of the social connections among residents in a community and that community's capacity to address local problems. Might this be part of what we were seeing in our data as well?

Looking for additional clues, we also pursued a second and very different tack: a broad empirical investigation of other available school community characteristics. Almost by accident, one factor caught our attention: stagnating schools had a relatively high percentage of students "living with nonparental guardians" as recorded in CPS records. This one piece of data, which we interpreted as a proxy for children living in a foster care arrangement, suggested another possibility. Might the concentration of students living under extraordinary circumstances—in foster care, homeless, neglected or abused, and/or living in a household marred by domestic violence—pose exceptional demands on schools that made attention to reform much harder to sustain? This represents a second, quite different potential explanation for the inequitable outcomes documented above.

Community Social Resources and School Improvement

A growing body of research in the area of urban community sociology focuses on the quality of social relationships in communities and how these relationships constitute a form of social capital shared among the residents of a neighborhood.[10] As James Coleman argued over two decades ago:

> If physical capital is wholly tangible, being embodied in observed material
> form, and human capital is less tangible, being embodied in the skills and

knowledge acquired by an individual, social capital is less tangible yet, for it exists in the relations among persons. Just as physical capital and human capital facilitate productive activity, social capital does as well.[11]

Not surprisingly, subsequent urban community studies have documented a wide range of positive consequences of social capital, including an enhanced ability of communities to mobilize for local problems,[12] sustain and maintain effective local democratic governance arrangements,[13] and control neighborhood crime.[14] On the more troublesome side, this research has also found that social capital can be in short supply in the poorest of urban neighborhoods. Beginning with William Julius Wilson's seminal work on the truly disadvantaged,[15] a body of evidence has now emerged that residents in the poorest communities are less likely to belong to community-based organizations, participate less actively even when they do belong, and report lower levels of collective efficacy in dealing with community problems. Many feel that they can do little to control the bad things happening around them. In addition, these urban residents are often quite isolated, with few meaningful contacts outside their neighborhood, thereby limiting their capacity to draw on external expertise to redress individual and local community concerns.[16]

Bonding social capital and bridging social capital. The research on social capital describes two forms of this resource, each serving a different purpose. Bonding social capital focuses on the density of supportive social ties within a neighborhood or community.[17] The existence of such ties affords group solidarity that makes achieving collective goals much more likely. Informal networks among residents in port-of-entry immigrant communities, for example, provide needed psychological and social support for new members. These social networks can ameliorate a range of social needs, such as helping the old and infirm, caring for children, and protecting one another from criminal elements.

In contrast, bridging social capital accrues as community residents have opportunities to engage with external individuals and organizations. These links to "different others" are valuable for just this reason. For example, bridging social capital can help job seekers in low-income communities benefit from acquaintances with individuals outside their community who can facilitate introductions to potential employers.[18] Similarly, tutoring and mentoring programs organized by churches can bring middle-class residents into extended relationships with low-income students and their families.[19] A special case of bridging social capital is the "constructive connections . . . between organized residents of poor communities and the officials and staff of public and private institutions."[20] In low-income, inner-city communities, churches and schools provide an essential training ground in this regard. Both institutions afford opportunities for residents to gain valuable civic experiences and to develop as local leaders with connections to powerful agents outside the community.[21] In fact, some proponents of Chicago's experiment in using democratic localism as a lever for school improvement envisioned decentralization as a potentially powerful community-building resource for these opportunities.[22]

In general, it is thought that bonding social capital is foundational for establishing bridging social capital, and both are necessary for establishing and maintaining viable local institutions that can take action on behalf of the community. Put succinctly, "bonding social capital constitutes a kind of sociological superglue, whereas bridging social capital provides a sociological WD-40."[23] Bonding social capital ties a community together, and bridging social capital helps lubricate its collective actions. It is worth noting that the framers of the 1988 Chicago School Reform Act assumed, at least implicitly, that sufficient social capital existed in every Chicago neighborhood to elect Local School Councils, secure external resources, and drive reform at the local level. Could gross inequities in the base of neighborhood social capital actually be part of the problem?

The special role of religious institutions as a moral resource for social action. Community institutions create a natural base for the formation and use of social capital, and religious organizations in particular can play an especially vital role. Like other neighborhood institutions, they afford an extant base of social capital (the existing relationships among church members) that can be appropriated to support some new collective action. Common to religious institutions, this collective action is infused with moral purpose, thereby adding a powerful catalyst for change.[24] Churches can foment a deep sense of collective responsibility for attacking neighborhood problems and vitalize a civic life with an "explicitly biblical second language."[25] One has only to recall the impassioned speeches of Martin Luther King Jr. to appreciate the mobilizing power that such language affords.[26]

This feature appears especially salient in urban African-American communities, which historically have had very high rates of religious participation, and where many churches have been actively involved in providing services and advancing community development and political action.[27] Unfortunately, in highly disadvantaged communities, these institutions, like most others, have been seriously weakened by the widespread dein-stitutionalization that Wilson documented. Their viability represents still another significant social resource whose presence (or absence) in a community could materially affect a neighborhood's capacity to improve its schools.

Crime and violence as a barrier to social capital formation. While certain social features of communities afford valuable resources for school improvement, other factors can create formidable barriers. Specifically, a high level of crime and violence can have profoundly debilitating effects on the formation and sustenance of social capital. Although the overall crime rate had been gradually declining in Chicago, high levels of violence and drug trafficking persist in many of its neighborhoods, particularly along the western and southern corridors. As we noted in the prologue about the Alexander Elementary School, a fear of victimization presented a serious barrier for scheduling evening meetings and other school community events aimed at local improvement efforts.

We are reminded on this account of de Tocqueville's classic observation about the essence of American democracy: the voluntary association of citizens to advance solutions to problems afflicting their life in the commons. This was the vitalizing spirit of Chicago's democratic localism: parents and community members coming together to improve their local schools. However, a fear of victimization can create a barrier to this civic participation. If so, highly disadvantaged school communities would be deprived of yet another significant resource for improving their local schools.

The Concentration of Students Living under Extraordinary Circumstances

As mentioned earlier, complementing this theoretical inquiry into how the social resources of a community affect its capacity for collective problem solving was a broad-based data exploration scanning empirical evidence that might suggest additional explanations. Our initial observation linking the proportion of children with "nonparental guardianship" and stagnation in students' reading and mathematics learning gains held up as we probed the data further. Subsequently, we were able to obtain information from the actual administrative records on students' placements in foster care, which allowed us to estimate directly the relationships with both individual student learning and overall school improvement.[28]

As anticipated from the nonparental guardianship data, foster-care children tended to be concentrated in certain schools, most of which were low performing. Specifically, one-fourth of children in foster care in Chicago were concentrated within 27 elementary schools, which represent only 5 percent of the system. We also learned that individual students in foster care made reasonable academic progress as they moved through the grades. However, the majority of foster-care students were substantially behind academically prior to their foster-care placement, and this gap did not close over time.[29] Taken together, these results suggested that the rates of nonimprovement in these schools could not simply be explained away as a consequence of having a large number of individual students who were "slow learners."[30] Students in foster care were not a major subgroup in any school, and they were learning at about the same rates as their other classmates in these schools. Even so, it also remained clear that schools with relatively high concentrations of such students were less likely to improve. These results led us to speculate that some form of a concentration or density effect might be at work here.

Bringing a school practitioner's perspective to bear on these findings suggested that we were probably looking at a phenomenon considerably broader than just foster care. An endemic concern for urban schoolteachers are the students in their classrooms with extraordinary personal and social needs.[31] Many urban children live under unstable home and community circumstances, including homelessness, domestic violence, abuse, and neglect. In such circumstances, a most basic need for healthy child development—stable, dependable relationships with caring adults—may not always be present. Not surprisingly, such children can make extraordinary demands on teachers when they appear in their classrooms. The natural inclination for school staff is to respond as fully as humanly possible to these heartfelt personal needs; but if the number of students presenting substantial needs is too large, even extraordinary teachers can be quickly overwhelmed.

Similar concentration effects can occur at the school level. Each student, receiving some form of external social services, may come with a different caseworker. School staffs have to interact with a large number of external service providers, and these providers themselves can turn over very rapidly. A Chapin Hall study found, for example, that on average, 45 percent of foster-care children have two or more caseworkers in a single year. Among schools with ten or more students in out-of-home care, the school staff had to interact with, on average, more than eleven different caseworkers in a single year.[32] And this is for only one social problem! If we factor in the full panoply of conditions under which some students live, and the attendant social services that they may in turn be connected to, a major problem of service integration, coordination, and communication presents itself. Moreover, this is all occurring in the context of an urban school district which significantly underfunds support for these social, psychological, and behavioral needs.[33]

In short, another possible mechanism sustaining school stagnation comes into clear focus. At both the classroom and the school level, the good efforts of even the best of educators are likely to be seriously taxed when confronted with a high density of students who are in foster care, homeless, neglected, abused, and so on. Classroom activity can understandably get diverted toward responding to these manifest personal needs. Similarly, it can be difficult at the school level to maintain collective attention on instructional improvement when the social needs of children continue to cry out for adult attention. It is easy to see how the core work of instruction and its improvement can quickly become a secondary priority.

Measuring Community Social Capital

To investigate how the social capital of a neighborhood and the density of students living under extraordinary circumstances might affect school improvement, we needed to develop good indicators for these potential explanatory factors.

Bonding social capital. We drew primarily on 1995 community survey data collected by the Project on Human Development in Chicago Neighborhoods (PHDCN). This interdisciplinary study, conducted by scholars at the Harvard School of Public Health, Columbia University, the University of Michigan, and the University of Chicago, sought to understand the causes and pathways that lead some children and youth toward antisocial behavior, such as crime and substance abuse, while others follow a more positive course. Included in this study was an intensive community survey, which provided in-depth information about the social conditions in each Chicago neighborhood.[34] This made it possible for us to characterize the social resources in the neighborhood around each elementary school.

Specifically, we drew on two PHDCN scales—collective efficacy and local religious participation—as indicators of bonding social capital. The collective efficacy measure taps the shared values and social cohesion of a community in responding to local problems that may arise. PHDCN researchers had previously found that communitywide collective efficacy can ameliorate the prevalence of a wide range of concerns, including delinquency, crime, and violence.[35] The scale includes items that asked respondents to

report on how likely it was that neighbors would intervene if they observed antisocial adolescent behavior such as graffiti painting or truancy.
A second set of more general questions inquired about whether neighbors
were willing to help each other, were trustworthy, and got along with
each other. (Appendix E provides further details on the PHDCN measures
used here.)

To form a measure of local religious participation, we combined residents' reports from four items in the PHDCN survey that asked whether
respondents belonged to a neighborhood religious organization, whether
someone in their household had spoken to a local religious leader about
a neighborhood problem, and their estimates of how many of their neighbors regularly attended church or some other religious assembly.

Finally, to round out our bonding social capital indicators, we added a
third measure based on data about the prevalence of neighborhood crime.
Specifically, we used Chicago Police Department beat statistics to estimate
the incidence of eleven different kinds of crime around each school and
in the neighborhoods where students lived (if different from the school
neighborhood).[36] We reasoned that a high incidence of neighborhood
crime can drive people behind locked doors, undermine mutual trust, and
foreclose opportunities to develop neighborhood cohesion.[37]

Bridging social capital. Finding good data to assess bridging social capital
proved more difficult. Fortunately, there was a single item in the PHDCN
survey that asked respondents to report on their own connections to others beyond the neighborhood. A report of a high number of friends outside
the neighborhood was viewed as an indicator of bridging social capital.
Answers to this question were averaged across respondents within each
neighborhood cluster to create an indicator of the amount of bridging
social capital in each community.

Measuring the Concentration of Students Living
under Extraordinary Circumstances

Beginning in the early 1990s, the Chapin Hall Center for Children at the
University of Chicago, working in collaboration with the Illinois Department of Children and Family Services, began a massive undertaking to
build a comprehensive, integrated database on social services delivered
to children and families in the state of Illinois. While it took considerable
time and effort to establish the necessary working relationships, understand the nuances of various administrative data structures, and work out

a myriad of problems involved in building a reliable analytic database from diverse administrative records, by the mid-1990s, quality data for selected social problems began to become available. Subsequently, through a collaboration of Chapin Hall with staff at the Consortium on Chicago School Research, and with the support and approval of both the Chicago Public Schools and the Illinois Department of Children and Family Services, a computerized record matching was undertaken to link students' school records to these administrative social services data. With these linked data, it became possible to compute indices of the proportions of students in each school exposed to different conditions. After examining the quality of these data for the time frame of interest to us, we eventually settled on using the percentage of students in each school who had been confirmed as abused or neglected as our overall index of the prevalence of children living under extraordinary circumstances in each school.[38]

Community Social Characteristics Link to School SES-Race/Ethnicity Groupings

Table 6.2 documents how the seven different subgroups of schools, formed by racial/ethnic composition and socioeconomic status, varied with respect to the community characteristics. These data align closely with the differential rates of school improvement and stagnation seen previously

TABLE 6.2. School community indicators for different subgroups of schools

	Truly disadvantaged	African-American, low-SES	African-American, moderate-SES	Predominantly minority	Predominantly Latino	Racially diverse	Racially integrated
Number of schools	46	95	74	45	39	34	57
Religious participation (in SD units)	−1.05	−0.40	0.28	0.04	0.78	−0.03	0.60
Collective efficacy (in SD units)	−0.86	−0.48	0.29	−0.03	−0.17	0.40	1.02
Number of crimes per 1000 residents per year	418	336	228	211	163	190	126
Density of outside connections (in SD units)	−0.38	−0.10	0.26	−0.45	−0.65	0.64	0.56
Percentage of students abused or neglected	23%	21%	17%	12%	7%	9%	7%

in figures 6.5 and 6.6. Truly disadvantaged schools are located in neighborhoods with the lowest collective efficacy and local religious participation, and also the highest crime rates. They are also second lowest, just ahead of predominantly Latino schools, on the bridging social capital index based on the density of friendship ties outside the neighborhood. All three of the African-American subgroups of schools have substantially higher percentages of abused or neglected children than the other four groups. In contrast, integrated schools have the most favorable reports on four of the five indicators, and rank second on religious participation.

In general, the five indicators move in tandem with one another as one moves from schools least likely to improve (truly disadvantaged schools, on the left-hand side of the table) to those most likely to improve (integrated schools, on the right-hand side of the table). The only exception to this is in predominantly Latino schools, where a community concentration of new immigrants breaks the pattern a bit. These schools have the highest religious participation rate of any subgroup, but have the least number of social ties outside the neighborhood.

We take special note of the density of students in Chicago schools living under extraordinary circumstances during the period of this study. In the average Chicago public school, about 15 percent of students had been substantiated by the Department of Children and Family Services as being abused or neglected, either currently or during some earlier point in their elementary career. In truly disadvantaged schools, this number swells to almost 25 percent of the students enrolled. This means that in a typical classroom of 30 in these schools, a teacher might be expected to engage 7 or 8 such students every year.

Moreover, as we factor in the presence of additional students who might be homeless or living in foster care, or in households with chronic domestic violence, one begins to develop a sobering picture of the magnitude of the overall personal and social needs facing some schools.

Examining the Linkage of Community Factors to School Improvement

The observed variability among schools on the five school community indicators appears generally consistent with the explanations sketched out above as to how the presence of social capital or the concentration of social problems can respectively facilitate or impede improvement. Before making any assertion about the plausibility of this proposition, however, some direct empirical tests are in order.

A First Look at the Evidence

We return to the basic analytic approach introduced in chapter 3, where we examined how a strength or weakness in each individual essential support was related to improvement or stagnation in student attendance, and reading and mathematics learning. Now we consider how a strength or weakness on each school community indicator links to improvement or stagnation on these same three outcome trends. We defined "high" and "low" on each school community indicator as consisting of those schools in the top and bottom quartiles, respectively, on that measure. A community classified as high in religious participation, for example, means that its indicator value placed it among the top quartile of communities within Chicago.

We first consider the relationships of school community factors with the likelihood of improvement (figures 6.7 and 6.8). The black bars now represent the outcome results for schools strong on each school community indicator, while the white bars represent results for schools weak on each indicator. If school community factors have no effects, we would expect 25 percent of the schools to demonstrate improvement just by chance alone.[39] To the extent that school community resources contribute to improvement, we should see the black bar extending beyond the 25-percent baseline and the white bars falling below it. The differences between these bars again represent the power of the indicator to discriminate between improving and nonimproving schools.[40]

Community factors and the likelihood of improvement. Our indicators of bonding social capital demonstrated broad associations with school improvement (see figure 6.7). Schools located in communities with strong religious participation were twice as likely to improve in reading and mathematics, as compared with schools in communities with weak participation levels. Community religious participation was also linked to a somewhat weaker degree with attendance improvement. Likewise, we see in figure 6.8 that neighborhood crime rate links to improvements on all three student outcome trends. In low-crime neighborhoods, one-third or more of the schools improved, in contrast to high-crime contexts, where only about 15 percent to 20 percent of the schools demonstrated progress. Differences in community collective efficacy, however, were limited to the mathematics outcomes. Over one-third of the schools in high-efficacy communities improved in mathematics, as compared with only 22 percent in low-efficacy neighborhoods.

In terms of bridging social capital, the strength of social ties outside the neighborhood predicts both reading and math improvement. One-third or more of the schools improved in communities with extensive connections, compared with 20 percent or less of the schools where such external social ties were weak. There was no evidence, however, that strong outside connections played a major role in attendance improvement.

Similarly, we found evidence that the density of students living under extraordinary conditions links to the likelihood of improvement. Less

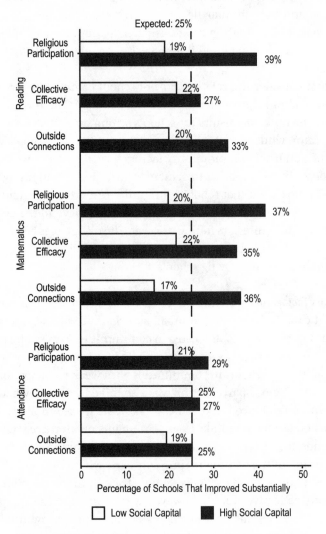

Figure 6.7. Likelihood of substantial improvement, given community social capital.

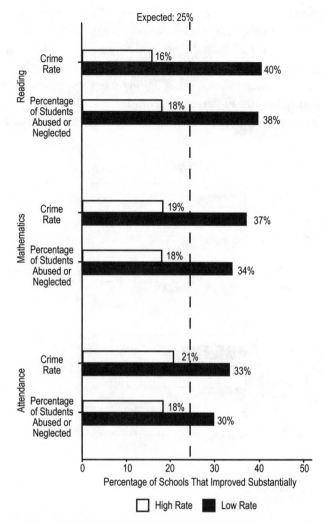

Figure 6.8. Likelihood of substantial improvement, given crime and density of abused or neglected students.

than 20 percent of the schools showed improvement on either attendance or student learning in reading and mathematics where the prevalence of abused or neglected children was high, as compared with 30 percent or more when these problems were less prevalent.

Community factors and the likelihood of stagnation. It is here where we found our strongest evidence of neighborhood effects on reform. The results presented in figures 6.9 and 6.10 document how the absence of social capital and the prevalence of crime and child abuse and neglect greatly increased the likelihood of school stagnation. School communities having weak reports on bonding social capital were typically twice as likely or more to stagnate as those having strong reports. For example, 35 percent of the schools in communities with weak religious activity stagnated in reading, as compared with only 14 percent in communities having strong reports on this indicator. Comparable results occurred for both the mathematics

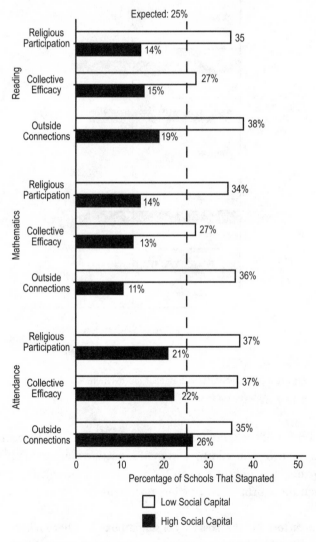

Figure 6.9. Likelihood of stagnation, given community social capital.

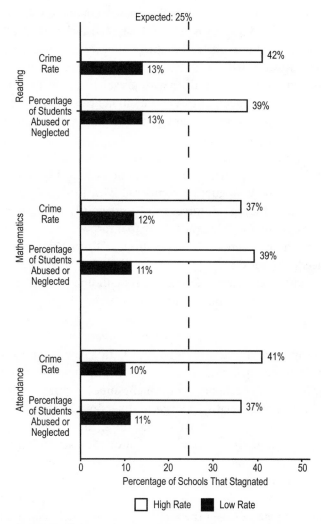

Figure 6.10. Likelihood of stagnation, given crime and density of abused or neglected students.

and the attendance outcomes. Similarly, in communities where residents had few outside connections, 36 percent of the schools stagnated in mathematics, compared with 11 percent of the schools in communities reporting strengths on this measure. The corresponding figures for reading stagnation were 38 percent and 19 percent, respectively. While the observed differences for attendance improvement were somewhat weaker, significant discrimination occurred here as well.

Most significant of all, high crime and prevalent child abuse and neglect were powerfully linked to school stagnation in reading, mathematics, and attendance (see figure 6.10). Schools located in such communities were three to four times more likely to stagnate than were schools in safer, less-violent communities with fewer social problems. Approximately 40 percent of the schools in communities with prevalent crime and child abuse or neglect remained "dead in the water." In contrast, only 10 percent to 13 percent of schools were stagnant in communities where the incidence of social problems was relatively low.

Also of note, a high rate of community crime was an especially strong predictor of attendance stagnation, with 41 percent of the schools in high-crime neighborhoods stagnating compared with just 10 percent in low-crime areas. This finding reinforces results previously reported in chapter 4, where we documented that the failure to improve attendance was more common in schools where students felt unsafe.[41] Given that safety is a basic human need, it is not surprising, then, that attendance problems persist in school communities where safety issues remain unaddressed both inside the school and out in the surrounding neighborhood.

Pulling this all together. These results strongly suggest that the level of bonding social capital and bridging social capital in a community plays a significant role in the capacity of a local school to improve student outcomes. Similarly, the work of school improvement appears quite challenging in communities serving relatively large numbers of children living under extraordinary circumstances. Of special note, these community social forces are more predictive of school stagnation than actual improvement. Taken together, these data paint a statistical portrait of a subset of troubled school communities where leaders are likely to be chronically stressed by pervasive social problems and in return have limited social resources to respond adequately. Given these circumstances, sustained attention to developing the essential supports for school improvement may simply be beyond their ken.

Strengthening the Empirical Warrant Connecting Community Factors to Schools' Capacities to Improve

To examine further this concern and strengthen the evidence base for our conclusions, we undertook additional analyses to discern how much of the observed differences in improvement and stagnation rates among the seven categories of school communities might actually be explained by measured differences in the level of social capital and the prevalence of social problems afflicting various neighborhoods. If each of these community factors does in fact influence the dynamics of local school reform, we would expect that the residual differences in improvement and stagnation rates across the school community types to diminish systematically as these factors are introduced into the analysis. Given the nature of the question at hand here, the discussion below is of necessity somewhat more technical. The reader less interested in these details might skip ahead to the conclusion to this subsection, "Pulling this all together."

We began by calculating the relative odds of improvement and stagnation for schools in each category, as compared with the performance of integrated schools. The white bars in figures 6.11 and 6.12 display these relative odds for schools in each racial and ethnic SES category, compared with integrated schools. Remember that integrated schools had the highest improvement rate and the lowest stagnation among the seven categories. As a result, the relative odds of improvement for each school community type as compared with integrated schools are substantially less than 1.0. Correspondingly, the relative odds of stagnation (figure 6.12) are substantially greater than 1.0 (in other words, these schools are much more likely to stagnate).

We then estimated a series of adjusted relative odds of improvement (or stagnation) after accounting for differences among school communities in (1) bonding social capital,[42] (2) bridging social capital, and (3) the density of students who were abused or neglected.[43] At each respective step, we estimated the expected improvement and stagnation rates that we would have observed had a school community type had the same level of bonding social capital, bridging social capital, and percentage of abused or neglected students as found in integrated school communities.

Accounting for improvement. Figure 6.11 displays the results of these analyses. Controlling for differences among school communities in bonding social capital brought the relative odds of improvement closer to even (a relative odds ratio of 1.0) for all schools, except those in the predominantly Latino category. Introducing the indicator for bridging social capital produced a small additional improvement in 10 out of the 12 comparisons. These adjusted odds of improvement were further homogenized as we took into account differences among school communities in the proportion of students who had been abused or neglected. In some cases, the adjusted relative odds exceeded 1.0, meaning that the observed rates of improvement in these subgroups were actually greater than we should have expected, given their school community characteristics.

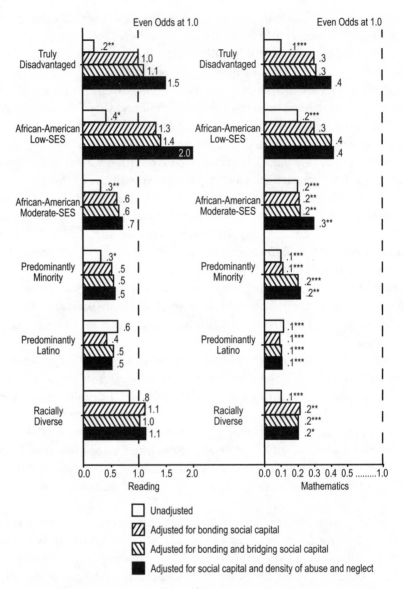

Figure 6.11. Difference in the relative odds of substantial improvement compared with integrated schools, unadjusted and adjusted. Note: In order to show effects clearly, the horizontal scale is expanded for the mathematics graph. Difference from integrated schools significant at *<0.05, **<0.01, ***<0.001.

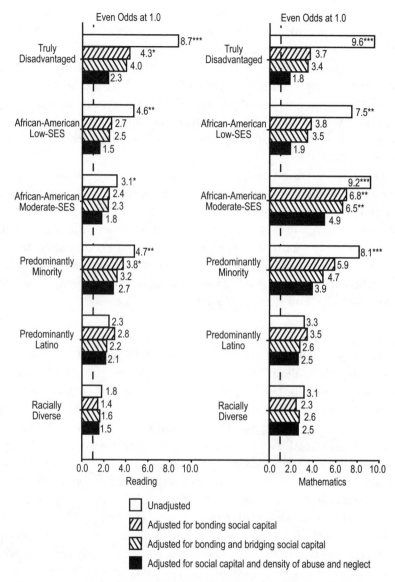

Figure 6.12. Difference in the relative odds of stagnation compared with integrated schools, unadjusted and adjusted. Note: Difference from integrated schools significant at *<0.05, **<0.01, ***<0.001.

In reading, the relative differences were fully explained away in truly disadvantaged schools, and African-American low-SES schools. The observed differences were partially explained in moderate-SES African-American and predominantly minority schools. The only anomaly on the reading outcomes was in predominantly Latino schools, where the adjustment for bonding social capital moved the estimated relative odds "in the wrong direction." (Recall from table 6.2 that the bonding social capital profile for these school communities was atypical as compared with the other six subgroups.)

A similar pattern occurred in mathematics, although the results here were weaker (see right-hand column of figure 6.11). While school community factors accounted for some of the observed differences in improvement rates, integrated schools were still more likely to improve in this subject area than we would have expected, given their community characteristics. Notice in this regard that even after all of these statistical adjustments, the estimated relative odds are all significantly less than 1.0, which means they still favor integrated schools.

Accounting for stagnation. Figure 6.12 displays comparable results for our analysis of the relative odds of stagnation. The impact of social capital appears especially significant here. For example, in truly disadvantaged schools, adjusting for bonding social capital reduced the relative odds of stagnation by more than half in both reading and mathematics. Adjusting for differences in bridging social capital reduced the relative odds a bit further for every category except predominantly Latino schools. Finally, the density of students who had been abused or neglected further cut the relative odds of stagnation by an additional significant amount. After taking into account all three factors, none of the relative odds of stagnation for any group on either the reading or the mathematics productivity trends were significantly different from 1.0. This means that the higher levels of stagnation observed in nonintegrated schools can be largely accounted for in terms of the lower levels of community social capital and higher density of abuse and neglect in these communities.

Pulling this all together. These analyses provide strong support for concluding that differences among communities in their social resources and problems significantly influence the capacity of local schools to improve. As we reflect on the institutional role conferred on public schools, these results should not be surprising. Sitting partway between families, indigenous communities, and the larger society, schools are intended to function as a bridge across the divides which may exist here. Our public schools aim to afford students the academic knowledge and social skill necessary to function in an increasingly complex modern world, and to nurture the habits of heart and mind necessary to maintain a civil democratic society. Inevitably, in carrying out this work, educators must engage parents and their local community. These connections often provide valuable resources for schools, but as our analyses suggest, they can sometimes act as significant impediments to change as well.

To the point, the job of school improvement appears especially demanding in truly disadvantaged urban communities where collective efficacy and church participation may be relatively low, residents have few social contacts outside their neighborhood, and crime rates are high. It can be equally demanding in schools with relatively high proportions of students living under exceptional circumstances, where the collective human need can easily overwhelm even the strongest of spirits and the best of intentions. Under these extreme conditions, sustaining the necessary efforts to push a school forward on a positive trajectory of change may prove daunting indeed.

School Community Factors and the Essential
Supports for Improvement

So far, we have shown that community factors link to a school's capacity to improve student outcomes, and that variations across school communities in this regard offer an account for some of the observed differences in rates of improvement and virtually all the observed differences in stagnation rates. We theorized in chapter 2 about the principal mechanism at work here. Basically, we argued that neighborhood context can affect a local school's capacity to take up and fully engage reform. That is, community factors matter primarily to the extent that they influence the development and maintenance of the essential supports, which in turn affect the probability of meaningful improvements in student outcomes. Moreover, we maintain that these relationships should hold broadly. While it may be harder for a highly disadvantaged community to develop the essential supports, we expect similar improvements in student outcomes when these essential organizational changes do occur. This suggests two final questions for us to examine.

Do Community Factors Affect the Likelihood of Developing
the Essential Supports for Improvement?

In this next set of analyses, we return to the summary organizational development indicator introduced previously at the end of chapter 3 (see
figure 3.4 and accompanying text). Recall that approximately 20 percent
of Chicago's schools demonstrated strength on three or more essential
supports; correspondingly, at the other end of the distribution, another
20 percent manifested weaknesses on three or more supports. If community social resources and the prevalence of social problems impact the
development of the essential supports, we would expect to find substantial
differences depending on these community characteristics. Figures 6.13
and 6.14 illustrate these results.[44]

Clearly, the social characteristics of a school community matter. A
broad base of organizational strength across the essential supports was
much more likely to occur in school communities with bonding social
capital—where neighborhood collective efficacy was strong, residents
were active in local religious institutions, and the incidence of crime was
relatively low. Strong essential supports were six times more likely to be
reported in such contexts. They were also more prevalent in communities with higher bridging social capital, where residents had significant
social contacts outside their neighborhoods. Most significant of all are
the observed differences among schools linked to the density of children
who live under extraordinary circumstances. Broad-based organizational
improvements occurred in 40 percent of schools where the incidence of
abused and neglected children was relatively low. In contrast, only 2 percent of the schools with a high concentration of abused and neglected
children reported strong essential supports.

A similar pattern was observed between the school community measures and manifest weaknesses in the essential supports. Weak reports
were more common in schools located in contexts with low levels of religious participation and collective efficacy, and few social connections
beyond the neighborhood. Similarly weak organizational reports clustered
in communities with high crime rates and relatively higher percentages of
abused or neglected children. In high-crime neighborhoods, for example,
33 percent of schools demonstrated broad-based weaknesses in the essential support indicators, as compared with only 7 percent of the schools
in low-crime communities. Similarly, 31 percent of the schools with high
densities of abused or neglected children were weak on the essential

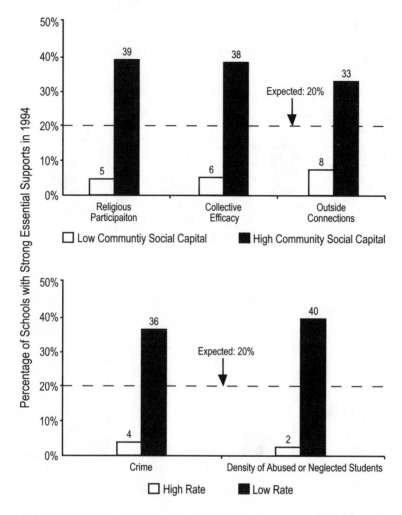

Figure 6.13. Likelihood of strong essential supports, given community social capital, crime, and density of abused or neglected students.

supports, compared with only 5 percent in school communities with relatively low incidences of abuse or neglect.

Taken together, these results provide compelling evidence that school community factors can act as potent catalysts for the broad-based organizational developments needed to improve student outcomes. The presence of community social capital facilitates the work of a school community at enhancing professional capacity, forging vital links to the parents, creating a healthy climate for children, and strengthening instruction. Absent

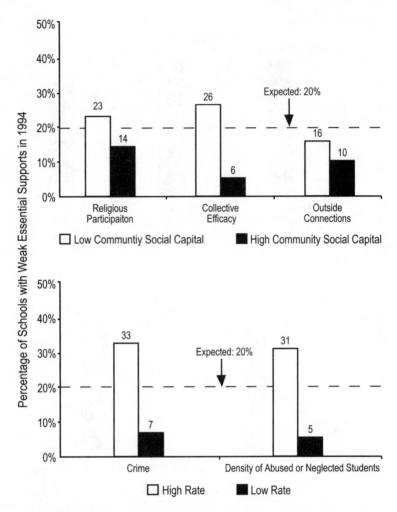

Figure 6.14. Likelihood of weak essential supports, given community social capital, crime, and density of abused or neglected students.

these social resources and confronting dense community problems, while it is still possible for schools to improve, as a few did in Chicago, the barriers appear almost insurmountable.

Do the Essential Supports Have the Same Effects across Different Types of School Communities?

At last, we turn to our final inquiry: what evidence is there that the five organizational supports are indeed essential in all types of school commu-

nities? Especially given the observed differences in improvement and stagnation rates between integrated and other schools, it seemed important to
examine directly the evidence on this account as well. Might it be possible,
for example, that the essential supports were not a route to improvement
in the more disadvantaged school communities?

To investigate this concern, we created a composite index of school
community conditions that combined the five indicators of religious
participation, collective efficacy, outside connections, the neighborhood
crime rate, and the percentage of abused and neglected children in the
school.[45] The bottom quartile on this composite index represents the most
disadvantaged community contexts. These communities have relatively
weak social resources and confront high social needs. In contrast, the top
quartile captures the more advantaged community contexts within Chicago where social resources are ample and social needs less extreme. For
assessing the overall strength of the essential supports, we used the same
composite index as above. We continued to define weak schools as those in
the bottom quartile on three or more essential supports. Similarly, schools
characterized as having strong supports had to be in the top quartile on at
least three components. For the purpose of this analysis, all other schools
were characterized as "average" on the essential supports.

Figure 6.15 displays the percentage of schools that improved or stagnated for various combinations of strengths and weaknesses on the essential supports and community contexts.[46] The left-hand panel shows the
percentage of schools that were in the top quartile on improvement trends
in reading, mathematics, or attendance. The right-hand panel provides
comparable percentages for schools that remained stagnant (or in the
bottom quartile) on these same three outcomes. The solid line represents
schools in more advantaged communities with higher social capital and
lower incidence of child abuse and neglect, and the broken line displays
the findings for schools in the most disadvantage contexts of low social
capital and higher rates of child abuse and neglect.

The results for reading and mathematics improvement are strikingly
similar. Schools in both advantaged and disadvantaged neighborhoods that
developed broad-based strengths in the essential supports were much more
likely to show improvements in reading and math than schools weak in
the essential supports. A corollary pattern of findings appeared for school
stagnation rates (right-hand panel of figure 6.15). About 35 percent of the
schools weak on the essential supports stagnated on reading outcomes in
both advantaged and disadvantaged communities. In mathematics, about
45 percent of these schools stagnated. In contrast, only about 10 percent

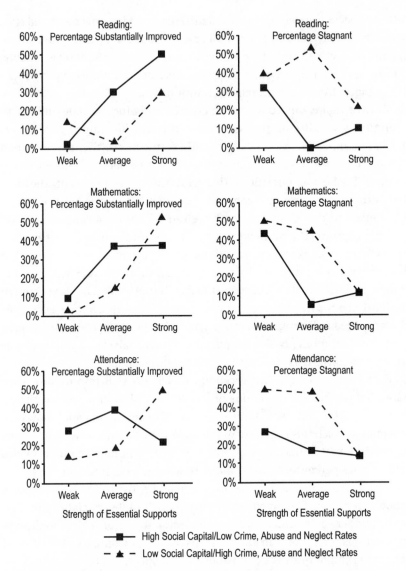

Figure 6.15. Likelihood of substantial improvement or stagnation, given strength in essential supports and level of community social capital/density of abused or neglected students.

of schools with strong supports stagnated in either subject, regardless of their community context.

Attendance trends were also associated with the essential supports, especially in disadvantaged community contexts (broken line). Approximately 50 percent of these schools improved attendance when the essential supports were strong, and only 10 percent remained stagnant. In comparison, almost 50 percent of the schools in disadvantaged contexts stagnated on attendance when the essential supports were weak, and only 10 percent of these improved. The trends in advantaged communities (solid line) appear different. Strength on the essential supports did not differentiate improvement rates within this subgroup. As noted earlier, there is a ceiling effect associated with the attendance indicator, since rates above 96 percent are virtually impossible to attain. Since many schools in advantaged communities began reform with a high level of attendance, the large improvements necessary to be categorized as "substantially improved" were not possible to achieve in these cases. On the other hand, the stagnation rates within advantaged communities did follow the expected pattern. Schools were three times more likely to stagnate on attendance when the essential supports were weak.

Clearly, achieving strength in the essential supports is important for all kinds of school communities. In their absence, comparable stagnation rates occur in both advantaged and disadvantaged contexts. To the point, even strong school community resources offer little buffer in this latter regard.

In contrast, large, significant differences emerged among schools with average levels of the essential supports. Little advantage appears to accrue to schools in disadvantaged communities in shifting from weak to average levels on the essential supports. (Notice that most of the slopes on these line segments are relatively flat.) Only genuine strength on the essential supports results in better improvement rates for these schools. (Notice the marked change in slope for the line segments connecting "average" to "strong" in disadvantaged communities.) More advantaged communities, however, did manifest some positive benefits with the more modest shift from weak to average levels on the essential supports.

There is cruel irony in these results. Schools in communities with weak social capital and high proportions of children living under exceptional circumstances have to achieve robust levels of the essential supports to increase their odds of improving student outcomes. In comparison, schools in more advantaged contexts can achieve measurable benefits through more modest levels of the essential supports. In short, the schools most disadvantaged by community context have to develop the strongest internal organizational supports to effect significant improvements for their students. Unfortunately, our data also indicate that achieving such organizational strengths is an exceedingly difficult task in highly disadvantaged community contexts. Out of 65 schools located in such communities that we considered in this analysis, only 10 achieved this level of organizational performance.

Hence a reform conundrum emerges. The schools that must develop strong essential supports will also often lack social capital in their school communities and may also confront an extraordinary density of student needs. These latter conditions make the development and maintenance of these essential supports quite difficult to attain in most cases.

Summing Up the Evidence and What It Means for Practice

By 1996, Chicago had begun to reap positive results from its decentralization reform. Student outcomes had improved substantially across many elementary schools. Unfortunately, an unintended consequence had also emerged: these improvements were inequitably distributed among the different kinds of school communities that make up the city. As we probed deeper looking for possible explanations, we identified two possible mechanisms at work in this regard: the level of social capital in a school community and the density of students living under extraordinary circumstances. Chicago schools varied substantially on both dimensions, and our analyses found that many of the observed differences in the rates of improvement and stagnation in both reading and math outcomes can be accounted for by the measured differences in these community factors. This evidence demonstrates that the neighborhood served by a school may offer significant social resources, or it may create formidable barriers to sustained development of the essential supports necessary to improve student outcomes. It sums up as a story of how community context fuels the development of school organizational supports that are essential for improving student learning.

This evidence offers new insights about issues often shrouded under the labels of neighborhood race, ethnicity, and social class. Community social capital is a critical resource for advancing school improvement. The presence of such social capital helps to explain why the essential supports took root in some schools and not others. Similarly, we have documented that the density of children living under extraordinary circumstances within a school community can create a significant barrier for improvement. Virtually none of the schools with high concentrations of such students managed to achieve broad-based organizational change during the seven-year period of our study. Taken together, a weakness in community social capital combined with a high density of student needs marks the social context of truly disadvantaged schools. These conditions define an extraordinary set of problems that no districtwide systemic reform initiative has yet been able to grasp fully.

So yes, 100-percent low-income and 100-percent minority communities can improve. But, we have also documented that even among such "disadvantaged schools," some confront much more adverse social conditions than others. These results offer a much-needed antidote to the rhetoric, fueled by accounts of successful change in "90/90/90" studies, that all schools can improve.[47] To be sure, we applaud such hopeful accounts, we endorse their spirit, and we would like to believe in their implications. Yet, we also now know that not all schools serving predominantly low-income and minority students are alike. For some the task of improvement is much more formidable than anyone has acknowledged to date.

Herbie Hancock Elementary School succeeded despite its location in a high-crime neighborhood with weak social resources. It is a story of exceptional leadership that created strong links with organizations both inside and outside the community, and built relational trust among school community members while pursuing a coherent program of improvement, both academic and social. On the academic front, Hancock sustained its focus on aligning curriculum with standards schoolwide, building common instructionally embedded assessments and regularly using them for internal accountability, and coupling this with extensive supports for professional development and attention to recruiting and nurturing capable new staff who were committed to teaching in this school community.

Complementing this and equally important was an unrelenting focus on garnering community resources to respond to the extraordinary needs present in this school. Establishing a sense of safety and organizational order was an essential first concern to address. Assembling a first-rate social services support team and accessing external program services that extended well beyond the meager ones offered by the school system itself was a key sustaining piece in the school's reform agenda. While instruction is the main business of schools, when 25 percent or more of the students live under extraordinary circumstances, as is typically the case in truly disadvantaged schools, a coherent, organized response is needed.

Reconnecting to families and supporting them in the education of their children was another interrelated element. As detailed in the prologue, Hancock School introduced a diverse array of parent education programs. It also launched a diverse array of initiatives to bring other family and community members into more active and supportive relations with students.

While it is unclear which, if any, of these programs had a direct effect on student learning, all of them helped to reweave the social fabric of a more supportive school community.

In short, in communities where there are few viable institutions, where crime, drug abuse, and gang activity are prevalent, and where palpable human needs walk through the school doors virtually every day, a much more powerful model of school development is needed—one that melds systemic efforts at strengthening instruction with the social resources of a comprehensive community schools initiative. Indeed, there are some notable developments in this latter regard.[48] The community schools model, for example, calls for schools to remain open after the regular day and on weekends to provide a locus for a wide variety of services, including healthcare, family supports, adult education, job training, recreation, and many others. Whether efforts like these prove sufficient in the end to respond to the complex problems detailed in this chapter remains to be seen. At a minimum, they at least recognize that the permeable boundaries between schools and communities need to be a major part of the reform equation.[49]

Over the long haul, diffuse social goods may well evolve from initiatives in this domain. While we have documented that a base of community social capital supports school improvement, it is also important to recognize that successful schools are core institutions of local communities. The social networks that form around schools give valuable resources back to the community. A robust elementary school affords an institutional base to strengthen the overall collective efficacy of a neighborhood. In the end, the whole community is what it takes to raise a child.

This book details the results of an intensive investigation of how the organization of schools and local communities affects their capacity to improve student engagement and learning. Our findings are based on analyses of student outcomes from several hundred Chicago public elementary schools over a period of seven years. A unique database has allowed us to rigorously test a framework of essential supports for school improvement. These data provided an extraordinary window to examine the complex interplay among organizational features and how they interact with aspects of local community context to alter dramatically the odds for improvement. Absent such detailed longitudinal data available on students, schools, and communities, these interconnections might easily have gone unnoticed.

The Empirical Warrant for a Framework of Five Essential Supports for School Improvement

We have brought an extensive array of evidence to bear on what we have come to call the five essential supports. School leadership sits in the first position. It acts as driver for improvements in four other organizational subsystems: parent and community ties, professional capacity of the faculty and staff, a student-centered learning climate, and an instructional guidance system. While it has been the practice of many districts and schools to concentrate reform efforts on just one or two elements within one or two of these subsystems (for example, improving the quality of teachers or mandating a common instructional curriculum), the evidence presented here attests that these systems stand in strong interaction with one another. As a consequence of this interactivity, meaningful improvement typically entails orchestrated initiatives across multiple domains.

We began our analyses in chapter 3 with a set of core indicators of the functional capacity of the five distinct subsystems that constitute a school's organization. We found that schools having strong indicator reports were up to ten times more likely to improve students' reading and mathematics learning than were contexts where three or more of these indicators were weak. Moreover, a low score in even just one indicator reduced the likelihood of improvement to less than 10 percent. While the results linking our indicators of the essential supports to improvement in student engagement with schooling were somewhat weaker, we found a powerful effect associated with safety and order on student attendance. Over half the schools that reported problems in this domain failed to improve student attendance over the seven-year period of our investigation.

Taken together, these statistical results provide a strong warrant that each of the five organizational subsystems detailed in chapter 2 plays a critical role in forming student outcomes. To the point, we found that a sustained weakness in any one of these subsystems undermined virtually all attempts at improving student learning.

These findings have important implications as school district leaders think about the tasks of strategic planning for school improvement and re-designing their central offices to support such work. Districts are unlikely to succeed in advancing student learning absent a sustained, integrated, and coherent focus on building their capacity to support school-level improvement across all five domains. Put succinctly, thinking about schools-as-social-systems must operate up, down, and throughout the district.

In a corresponding fashion, school community leaders drawing on district-level support must attend to strengthening the ties among school professionals, parents, and the local community and to expanding the professional capabilities of the school's faculty. Adults within the school community must join together to foster a normative environment that promotes pupils' engagement with more challenging academic work in classrooms. Finally and most important, a coherent schoolwide instructional guidance system must scaffold and integrate all academic activity.

In sum, strengthening these five organizational subsystems is essential work for individual school improvement. Consequently, building a district's capacity to support each of these represents the essential work of an effective district.

In chapter 4 we probed more deeply the interconnections among the five organizational subsystems and the outcomes that ensued as a result. We found evidence of powerful effects associated with the day-to-day social dynamic operating among school professionals, community leaders, parents, and students. We saw that schools with robust ties to parents and the local community benefited greatly as they sought to create a safer and more orderly environment. Such contexts enhanced students' participation in schooling, and pressed and supported students toward more rigorous academic work. These findings substantiate a long-standing observation about urban school improvement and one central to Chicago's 1988 reform legislation: reconnecting local schools to the parents and community that they are intended to serve is central for reform.

We also considered in chapter 4 the organizational mechanisms at work in both improving and stagnating schools. Schools in the latter group manifested weak instructional guidance systems. Poor curriculum alignment coupled with an overemphasis on teacher-directed didactic instruction undermined student interest and engagement in schooling. These instructional system weaknesses combined, in turn, with limited human resources among the school's faculty and few opportunities for social learning across a feeble school-based professional community. Undergirding all of this was an anemic social activity structure for interconnecting students, parents, and teachers.

A complementary set of mechanisms was at work in improving schools. We found evidence attesting to the importance of the organizational subsystems most directly tied to classroom instruction. Key in this regard was quality professional development. Interestingly, the estimated effects of professional development on school improvement, taken alone, were modest. In contrast, maximum leverage was achieved when this activity occurred within a supportive professional work environment, and where teaching was grounded within an aligned instructional guidance system.

Finally, our empirical results also attest strongly to the centrality of school leadership as a catalyst for change. Efforts to strengthen school-community ties and the professional capabilities within a school's faculty demand a dynamic blend of both instructional and inclusive-facilitative leadership. Principals in improving schools encouraged the broad involvement of their staff in reform as they sought to guide and coordinate this activity by means of a coherent vision that integrated the diverse and multiple changes which were co-occurring. The strength of these statistical findings is highly consistent with our own field observations—we know of not even one case of sustained school improvement in Chicago where local leadership remained chronically weak.

A Further Bit of Replication Evidence

Replication of findings represents a fundamental principle for disciplined inquiry. In our case this would mean subjecting our framework to replication studies over time and with data from other districts. Unfortunately, no other district or reform group has engaged in a similar large-scale lon-gitudinal investigation of school improvement, so this form of replication was not possible. However, we were able to undertake one additional test of our findings by examining related data from subsequent reform periods in Chicago from 1997 through 2005.

In the eight-year period following our study, the Consortium on Chicago School Research (CCSR) began to compute annual estimates of the value-added to student learning in each school. Survey data were also collected biannually on a subset of the school indicators used in this study for four of the five essential supports and for relational trust. Taken together, these data allowed us to examine the relationship between this subset of orga-nizational indicators and value-added test score improvements from 1997 through 2005. We note that during this period, the CPS introduced a num-ber of highly structured, centrally developed initiatives to improve failing schools as well as some broader-based professional development programs in both literacy and mathematics. In principle, controlled initiatives of this sort might be expected to reduce the influence of local school factors on variation in improvements and thereby create a more conservative set of conditions for testing the significance of the essential supports.

Even so, we again found strong evidence of the influence of the es-sential supports on gains in student learning. For 10 of the 11 indicators, where we had comparable data over time, the base level on each organi-zational measure predicted subsequent improvements over the next two years in the school's value-added to student learning. This is precisely what we expect to see if the base level of an organizational support conditions a school's capacity to improve productivity over the next period. Similarly, for 9 of the 11 indicators we found that observed improvements in the academic productivity of schools occurred in tandem with school reports about improvements in the core supports. Again as expected, as schools strengthened their organizational capacity, their overall productivity im-proved as well. (See appendix G for further technical details on these analy-ses.) Thus, findings from these replication analyses add one more piece of evidence warranting our conclusions.

Two Puzzling Results

In general, the evidence presented here strongly supports the idea of five essential supports for improving student learning. In two subconcepts, however, the empirical results were not as robust as we had hypothesized. In each case reasonable questions can be raised about the quality of the available indicators in the domain, and some further elaboration may also be in order as to the conditions necessary for significant effects to be manifest.

Relatively weak effects associated with teacher background differences among schools. Arguably, teacher quality is the single most important predictor of differences among classrooms in student learning. A growing body of research documents that it is quite possible to find students gaining twice as much per year as others within the same school, depending on the particular teacher and classroom they are assigned.[1] Why, then, did we find only modest differences in improving the academic productivity of schools associated with our indicators in this domain?

As we acknowledged in chapter 2, a lack of good measures of teacher quality poses a general problem for both research and school practice. Put simply, variations in teacher effects appear large and therefore the assignment of teachers to students matters a lot, but we do not know how to assess teacher quality reliably. Traditional indicators such as years of experience, advanced degrees, and special courses taken typically account for little of this observed variation. Even such high-profile initiatives as Teach for America and National Board Certification have only relatively modest effect sizes when compared with findings from several recent studies about the overall variability in student outcomes associated with teachers.[2]

This phenomenon leads some to advocate that we use direct measures of student learning at the classroom level as a proxy for teacher quality— regardless of the fact that such learning is the joint product of teachers' and students' work together, and involves a mix of knowledge, skill, and effort from all parties involved. While this approach offers some promise for a variety of research and policy analytic purposes, it still leaves the precise practices of effective instruction, including the specification of what teachers need to know and be able to do, as essentially a black box. Developing greater specificity in the latter regard, however, remains critical, as this constitutes the immediate objectives of teacher preparation and professional development programs, both of which are big-ticket budget items. It is hard to envision how these activities could actually improve without reliable and valid information about what truly matters for strengthening instructional practices.[3]

In addition, it is important to remember that we have focused on the school as the unit of change. As such we are inquiring about the quality of a school's overall faculty and its relationship to schoolwide improvements in student learning. Both our indicators and other extant research document greater variability in quality among teachers within schools than between schools.[4] As a result, for this reason as well, it is less surprising that our teacher quality indicators account for only modest variability in school outcomes.

So the bottom line is straightforward. Readers should not interpret our results as in any way suggesting that teacher quality does not matter. Rather, the state of the art for measurement in this domain is weak, and our study was not designed with this as a primary inquiry objective.

Relatively weak effects associated with academic press and student support. We also argued in chapter 2 that the nature of a school's normative environment can have profound effects on student motivation, engagement with schooling, and ultimately learning. We hypothesized that a school's press on students toward higher academic standards must be accompanied by active faculty outreach to know each student well and support each student as he or she pursues the demanding work entailed in responding to heightened academic expectations. Evidence on this point turned out mixed, however.

Recall that the measures developed for academic press and personalism in this study relied primarily on data from students, but our analyses raised some doubts as to whether students are good informants in this regard. Although mobility is high in urban contexts like Chicago, and as a result many students have experiences in multiple schools, students are typically shifting among very similar kinds of schools.[5] As a result, students may simply lack a well-developed frame of reference for offering comparative judgments about the degree of academic press and personalism in any given school. Consistent with this speculation, we found significantly less variability among schools in these student-based indicators as compared with our teacher-based measures. While student reports did discriminate within schools as we expected (for example, individual students who reported stronger press and support tended to do better academically than classmates offering weaker reports), aggregated student data did not differentiate much among schools. In retrospect, these survey items may be better indicators of the social-psychological phenomena operating on individual students within schools than of normative differences among schools. While we continue to posit that academic press and personalism matters, better empirical evidence to fully test this hypothesis is still needed.

Even so, a cautionary note merits mention. It is important to recognize that the significant results found in chapter 4 for academic press and personalism were primarily as predictors of stagnation in attendance and academic productivity. We found only weak or no association with improvement rates. This pattern of findings lends itself to a more nuanced interpretation than a simple declaration that academic press and personalism matter. The stress of a negative environment, as sensed by students, clearly signifies a troubled context, and redressing this is surely an important part of a larger effort to improve learning. By itself, however, an improved environment remains insufficient. In fact, schools can create environments that feel good but where little meaningful academic work is actually occurring. The presence of a supportive normative environment may well condition or facilitate other needed improvements across the school organization. Absent sustained, coordinated efforts in these other domains, however, a stronger social environment taken in isolation remains an inert or untapped resource for improving student achievement.[6]

Revisiting the Analogy of "Baking a Cake"

We argued in chapter 2 that the five organizational subsystems of a school stand in dynamic interaction with one another. As a consequence, improvement entails an orchestrated set of mutually reinforcing activities over time across these domains. We suggested that these processes of improvement are akin to baking a cake. Taking this analogy further, four of the organizational supports—parent-community ties, professional capacity, student-centered learning climate, and the instructional guidance system—can be conceived as a list of essential ingredients. Should a core ingredient be absent, it is just not a cake. By the same token, if there is a material weakness in any core organizational support, school improvement won't happen.

Continuing with this culinary analogy, the overall coherence of improvement efforts, as detailed further below, is akin to a recipe. It provides guidance about how one should mix and blend the ingredients—the diverse array of initiatives across the four core organizational subsystems—to make reform truly add up to systemic change. Similarly, we can think of relational trust as the oven heat that transforms the blended ingredients into a full, rich cake. Finally, standing behind all of this is the head chef. In our case, this is the school principal, who orchestrates the collaborative processes of school transformation.

Detailing the essential list of ingredients has been the prime focus of this book, and we have summarized our results on this account. We now shift to consider in a bit more detail the implications of our inquiries for the chef, the recipe, and the oven's heat.

Local School Leadership as the Catalyst for Change

Through both field studies and school surveys, the research programs of
the CCSR have had multiple opportunities to examine the dynamics of local leadership for change. Taken together, these investigations have led us
to a major practical "take-away": the centrality of principal leadership in
initiating and sustaining the organizational changes necessary to improve
student learning. Quite simply, school improvement is highly unlikely to
occur in its absence.

In chapter 2, we carved the organizational dynamics of schooling into
four core subsystems in an effort to understand how each distinct subsystem influences classroom teaching and student learning. In supporting
principals to think like a leader, however, we now need to reassemble the
separate components into a more integrative frame that can guide principals as they reflect on their everyday actions and engage in longer-term
strategic planning.

Basically, our research suggests that effective leadership attends to two
key ideas.[7] The first is a strategic focus on improving the technical core of
teaching and learning. Leaders must make many decisions about core programs, supplemental supports, the hiring and development of staff, and
setting strategic priorities for where marginal resources (including time)
are to be spent, as well as buffer externalities that might distract from
a coherent course for reform. Orchestrating effectively across these and
numerous other acts of improvement requires sustained attention to what
we have come to call *program coherence*. This framework guides leadership
thinking regarding the technical layer for reform.

Second and working in tandem with this, improvement initiatives
must be grounded in continuing efforts to build trusting relationships
across the school community. Quite simply, the technical activities of
school improvement rest on a social base. Effecting constructive change in
teaching and learning makes demands on the social resources of a school
community. In the absence of these resources, individual reform initiatives
are less likely to be engaged deeply, build on one another over time, and
culminate in significant improvements in a school's capacity to educate
all its children. So building *relational trust* remains a central concern for
leadership as well.

A principal's daily work entails a dynamic interplay between these
two key ideas. Effective leadership requires taking a strategic approach
toward enhancing performance in the four core subsystems while simultaneously nurturing the social relationships embedded in the day-to-day

work of schooling and its improvement. In carrying out their daily activities, school leaders are advancing instrumental objectives while at the same time seeking to develop a supportive followership for change. In the process, they are cultivating a growing subset of leaders (teachers, parents, and community members) who can help expand the reach of this work and distribute overall responsibility for improvement.[8]

Program Coherence: The Strategic Lens for Guiding Change

A focus on program coherence directs attention to aligning all elements of the instructional guidance system; securing the necessary human resources to execute this activity; and strategically allocating scarce resources to enable reform activity and maintain direction over time.

The instructional guidance system and closely related supports. The instructional guidance system begins with a curriculum framework that details the subject matter to be taught. Encapsulated here are the scope and sequence of instruction, which coordinate learning objectives among classrooms both within and across grades. Accompanying this is a common pedagogy: the core practices and social routines that teachers use to engage students in the subject matter. Key here is that the practices and routines of instruction are shared across a faculty, rather than being purely matters of individual choice. This is essential if social learning regarding instructional improvement is to occur. Effecting this collective cognition requires a common language for instruction accompanied by a reservoir of teacher experiences in confronting the same work tasks in their classroom. Minus this resource, improvement conversations would resemble a Tower of Babel.

Next are the assessment systems that operationalize what it is the faculty wants its students to know and be able to do. These data streams create the information feedback loops needed to support a continuous improvement regime. These tools must be shared if a community of practice, organized around evidence of student learning, is to form. Absent shared evidence of student learning associated with common pedagogical practices, there is little basis for collective exploration of the cause-and-effect linkages at the core of improving teaching and learning.

Moving beyond the classroom walls, a coherent instructional guidance system also requires attention to the vast array of supplemental academic support programs common in urban schools. These programs demand coordination among themselves and with core classroom activities. Achieving this is essential if the programs' intent—accelerating student learning—is to materialize. Included here is a conscious focus on how parents and other leaders in local school communities can become more supportive agents in advancing student learning.

Finally, and undergirding all the above, are the assumptions that the instructional guidance system makes about the requisite normative environment for effective teaching and learning to occur. Every approach to instruction imposes certain expectations about how adults should interact with students and how students should engage their classmates. So, these requisite normative aspects must be identified, aligned, and in most instances, refined as well.

Securing the professional capabilities needed to vitalize the instructional guidance system. Too often, choices about instructional systems are made with little regard for the human resources necessary to make the system actually work. At base here is a problem of execution. One may have a compelling vision for instruction, but simply lack the people necessary to make it a reality.[9] To combat this problem, prospective hires must be carefully evaluated for their commitment to and competence in the specific instructional system that has been adopted. More generally, strengthening everyone's work within the instructional system becomes a sustained, targeted focus for professional development. In corollary fashion, teachers' continuing efforts to enhance their expertise within this system become the guiding principle for internal accountability and for individual teacher evaluation.

Accompanying this, school leaders must nurture over time new norm formation where continuous individual and collective efforts at improvement within a shared instructional guidance system are "what we do here." At base are considerations regarding how teachers think about their individual work and their social interactions with colleagues. For example, the successful implementation of many reforms demands sustained collaborative activity among school professionals. Is such collegial activity already normative in the school? If not, developing this capacity becomes another important objective.

Strategically allocating limited school resources to nurture the adoption, use, and continued development of the instructional guidance system. Principals need to provide time and fiscal support for initiatives that advance a school's instructional system. They must create the organizational flexibility necessary for teachers to experiment with new instructional practices, and nurture a safe zone in which this trial-and-error activity can occur. In addition, since teacher learning is typically a long-term process, assuring stability in teacher assignments is a key consideration, because it enables teachers to stay the course within a specific domain of the instructional system [10] so that genuine expertise can develop. And finally, because staff attention is also a scarce commodity, effective principals remove competing agendas so that work on strengthening the school's instruction remains at the forefront.

On balance, we recognize that actually effecting an integrated improvement plan of the sort described above may present daunting challenges for many principals. Advocating instructional coherence at the school-site level entails a frontal assault on long-standing norms about teacher autonomy in the classroom, the privacy of individual practice, and a laissez-faire orientation toward professional development and practice innovation. Not surprisingly, then, cultivating teacher buy-in and commitment becomes a central concern in promoting the deep cultural changes that such an initiative entails. At this juncture, concerns about building relational trust come forcefully into play.

Relational Trust: Building the Social Resources for Improvement

Some of the most powerful relationships found in our data are associated with the effects of relational trust and how it operates as both a lubricant for organizational change and a moral resource for sustaining the hard work of local school improvement. Absent such trust, it is nearly impossible for schools to develop and sustain strength in the essential supports. More specifically, our analyses document that in schools where the base level of trust was high, improvements occurred in subsequent years in teachers' orientation toward innovation and commitment, parent involvement, and safety and order. The reverse was also true: low trust was linked to weaker developments across all organizational subsystems.

Given the asymmetry of power in urban school communities, principals' actions play a key role in nurturing trust formation. Principals establish both respect and personal regard when they acknowledge the vulnerabilities of others, actively listen to their concerns, and eschew arbitrary actions. If principals couple this empathy with a compelling school vision, and if their behavior can be understood as advancing this vision, their personal integrity is also affirmed. Then, assuming principals are competent in the management of routine school affairs, an overall ethos conducive to trust formation is likely to emerge.

The actual dynamic of such leadership entails the constructive use of power to jump-start change.[11] One does not advance trust in a troubled school community simply by assuming its existence. Here it is especially important to distinguish between the ends and means of reform. While the ends are clear—an environment of high relational trust rooted in professional colleagueship, expert practice, and mutual commitment—attaining these may require significant use of role authority.

In the initial stages, school leaders would do well to cultivate low-risk collaborations (consistent with the coherence agenda described above) among subgroups of faculty that may emerge serendipitously and are predisposed to working together. School-based professional development activities should be carefully designed not only to advance the instructional improvement but also to create occasions that enhance a sense of community and shared commitments among the faculty. Similarly, principals must engage parents and other community members in meaningful activities where participants are likely to experience a sense of efficacy in contributing to the school and/or advancing the learning of their own children. Considerable thought is needed to assure that these initial forays are "small wins" for all involved, as these successes gradually build the school community's capacity for the greater challenges (and higher-risk social exchanges) that may lie ahead.[12]

On balance, as principals seek to initiate change in their school, not everyone is necessarily affirmed, nor is everyone afforded an equal voice in shaping the vision of reform. Teachers who are unwilling to take on the hard work of change and align with colleagues in a common reform agenda must leave. It is only as participants demonstrate their commitment to engage in such work, and see others doing the same, that a genuine community grounded in relational trust can emerge. Principals must take the lead and extend themselves by reaching out to others. On occasion, they may be called on to demonstrate trust in colleagues who may not fully reciprocate, at least initially. But in the end, they must also be prepared to use their role authority to reform the school community via professional norms. Interestingly, such authority may rarely need to be invoked thereafter once these new norms are firmly established.

Securing the General Managerial Base

Finally, we would be remiss if we did not return to the observation, noted in chapter 2, that strong school leadership is anchored in the effective management of everyday operations. This aspect of school organization tends to be taken for granted when schools work well; in contrast, the negative consequences associated with its absence are highly manifest. Moreover, school operations in highly disadvantaged communities typically place extra demands on managerial capacity. Exacerbating this pressure are the large, often inefficient central bureaucracies in which the leaders' work must be carried out. In short, the stress caused by the general managerial aspects of urban school leadership should not be underestimated.

Consequently, as we exhort principals to be instructional leaders, we must also recognize the demands they face, sometimes quite heavy ones, in executing the basic managerial affairs of a school community. Urban schools are typically under-resourced and overextended in this regard, yet somehow these pressing, daily operational needs must be addressed. To simply say that principals must now be instructional leaders and spend at least half their time within classrooms, while simultaneously enhancing their school's ability to manage its day-to-day affairs, is an educational pipe dream. Yes, a few heroic individuals of exceptional talent may somehow carry this out, but the vast majority are destined to fail.

Revisiting the Interplay between the Essential Supports and Community Context: The Unrecognized Challenge of Truly Disadvantaged School Communities

In many discussions about school reform lately, ideas about parent involvement and school community contexts fade into the background. For some school reform advocates, it's all about instruction and instructional leadership. This perspective presumes that the public schools' social and personal connections with local families and communities have little role to play in reform. The evidence presented in this book, however, offers a strong challenge to these oversimplifying assumptions. To be sure, instruction matters and it matters a lot; but so does the social context in which it is embedded. We have documented that strength across all five essential supports, including parent-school-community ties, is critical for improvement to occur in all kinds of urban schools. Unfortunately, we have also learned that this organizational development is much harder to initiate and sustain in some community contexts than others.

Specifically, we saw in chapter 6 that the essential supports must be very strong for significant improvement in student learning to occur in truly disadvantaged communities where social capital is scarce. This finding raises troublesome questions about our society's capacity to improve schooling in its most neglected communities. For these school communities, it is a "three-strike" problem. Not only are the schools highly stressed organizations, but they exist in weak communities and confront an extraordinary density of human needs that walk through the front door every day. Not surprisingly in retrospect, many in this group were left behind under Chicago's decentralization, and for that matter, few faired especially well under the more centralized initiatives that followed.[13]

Our findings about schooling in truly disadvantaged communities offer a sobering antidote to a heady political rhetoric arguing that all schools can be improved. Our evidence suggests a need to temper this enthusiasm with a realistic appraisal of the extraordinary problems confronted by some schools. To be sure, this comment should not be read as an excuse to let some places off the hook. But it does require us to recognize that few reform efforts to date have adequately acknowledged the full scope of problems that must be confronted.

One of the main purposes of this book is simply to shed light on these extraordinary needs. In the city of Chicago alone, some 40,000 students are educated every day in truly disadvantaged schools. We must do better. The first step in this direction involves recognizing that we have a critical problem here, one that requires deliberate attention.

How might we think about developing more effective schools in highly disadvantaged communities? One obvious answer is that this is not solely a school improvement problem but rather a broader community development problem. Our results actually provide some support for this idea in that stronger communities resourced the development of stronger schools. At least in the near term, however, this finding offers little solace for the thousands of children and families who reside in neglected neighborhoods, and the thousands of teachers who labor in those communities every day.

One promising alternative approach conceives of transforming schooling in these contexts through a comprehensive and integrated set of community, school, and related social program initiatives. This strategy is anchored in efforts to cultivate local leadership and more productive working relationships among school staff, parents, and local neighborhood services and officials. Building on this human and social resource development is an expansion of student learning opportunities through increased instructional time, coupled with sustained programmatic activities in all the essential support areas so that this expanded learning time is more productive. Also included is a strong programmatic focus on the myriad of social, emotional, and physical health needs that impede the learning of many children.[14]

Others when confronting the enormity of this problem might reasonably ask instead, Do we actually have the right model for schooling in these contexts? There is reason to worry that in some situations, it may simply not be realistic to bank on communities as resource partners for school improvement, because extant local institutions are weak themselves and similarly overwhelmed by the same density of social demands confronting their schools. Might new designs for exceptionally strong schools be needed? Perhaps we should be aiming toward something more akin to a total institution that creates an island of safety and order, established social routine, and new norms for academic effort in order to counter the external forces pushing students in very different directions.[15]

While there are some good examples now of initiatives pursuing one or the other of these strategies, effectively enacting reforms of this sort remains a daunting task. Moreover, as we bring broader attention to the problem of truly disadvantaged schools and engage in a deeper scrutiny of such initiatives, tough and sometimes uncomfortable questions may need to be asked. Eschewing such conversations is a natural response, but in doing so—in being unwilling to put all plausible ideas for educational improvement on the table and seriously consider each—we will continue to relegate many of our students and their teachers to failure.

Revisiting Our Approach to Inquiry

The findings summarized above evolved out of a longitudinal natural experiment that allowed us to probe the organizational demands entailed in advancing local school improvement. Our research involved melding social science theory that deepened our conceptualization of the organization of schools, social science methods that powered our analyses and disciplined how we inquired, and extensive direct experiences in day-to-day reform activity. Interweaving these multiple strands deepened our understandings of the basic phenomena that were focal to the inquiry and allowed us to hear and give voice to a broader set of concerns than might have otherwise arisen if we attended only to policy audiences or disciplinary colleagues. In a very practical sense, this melding of perspectives helped us to design more-sensitive field studies, craft better interview protocols, and draft survey items that were more likely to be in tune with how practitioners actually thought about their work.

Applied social research of this sort is a creative act of identifying the best tools for inquiry: both theoretical ideas and analytic methods. We had to make critical choices during the course of our work—for example, about conceptualizing the systemic nature of schools as organizations and how to empirically test whether a concept of essentiality characterized the organizational dynamics operating among a school's subsystems. Guiding all of this was a simple principle: choosing appropriate methods follows from the primary research questions of interest. In most general terms, both theory and methods are simply tools; and the choice of the right tools is central in the craft of bringing applied inquiry effectively to bear on social problem solving.

Questions, Methods, and Evidence

It is increasingly common in education research to judge all findings against the gold standard of randomized clinical trials (RCTs). In this context, it is argued that great care should be exercised in drawing inferences from a natural experiment such as ours. While this is sage advice, like any working principle it has its limits. It is important to recognize that the "RCT gold standard" actually sits within a larger network of principles for assuring the validity of research findings.[16] In general this larger framework argues that the capacity to draw substantive inferences from any study depends on the generalizability of the populations and contexts under investigation, the disciplined character with which the inquiry is conducted, the size of the effects estimated, and the questions that the inquiry is intended to inform. On each of these accounts, we have good reasons to conclude that the findings presented here are both robust in size and likely to generalize broadly across urban school community contexts.

First and most important, decisions about research design are especially critical when investigating small effects. In these instances, different choices among alternative analytic methods and models can easily lead to drawing different conclusions. In contrast, we have focused our presentations in this book on effects that are both consistent (found in both the 1994 and the 1997 data) and large in size. In fact, they are akin to "interocular effects," so big that they hit you right between the eyes! Concerns about possible confounding inferences due to design artifacts typically fade in the presence of such large effects.[17]

Second, and at a practical level, it is inconceivable to us how one might actually attain RCT evidence, given the core propositions under study here. One cannot assign better and worse levels of safety and order to schools, or different degrees of parent involvement, or an incoherent instructional guidance system. More generally, the subsystems that form the organization of a school are not treatments in the conventional sense that they can be externally defined and assigned to units. Rather, they are largely social phenomena created by the particular group of individuals who form the organization through their work together. Of necessity, we need other methods to explore such naturally developing phenomena.

This, in turn, closely connects with a third consideration: the epistemological nature of the core questions focal to our inquiry. Specifically, we sought to ascertain fundamental features that constitute the organization of schools and affect their capacity to improve. Toward this end, we were concerned about the variability in outcomes and how local school and community conditions contributed to this. In reporting on the results of this inquiry, we have focused on distilling a set of core, robust, replicable findings that warrant an empirically grounded theory of how school context and organization interact with efforts to enhance student learning. This is quite different from the objective of the typical RCT, which seeks to establish a precise estimate of some "average effect" associated with a particular intervention protocol in some set of sites. Such an RCT may remain agnostic about questions concerning how and why and when these effects accrue. Yet these were the central questions for our study as we sought to develop sturdy knowledge to inform subsequent reform activity.

Finally, the strength of a large natural experiment of the type that we have exploited in our research is precisely that it is large and natural. It provided us with a rare opportunity to examine organizational change as it played out over time across many different school and community conditions. To this point, our results are not from some small, possibly atypical sample of schools who volunteered to participate in a structured experiment, but rather from a whole system of schools attempting to improve themselves under local control. Some of these were willing participants, but others much less so. This combination—the diversity of the school community considerations that we were able to study and the naturalness of the schools' reform effort—adds considerably to the overall generalizability of our findings.

Research on School Improvement as Disciplined Inquiry

In addition, even though our objective was a very practical concern—the improvement of schooling—we operated from a standpoint that the basic principles of scientific inquiry can and should apply.[18] Throughout the conduct of our research, we brought scientific rigor to bear in conceptualizing the basic phenomena to be studied; assessing the reliability and validity of the measures; making the data, our analyses, and the processes of interpretation public; investigating whether our findings replicated over time; and vetting this work along the way through a diverse set of research, practice, and policy stakeholders.

Especially important in this regard was the ongoing, constant scrutiny that this activity received from the Steering Committee of the Consortium on Chicago School Research. It initially inspired the investigation, challenged the work in progress, offered alternative explanations for emerging findings, and pushed us toward greater levels of rigor and specificity. The voices within this dynamic, multipartisan mix of researchers, policy advocates, community activists, and school system and professional organization leaders formed a vigorous, social-proof network for our work, and to them we remain deeply grateful. Their intensive peer review provides the strongest assurance for the validity of our findings and the substantive generalizability of these results.

These interactions also pressed us to reflect on our own internal ethics. It forced us to constantly ask: What do I *believe* by virtue of my background, upbringing, and personal ideology; what do I think I *know* by virtue of my professional work experiences; and in contrast, what assertions can I *warrant* with a large body of empirical evidence? Since we were actors within the social phenomena that we sought to study, being vigilant about these distinctions was critical to preserving the special role that inquiry of this sort can and should play in social problem solving. Absent these questions and this vigilance, we may well capture the public's ear, but have nothing really special to say.

Revisiting Decentralization and School Improvement

The main focus of this book has been exploring how efforts to improve the organization of schools can advance student engagement and learning. We have capitalized on Chicago's natural experiment in decentralization to probe a set of interrelated propositions about school organization and change. Along the way, we have also documented that decentralization had broad, positive effects on many of Chicago's elementary schools. We would be remiss in concluding this book if we did not offer at least some perspective on these overall results as well.

Returning to basic descriptive findings in chapter 1, over 80 percent of Chicago's elementary schools showed at least some improvements in mathematics learning and close to 70-percent improvement in reading. The average elementary school increased student-learning gains in reading by 4 percent and improved in mathematics by more than 12 percent over a six-year period. In the top quartile of schools, which we character-

ized as improving, learning gains jumped by 10 and 20 percent, respectively, in reading and mathematics. To put these results in perspective, a
10-percent increase in academic productivity from kindergarten through
grade 8 would amount to almost an extra year of learning accumulating
over a student's elementary school experience. So the average gains under
decentralization were not trivial, and in many schools the improvements
were quite significant.

In short, as the decentralization phase in Chicago's reform came to
a close, widespread gains in student learning had materialized in many
but not all schools. While these gains were clearly insufficient, given how
far behind the city's students were as reform began, this is nonetheless a
compelling account of broad-based improvement. To say that decentralization doesn't work, as some policy pundits have proclaimed, is simply
inconsistent with the data from Chicago during this period in its school
reform history.

Now one can reasonably ask whether what was accomplished represents a lot or a little. To really answer this question, we would need information from other school systems on the distribution of schools' trends
over time in their value added to student learning. Unfortunately, we know
of no other similar distribution of improvement results against which to
judge Chicago's outcomes.

Moreover, in attempting to compare the magnitude of effects over time
across different school districts, it is important to remember that Chicago's outcomes were measured against a norm-referenced rather than a
criterion-referenced test. Additionally, these gains accrued during a reform
period that was neither high stakes nor assessment driven. In comparison,
many cities and states are now using criterion-referenced tests as part of
assessment-driven, high-stakes accountability reforms. It seems quite reasonable to assume that if districts create strong incentives to teach particular content knowledge and skills, as operationalized in the accountability
assessments, these test scores will surely increase over time. Whether these
results generalize across other subjects and forms of assessment, however,
is far less clear.[19] In addition, we now know that assessment-driven reforms
simultaneously increase the incentives for cheating, gaming the testing
system, deliberately forcing out students who hurt a school's accountability standings, and ignoring instruction in academic subjects not directly
included in the assessment system. Yet there is no evidence that any of this
came into play during Chicago's decentralization—although it did occur
immediately thereafter as higher-stakes, more-centralized reforms were
put into place.[20]

How a Governance Reform Can Improve Student Achievement

A general critique of governance reforms, of which decentralization is one instantiation, is that they do not directly address the technical core of instruction in classrooms, where teachers interact with students around subject matter. Given this fact, a finding of overall positive effects for decentralization still leaves open a question as to how these effects actually accrued. The analyses presented in this book, taken in combination with other research findings on Chicago's decentralization, now allow us to offer at least one empirically grounded account as to how such reforms can make a difference.[21]

Specifically, Chicago's governance reform reshaped the power relationships among principals, teachers, parents, and local community leaders. First, the introduction of Local School Councils created opportunities to change the connections of parents and community members to their local school. Second, by shifting decisions about the hiring of principals and teachers to the individual school site, subsequent professional work assignments to schools became a matter of voluntary choice rather than central office control. Thus, reform increased the likelihood that a school's professional staff really wanted to work in a particular community, connect to its parents, and educate its children. Third, by devolving significant authority to innovate locally, and providing new resources to support this activity, a genuine empowerment for local action was enjoined. Taken together, these reform elements created a new force field, much more horizontal in its press extending into local communities rather than vertical into a central bureaucracy. The ensuing social processes restructured the interpersonal ties among the adults in school communities. Chicago's decentralization pushed everyone involved to revisit their expectations of one another and to reconsider their own sense of obligations toward one another. In many instances, governance reform resulted in constructive new dialogue, and opened up possibilities for new social resources to develop at the school-site level.[22] Clearly, this did not happen in every Chicago elementary school. Even so, there is ample evidence that this did happen in many schools, and many of these schools substantially improved student learning.[23]

In sum, our research suggests relational trust as the one mechanism that makes governance reforms matter by catalyzing a redress of the dysfunctional understandings that may now operate among adults and impede educating all children well. Consequently, we can reasonably expect significant improvements in student learning to result from other governance reforms—*if* the power distribution reshaped by these reforms actually culminates in a renewal of relational trust at the school level. Absent such trust building, broad-based improvements remain unlikely.

In this regard, our results should also be read as a caution to instructional reform advocates. Clearly, teachers' interactions with students around subject matter must improve if major advances in learning are to occur. Even so, reform remains a stereoscopic strategy. Regardless of the quality of human resource development initiatives, new instructional materials purchased, or technological resources provided, little of value is likely to accrue unless some collective social capacity emerges to engage these resources in meaningful ways.

A New Case for Decentralization as a Principle in Large District Reform

At a minimum, the evidence assembled here gives reason to revisit some of the quick pronouncements of educational policy advocates—chief among them, that decentralization strategies failed to deliver the goods. The fact is that most other decentralization efforts, for example school-site decision making and school-based management, were deficient by design in that few resources and little authority were ever delegated to the local school site, and no viable accountability system ever assembled to create incentives for improvement. Chicago's efforts in comparison remain the most extensive to date in U.S. schools. Substantial discretionary resources (in other words, real money to spend) were allocated to local schools, and principals were placed on performance contracts, hired at the local school community level, and granted authority over the hiring of new teachers without regard to system seniority considerations.

Even so, the reform was weak in other ways. No provisions were made to facilitate the removal and/or transfer of problematic teachers and others resisting reform. No assistance systems were assembled to support local actors as they pursued instructional improvement. No viable secondary accountability mechanism was put in place until after 1996 to complement the primary accountability through locally elected school councils. As a consequence, in some school communities the intended local governance arrangements were never effectively engaged, no sustained efforts to strengthen the essential organizational supports ever emerged, and these schools atrophied. Absent was any system-level capacity to identify, assist, and, where necessary, jump-start improvement in these contexts.

Regardless of these manifest weaknesses, significant improvements still occurred in a large number of Chicago elementary schools. (The nonimprovement in the city's high schools is a story for another day.) All of which brings us to an interesting question: given the choices facing Chicago in 1988, and the local capacity then available in the CPS, could the city have done better under some other type of reform? Specifically, as we consider the major alternative now being embraced by many districts and states— centrally driven systemic improvement efforts—it may well be that Chicago actually chose a prudent course, given its local circumstances at the time.

Specifically, systemic reform demands a broad array of expertise among senior system staff members as they craft new policies and procedures and seek to offer meaningful day-to-day guidance to school-level leaders. It also presumes a broad confidence and trust in this central expertise and the individuals who have been authorized by government to use it. Yet such expertise and institutional trust was in very short supply in Chicago in the late 1980s. The unpolished gem in decentralization was that many school communities were able to innovate and improve on their own, even though the central system had little capacity to support this activity and little likelihood of "getting it right" even if they tried. We speculate that similar conditions may still be the case in some other large school districts today.

In addition, there are at least three other arguments in the political economy of public education that support reconsidering the merits of re-form initiatives that seek to localize authority, create conditions more responsive to diversity, and provide resources and incentives for local school community improvement.

Designing for the politics of educational pluralism in large urban districts. No matter how thoughtful and compelling a given plan for district improvement might seem, anyone who has a different view about the appropriate processes of teaching, the appropriate goals for schools, or the appropriate mechanisms for transforming the current enterprise immediately become the opposition for this systemic plan. Given this political reality, district leaders inevitably spend valuable time and energy fending off their attacks and far too often ultimately falling victim to them. School systems then look for a new heroic leader to take up this same charge, and the cycle repeats itself.

One significant consequence of decentralization in Chicago was that many issues that previously dominated the attention of the central school board—for example, how a multicultural curriculum should be handled, which texts students should read, and which reading program is best— could now be answered somewhat differently in varied local school communities. Policies such as these, which are inherently contestable, tend to be easier to resolve locally than centrally. In principle, this frees leadership resources at the district level to maintain a sharper focus on how better to support its system of schools.

This perspective on the politics of educational pluralism leads us to a general district design principle. In shaping the reform of large urban public school systems, a core objective should focus on transforming the energy currently used to resist and overturn centrally driven reforms into new local energy for improvement. A largely unrecognized value of local school enablement, whether of the Chicago variety or in school systems anchored in charters, contracting, or some other similar strategy, is that it does precisely this. In the end, the energy typically expended in resisting now gets redirected toward actually making one's ideas work in local communities of practice.

Stated somewhat differently, school district politics is not a "problem to be managed" as one seeks to implement some vision of systemic reform. Rather, it is central to the very design of effective district improvement. Moreover, for reasons detailed next, the problems associated with the politics of educational pluralism may well increase in the years ahead.

Responding to the "development of taste" about schooling. How happy would we be if suddenly we were mandated to eat in the same restaurant chain every night; drink the same wine from the same vineyard; receive our medical care from the same service; or attend the same public events? In every regard the development of individual taste and choice is quintessentially American.

This "American perspective" is increasingly salient for schools as we come to appreciate that a good education matters more now than ever— whether we think about this from the point of view of "who gets ahead," the welfare of cities and states, or global economic competition. Given this increased valuation placed on education and the American penchant for choice, it seems likely that we will develop more distinct and varied views about how we would like our children to be educated. At base, many issues surrounding educational goals and methods are inherently contested. To be sure, conversations about these issues can be informed by scientific evidence, but are rarely fully resolved by such evidence. In the absence of an overwhelmingly powerful empirical argument, differences of opinion will abound. Consequently, as our views about the social significance of education increase, the debates concerning how to educate are also likely to multiply and become more vociferous.

This perspective, too, encourages us to think about a more diverse system of schools characterized by voluntary association for both parents and staff. Ironically, it may only be through fully embracing our diversity that we can ultimately come to understand and advance the common ground essential for educating all children well. Otherwise, the conflicts in our larger civic society are likely to propagate in the petri dish of public education policy. The resultant system stagnation is a sure recipe for losing ground in the global competition now challenging leadership in a knowledge economy.

A potential market advantage for urban contexts. The out-migration from urban centers begun in the late 1950s, coupled with the changing structure of our economy, has left many cities struggling for survival. Of late, a revival has emerged in many of them, but the relatively poor quality of their school systems remains a major impediment. Urban centers, however, have extraordinary untapped cultural and other institutional resources (colleges and universities, for example) that could be appropriated to support a more diverse system of schools. Moreover, from this point of view, system size—normally viewed as a serious impediment to district reform— suddenly becomes an asset. Interestingly, this is the one place where urban districts, by virtue of their size and the diversity of cultural and other intellectual resources that can be drawn on, have a distinct market advantage relative to both suburban and rural districts. For the same reason that folks regularly travel to the city for dining and entertainment, cities could become a mecca for distinct educational tastes as well.

A Closing Perspective

Building a diverse system of good schools, like its major alternative of centrally driven systemic reform, requires a critical realism about the base capacity available to initiate reform in a district and the new capacities that must be developed to sustain and extend these initial efforts over time. Like the design of a good school, the design of an effective district entails stereoscopic thinking. It must blend a coherent theory for improving schools (and establishing new ones) with a relationship-building strategy that expands social resources for individual schools, and builds trust up and down the system as well as out into the larger community. Moreover, this systems thinking must remain rooted in a clear understanding of the desired goals at the classroom and school levels and the means to reach these aims. The research reported in this book is intended to inform precisely these considerations.

Lessons for School Systems Design

It is important to recognize that a complex trust relationship, with its attendant vulnerabilities and mutual responsibilities, exists between the school system center and its local school sites. While formal responsibility and power for school improvement resides in the board of education and the central office that administers its policies, improving teaching and learning must occur out there in schools and classrooms. Ultimately, accountability for improvement resides in the habits of mind and heart of local school professionals as they engage their particular community. Correspondingly, the design of an effective system of schools must aim to nurture in every school community, and in each of the school professionals who work there, the responsibility to educate every child well and to support their parents well. Advancing this principle is the firmest assurance that the complex tasks of improving schooling might occur with some consistency at scale. Consequently, figuring out how to shape an overall system of finance and governance that creates environments and incentives, which push in this direction, is a major institutional design consideration.

A key lesson from Chicago's reform is that no single organizational control mechanism will likely carry the full freight. To be sure, democratic localism was a lever for change in many Chicago schools, but it was never activated in still others. Similarly, there is ample evidence now that market failures abound among charter schools and charter management organizations, and systemic reform, driven by central bureaucracies, continues to leave some schools behind as well.[24] Variation is the natural state of human and social affairs and of efforts to improve these affairs. In this regard, it is important to recognize that the basic school and community factors that impeded improvement in the context of Chicago's decentralization are likely to manifest themselves in the contexts of other reforms as well.[25]

In short, that some school failures occurred in Chicago under decentralization does not signify a weakness per se in the basic reform principle. The real institutional design failure lies in not recognizing that such differentiated outcomes are likely to occur, in not developing appropriate mechanisms to identify these failures and intervene when and where they do occur, and in not developing the organizational capacity to learn from these problems so that systems gradually become more effective in managing their own performance improvement. Improving social systems entails improving the social learning that pulses through them. This, too, requires deliberate design.

Living on the Boundary of Belief and Doubt

Our work has been motivated by a deep belief that our schools can and must do much better if we are to revitalize for the next generation the American dream of opportunity for all. A good education is now more important than ever in creating the pathway to this opportunity. Unfortunately, for far too many this pathway is now closed, and opportunity dies early on. Thomas Jefferson's long-standing observation about America's noble experiment in democracy—ignorant and free, is a state of affairs that never was and never will be—is truer today than ever before.

However, a belief in the power of schooling and in our ability to improve this institution must also coexist with a modicum of doubt—a critical perspective—about the wisdom of any particular reform effort. Virtually every reform involves at least some zone of wishful thinking,[26] and even good designs typically require executing a strategy for which there is no established game plan. We now know, for example, that improvements under decentralization in Chicago were inequitably distributed. Some schools, especially in poorer African-American neighborhoods, were disproportionately left behind. This is a brutal fact that had to be told; our role as an agent informing reform meant bringing it to light. Absent our inquiry, this result could easily have remained hidden in a more casual accounting of the overall positive test score trends.

But we must also do more than just "tell the facts." We must seek to understand, and we must also ask why. As we argued in chapter 6, to see race and class differences in rates of improvement and to just stop there without probing deeper simply creates more fodder for conflict among critics and apologists of the current state of affairs. This dysfunctional discourse advances no common understandings and helps no children and no families. What is really going on in these school communities, and why are the important tasks of improving schools so difficult to advance? Asking these questions, bringing evidence to bear on them, and in the process advancing public discourse about the improvement of public education is a vital role that applied social inquiry can and should fill in a technically complex and politically diverse democratic society. In the end, melding strong, independent disciplined inquiry of the type detailed in this book with a sustained commitment among civic leaders to improve schooling is the only long-term assurance that an education of value for all may finally emerge.

APPENDIX A SOCIOECONOMIC STATUS FACTOR

Two socioeconomic status (SES) measures were developed using factor analysis. The first was School SES, which reflected the socioeconomic characteristics of the census block group surrounding each elementary school. The second was Student SES, which included the average value of socioeconomic characteristics of the census blocks in which the students lived. Since school and student neighborhoods largely overlap and are highly correlated ($r = 0.86$), it was logical to combine these measures through a single factor analysis. The table on the following page shows the 1990 census data and other data used in developing the SES factor. Information regarding geographic level of the data is included to distinguish data obtained for the residential census block from data obtained for the school.

TABLE A.1. Socioeconomic status (SES) factor

Name of measure	Description	Source of data and year collected	Geographic level	Factor loading
Concentration of poverty	The following two census measures were combined and reverse coded to create a measure of neighborhood poverty: • Percentage of male residents over age 18 employed one or more weeks during the year • Percentage of families above the poverty line A measure was created for both the location of the school and students attending the school.	1990 United States Census	Census block group	Student addresses: 0.88 School location: 0.85
Social status	The following two census measures were combined to create a measure of neighborhood affluence: • Percentage of employed persons aged 16 years or older who are managers and executives • Mean level of education among people over age 18 A measure was created for both the location of the school and students attending the school.	1990 United States Census	Census block group	Student addresses: 0.83 School location: 0.77
Percentage low income	Percentage of students attending an elementary school who received a free or reduced-price lunch in the 1993–94 school year	1993–94 Chicago Public Schools	School	0.70
Percentage of students living in a public housing project	Percentage of students attending an elementary school who lived in a large Chicago Housing Authority residential project	Chicago Housing Authority, 1994	School	0.60

APPENDIX B A VALUE-ADDED INDICATOR: A SCHOOL'S ACADEMIC PRODUCTIVITY PROFILE

In developing a productivity profile for each school, we sought to focus directly on the amount students learn each year and whether these learning gains increase over time. According to this standard, improving schools should show greater learning gains at the end of our study, the 1995–96 academic year, than in the base period of 1990–91.

Our productivity profile, which captures this feature, is built out of two basic pieces of information for each school grade and year: the input status for the school grade, and the learning gain subsequently recorded for that group. The input status indicates the level of prior achievement that students bring to their next year of instruction. To calculate this input status, we began by identifying the group of students who were enrolled for a full academic year in each grade in each school, and then retrieved their test results from the previous spring.[1] The illustration in figure B.1 considers the productivity profile for grade 6 at a randomly sampled Chicago school. We began by retrieving the end of grade 5 test scores from spring 1990 for all sixth-grade students who were enrolled in the sample school in October of 1990 and were eventually tested in the spring of 1991 at that same school. The average of these students' previous-year test scores, from spring of 1990, is the input status for that school grade. This input status is the skill base that the sixth-grade teachers had to build on during the school year to advance further the learning of these students.

The actual learning gain is the amount that the students' end-of-year results in grade 6 improved over those from the previous spring. If we add this learning gain to the input status, we obtain a third important piece of information: the output status. This tells us the skill level that students at this school grade reached after another year of instruction.

Panel A in figure B.1 shows the input status, learning gain, and output status for the students in grade 6 at our example school in the base period of the

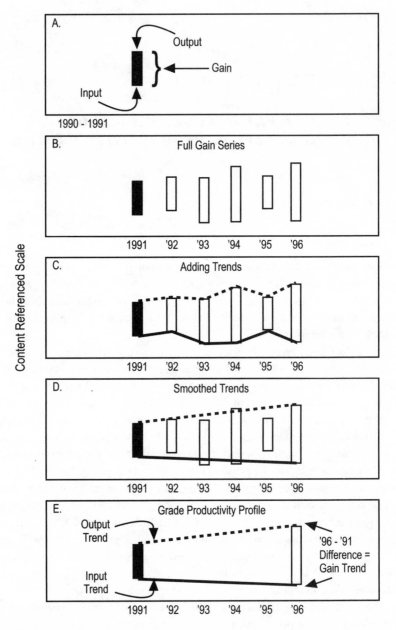

Figure B.1. Constructing a sixth-grade productivity profile for Prairie School, 1991–96.

1990–91 academic year. Panel B then shows similar data for all the years in our study, 1990–96. We use a basic data series like this to estimate the academic productivity for each grade at each school. Our interest in assessing changes in productivity directs attention to the time trends reflected in these data. A quick examination of panel B suggests that the inputs to grade 6 at this school may be declining over time. That is, each year students are entering grade 6 with somewhat lower levels of prior achievement. However, the learning gains seem to be increasing, and the output trend rising as well. To make these trends clearer, panel C adds an input trend and an output trend to the profile. Even with these trend lines added, considerable noise remains, which tends to obscure the overall pattern in the data. To adjust for random variation, we computed smoothed trends that represent the best summary lines that fit these data. These are displayed in panel D.

These trends are based on a multilevel statistical model that uses all the available student information to generate better estimates of

- *initial status* (the average prior achievement level of students entering a particular school grade in the base period of 1990–91);
- *base gain* (the amount these students learned in the 1990–91 school year);
- *input trend* (the change over time in the prior achievement of students entering each grade at each school); and
- *gain trend* (the change over time in the learning gains recorded in each grade at each school).

This multilevel model also allows us to adjust for other factors that may be changing over time, which can confound interpretations about productivity improvements at particular schools. Of key concern here are possible demographic shifts in student enrollments due to either changing neighborhood characteristics or school feeder patterns. In the latter regard, a school might, for example, add a selective admissions magnet program, which would suddenly improve their input trends. Alternatively, as was the case at Hancock, the school began to enroll, partway through our study, increasing numbers of low-achieving students in grades 6, 7, and 8 who transferred in from other neighborhood schools. Basically, we sought to assure that we were actually measuring real changes in school productivity, and not other spurious factors. (Appendix C provides further technical details on the actual statistical models and variables employed in these analyses.)

The final grade productivity profile, with the data bars removed, appears in panel E. This geometric graphic highlights the essential time trend characteristics in the achievement data for each school grade. The profile clearly depicts a situation in which learning gains are increasing over time, as evidenced by the fact that the right side of the trapezoid is larger than the left side. This means that each new cohort of students appears to be learning a bit more than prior cohorts in grade 6 at our example school.

Estimating Trends in School Productivity

Estimation Model

1. We denote the Rasch estimated scale score (that is, the equated metric) obtained for student j from school k at time point t by y_{jkt}. Also available is an estimate of the precision, $1/s_{jkt}$, associated with each scale measure. This is based on the real standard error of measurement, s_{jkt}, which is the nominal standard error inflated for scale misfit. Students at school k are subscripted $j = 1, 2, \ldots, n_k$. Schools are indexed $k = 1, 2, \ldots, N$. Each time point, t, may run from 1988 to 1996. Only students with at least two consecutive time points, a test score (y_{jkt}) at time t and an input score $(y_{jk(t-1)})$ at time $t - 1$, are included in our analysis.

2. Given the student's test scores, we proceed with a parameterization at level 1 of a measurement model that estimates a student's true input ability and true gain for year t:

   (1) $y^*_{jkt} = a^*_{1jkt} \pi_{1jkt} + a^*_{2jkt} \pi_{2jkt} + e^*_{jkt}$.

   Note that: $y^*_{jkt} = \dfrac{y_{jkt}}{s_{jkt}}$. Furthermore,

   $$a^*_{1jkt} = \frac{1}{s_{jkt}} \text{ and } a^*_{2jkt} = \left\{ \begin{array}{l} 0 \text{ if } t \text{ is the input data} \\ \dfrac{1}{s_{jkt}} \text{ if } t \text{ is the test year data} \end{array} \right\}.$$

   Thus, $e^*_{jkt} \sim N(0,1)$ and e^*_{1jkt} is the student's *true input ability*, while π_{2jkt} represents the *true gain*.

3. For all students in a given grade $j = 1, 2, \ldots, n_k$ at all k schools, we estimate the school input and gain trends at level 2 by

   $$(2) \begin{array}{l} input \\ gain \end{array} \begin{bmatrix} \pi_{1jkt} \\ \pi_{2jkt} \end{bmatrix} = \begin{bmatrix} 1(t-1991)0 & 0 \\ 0 & 0 & 1(t-1991) \end{bmatrix} \begin{bmatrix} \beta_{11k} \\ \beta_{12k} \\ \beta_{21k} \\ \beta_{22k} \end{bmatrix} + \begin{bmatrix} r_{1jkt} \\ r_{2jkt} \end{bmatrix}.$$

In this model, we center t at 1991, so that β_{11k} estimates the average input in 1991. Similarly, β_{21k} is the average value-added in 1991. β_{12k} is the input trend for the grade, and β_{22k} is the gain trend for the grade. We assume that the errors in (2) are correlated, $r_{jkt} \sim N(0, T_\pi)$. Equation (2) is sometimes called a "cross-domain" growth model, because it tracks two closely related short time-series simultaneously.

Student-level covariates. In addition, we adjust the school effect vector, β_k, for five student composition characteristics that might be changing over time. The five student characteristics are bilingual "C" status; too old for a grade; if the student is retained; if the student is white; and if the student is African American. Each of these covariates is deviated around the school mean for 1988 and 1989, or generally $(X_{sjk,t} - \overline{X}_{s \cdot k,0})$, where $\overline{X}_{s \cdot k,0}$ denotes the 1988–89 baseline. The associated coefficients estimate a time-varying school composition effect. We assume that these level 2 coefficients are constant across years and across schools.

Form-effect adjustments. The final version of this model adjusts for form effect associated with 1988 and 1989 tests (form 7) and for 1990. This is accomplished by incorporating two additional dummies. The first takes on a value of "1" if the test year for a student is 1988 or 1989 and "0" at all other times. Similarly, a second dummy variable is coded "1" if the test data are for 1990 and is coded "0" for all other times. In summary, we adopted the following coding scheme for the trend component (slope) and the form effects (form 7 and CPS 90):

	Year								
	88	89	90	91	92	93	94	95	96
Slope (1991)	−2	−2	−1	0	1	2	3	4	5
Form 7	1	1	0	0	0	0	0	0	0
CPS 90	0	0	1	0	0	0	0	0	0

This results in a final level 2 model for π_1 and π_2 of

$$(3) \quad \pi_{1jkt} = \beta_{21k} + (t - 1991) \cdot \beta_{22k} + FORM7 \cdot \beta_{23} + CPS90 \cdot \beta_{24}$$
$$+ \sum_s (X_{sjk} - \overline{X}_{s \cdot k,0}) \cdot \beta_{25} + r_{2jkt}$$

4. School input and gain trend estimates, $\beta_{k,}$ are expected to vary from one school to the next as follows:

(4)

1991 input	β_{11k}	1	0	0	0	γ_{11}	u_{11k}
Input trend	β_{12k}	0	1	0	0	γ_{12}	u_{12k}
1991 gain	β_{21k}	0	0	1	0	γ_{21}	u_{21k}
Gain trend	β_{22k}	0	0	0	1	γ_{22}	u_{22k}

Here, the quantities in γ are the systemwide input and gain trend estimates. Across schools, $\mathbf{u} \sim N(\mathbf{0}, \mathbf{T}_\beta)$.

Equation (4) yields *empirical Bayes* estimates of β_k for each school. They are weighted composite estimators that take into account information about school k relative to other schools in the system. If the information for school k is relatively weak, β_k is *shrunk* toward the system average γ. This estimator thus efficiently utilizes all the available information to provide predictions for each school.

Discussion of the Estimation Model

Appropriate techniques for research on change have long perplexed behavioral scientists (see, for example, Harris [1963]). The methodological studies of Rogosa, Brand, and Zimowski (1982), Rogosa and Willett (1985), and Willett (1988) have greatly clarified these problems. Briefly, they demonstrate that if individual growth is linear (or approximately so), then the gain score is the unbiased estimator of the instantaneous growth rate. Even if the underlying growth demonstrates some curvature, the gain score will estimate the average growth rate over the time period of study. In contrast, the covariance model can be seriously biased in studies of school and program effects on individual growth (Bryk and Weisberg 1977).

For these reasons, the analysis model employed in this research is based on gain scores rather than a covariance adjustment approach. It develops out of the growth-modeling strategy explicated in Bryk and Raudenbush (1992). Since we are studying students' academic development over a one-year period, the use of a gain score seems quite appropriate. We note that over the full 100-point metric, individual growth displays some deceleration at the upper ability levels. Within any grade slice, however, we found no evidence of nonlinearity in an analysis of a subset of eight-year longitudinal data on students at the same schools.

A key to use of a gain score strategy is an appropriate quantitative metric for measuring change. The content-referenced scale developed in this research is critical in this regard. Unlike grade equivalents, the equated test score metric yields an interval measurement scale based on the relative difficulty of the items. Such interval measurement is necessary for quantitative studies of change.

We also note that our analysis is based on the latent initial status and gain scores rather than the observed data. This is accomplished by the use of a measurement model at level 1. The problems of statistical artifacts due to correlated errors in observed input status and gains are thus eliminated. Also, unlike a covariance model, all the test data appear on the left-hand side of the equations; as a result, we also avoid the problems of key adjustor variables that are fallible covariates. This is another strength of this modeling approach.

APPENDIX C OVERVIEW OF THE FOURTEEN
INDICATORS FOR THE FIVE ESSENTIAL SUPPORTS

Figures C.1 through C.6 provide summary information about the measures we developed for each organizational subsystem. We include information on the number of questionnaire items that comprise the measure, a sample of items from each measure, and the year(s) in which the questions were asked. For further details on the exact wording of the survey questions, see "Survey Measures, Factors, Composite Variables, and Items Used in Organizing Schools for Improvement" (http://ccsr.uchicago.edu/publications/measures_in_organizing_schools .pdf). In the text below, the individual measures are denoted in italics, and the fourteen overall indicators are highlighted in bold italics.

School Leadership. We developed three measures each for the inclusive-facilitative and instructional leadership dimensions of this subsystem. For inclusive-facilitative leadership, one measure, *inclusive principal leadership,* focuses on the principal's efforts at reaching out to faculty and encouraging parent and community involvement. A second measure directly assesses the extent of *teacher influence* across a range of local school decisions. Similarly, the third measure, *LSC contribution,* examines the degree of parent and community influence on improvement efforts through their Local School Council. As expected, these teacher reports clustered strongly together. This is highly consistent with our field observations that inclusive principal leaders nurtured meaningful engagement among teacher, parent, and community members in local school improvement.

The measures for instructional leadership were anchored in teachers' assessments of their principal's initiatives in setting high academic standards, visiting classrooms, and other activities directly associated with instruction (*principal instructional leadership*). This is further supplemented by a measure of *program coherence,* which focuses on the quality implementation of new school programs and the integration and coordination of instructional programs and services within the school. Finally, the third measure in this domain, *SIP implementation,*

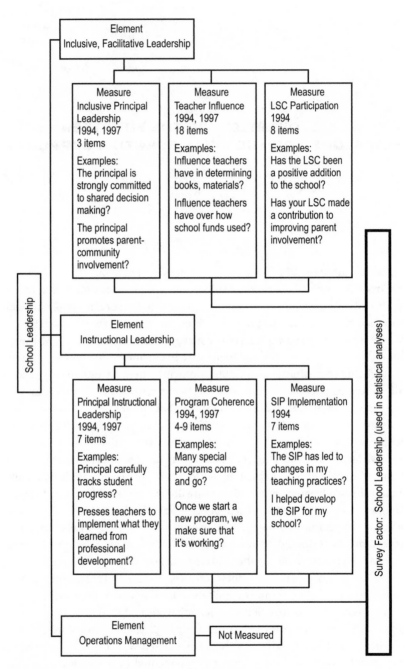

Figure C.1. School leadership. Note: All questions were asked of teachers.

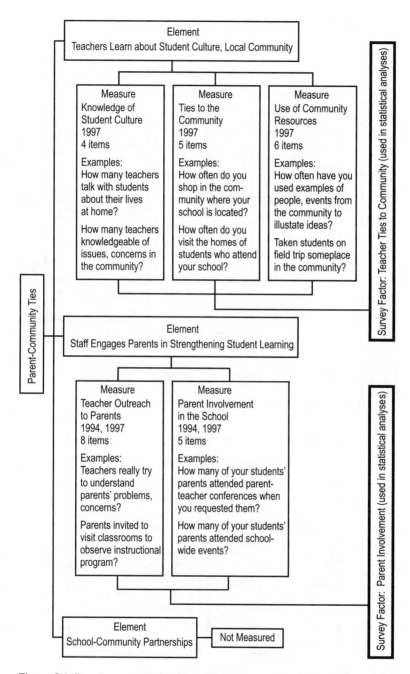

Figure C.2. Parent-community ties. Note: All questions were asked of teachers.

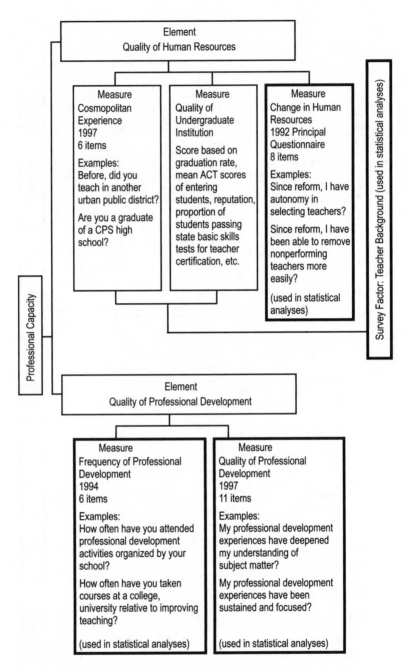

Figure C.3. Professional capacity. Note: All questions were asked of teachers, except Change in Human Resources.

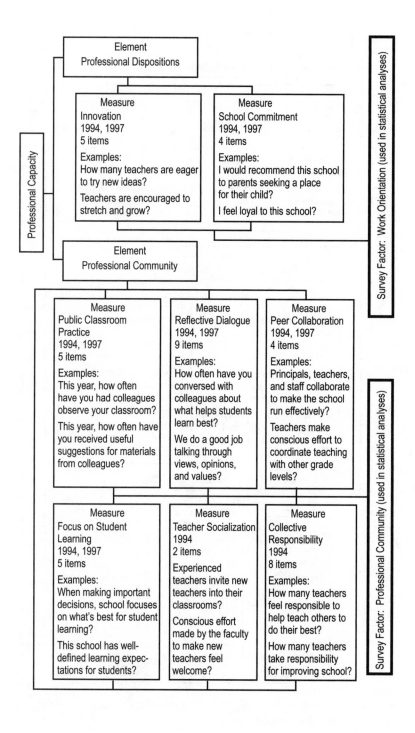

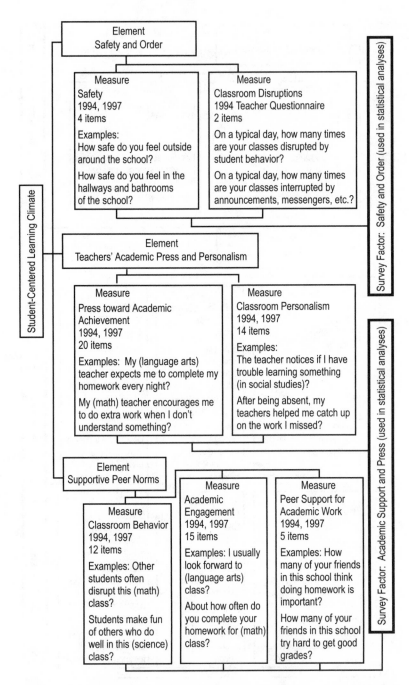

Figure C.4. Student-centered learning climate. Note: All questions were asked of students, except Classroom Disruptions.

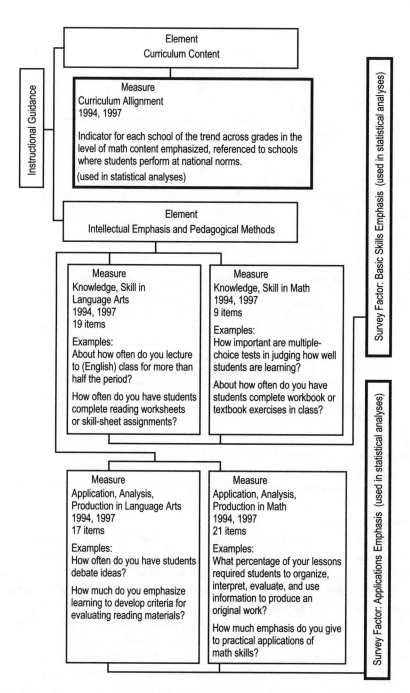

Figure C.5. Instructional guidance. Note: All questions were asked of teachers.

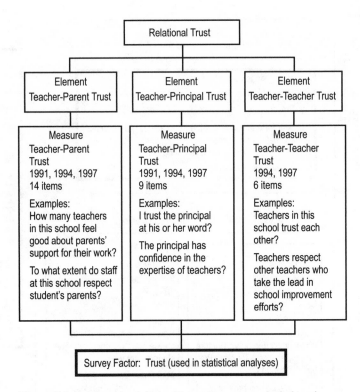

Figure C.6. Relational trust. Note: All questions were asked of teachers.

assesses whether the school improvement plan developed by the LSC was a living, guiding document for local reform or just "shelfware."

For most of our analyses, we combined these six measures of inclusive and instructional leadership into an overall composite indicator that we simply termed *School Leadership.*

Parent-Community Ties. The first three measures in this domain focus on teachers' *knowledge of the community,* the depth of their *personal ties to the community,* and their *use of community resources* in their instruction. The survey items that comprise these measures focus on teacher reports as to how knowledgeable they are about issues in their local school community, how much time they actually spend out in the community, and whether they try to use various institutions, people, and concerns from the community in their instruction. We combined these three measures into a composite indicator of *Teachers' Ties to the Community.*

The second composite indicator in this domain, *Parent Involvement,* is composed of two measures: *teachers' outreach to parents* and *parent involvement in the school.* The first of these focuses on the teachers' proactive efforts to invite parents into their classroom, understand parental concerns, and embrace parents as partners in their children's education. The second measure focuses on the extent to which parents reciprocate by being involved in school activity and responding to specific concerns that teachers may raise about their child's schoolwork. Both of these are based on teacher survey reports aggregated to the school level.

Professional capacity. This was the most extensively measured subsystem within our framework. Some thirteen measures eventually formed six overall indicators for this domain. The composite indicator of *Teacher Background* was formed from two measures of teachers' *cosmopolitan experience* and the *quality of the undergraduate institution* that they attended. The latter, based on multiple sources of data about the selectivity of a teacher's undergraduate institution, is a proxy for an individual teacher's overall academic background. This was then averaged across teachers to form a school-level indicator. The cosmopolitan measure focuses on the extent to which teachers bring a diverse set of prior experiences into the classroom. Its formation was motivated by earlier research that described a troublesome phenomenon in Chicago where poorly educated CPS graduates attended weak undergraduate institutions in Chicago and then return to teach in the CPS.[1] Teachers who had experience in private schools or schools outside Chicago were characterized as "cosmopolitan," and the proportion of those within a school became our organizational measure.

Our next two indicators in this domain, the *Frequency of Professional Development* and the *Quality of Professional Development,* were directly measured from teacher reports about the extensiveness of their participation in such activities and the degree to which these activities formed coherent, sustained programs relevant to local improvement efforts. Similarly, another indicator drew on principals' reports about their capacity to hire quality teachers and remove problematic teachers, and the intensity with which they pursued both of these activities during the initiation of reform in Chicago. In our earlier book, we had identified such school-based *Changes in Human Resources* as a leading indicator of systemic school improvement.[2]

The professional dispositions element was operationalized in two measures of teachers' orientation toward *innovation* and *school commitment*. These teacher survey responses capture critical aspects of teachers' willingness to try out new instructional practices in their classroom, maintain a can-do attitude, and internalize responsibility for improving their school. We combined these two measures into an overall indicator called *Work Orientation.*

Finally, the concept of school-based *Professional Community* was captured in six separate measures that combined to form one overall composite indicator by the same name. Four of the measures focus on specific practices: *public classroom practice,* where teachers observe one another and offer suggestions for improvement; *reflective dialogue,* where teachers engage in critical conversations with one another about the improvement of instructional practice; *peer collaboration,* where teachers work together on developing curriculum and other school improvement activities; and *teacher socialization,* where faculty are proactive in supporting new members and incorporating them into the school community. The final two measures in this domain consist of a set of teacher survey items that probe whether teachers embrace norms of *collective responsibility* for school improvement, with a specific focus on *student learning.* This combination of norms influences how teachers enact their daily instruction and engage with colleagues in the four work practices enumerated above.

Student-Centered Learning Climate. The safety and order element in this domain was assessed with two measures: student reports about their perceived *safety* in and around school, and data from teachers on the incidence of *classroom disruptions* due to student misbehavior and other events. We combined these two measures into an overall indicator of *Safety and Order.*

The next two survey measures are based on student reports about the *press toward academic achievement in their classrooms* and whether this is coupled with the personal support from teachers that students need in order to succeed at this academic work (*classroom personalism*). Students were asked a variety of questions about whether teachers press them to work hard and do homework, and whether teachers notice when they are having trouble and can be counted on to reach out and help. Together, these items provide a window onto the nature of teacher norms toward student instruction at the school. The next three measures—*classroom behavior, academic engagement, and peer support for academic work*—focus on the presence of supportive school norms among peers. Students were asked questions such as how often students make fun of their classmates, disrupt one another, and work hard at getting good grades. While teacher and peer norms are conceptually distinct elements within a student-centered learning climate, the five measures described above loaded together in our factor analyses. For this reason, we combined these five measures into one overall indicator of *Academic Support and Press.*

Instructional Guidance System. The nature of the school's curriculum content map—the subject matter that students are exposed to as they move across grades—constitutes the first element in this subsystem. We were able to develop a school indicator based on teacher reports about the content emphases in their mathematics instruction. At each grade level, we asked teachers how much time they spent teaching some fifty-four different topics in mathematics during the school year, ranging from simple arithmetic to algebraic equations involving two unknowns. By combining this information across teachers at various grade levels within a school, we could assess the pacing with which new topics were introduced into the curriculum at that school. We then compared this to a content analysis of the subject matter demand (and how this varied by grade level) in the standardized mathematics tests used by the CPS. Taken together, these data provided us with an overall indicator that we called *Curriculum Alignment.*

Our indicator system also focused on the instructional emphases in a school's curriculum and the related pedagogical methods used to advance these. While each teacher regularly makes decisions about these emphases within his or her classroom, these decisions are structured by the set of available school resources and accountability press (if present).[3] To operationalize this combination of resources and pressure, we chose to aggregate information from teachers' reports about their instruction in both reading and mathematics and the extent to which they emphasized basic skills and/or applications work in their classrooms. We developed four measures—two each in math and language arts—based on teachers' reports about the nature of their assignments (for example, completing worksheets versus longer term projects), classroom pedagogies employed (for example, extensive teacher lectures versus facilitated classroom discussions), and the types of student assessments used (for example, reliance on standardized tests versus analysis of students' written work products from project-based activities). Two of the measures combined survey reports to assess the degree of didactic teaching with a basic skills emphasis in the school, and the other two focused on students' active engagement in tasks that required applications of knowledge and skill. We eventually combined these four measures from language arts and mathematics into two overall indicators of the school's *Didactic Teaching Focus on Basic Skills* and *Active Student Applications Emphasis*. We refer to these simply as a basic skills and applications emphasis or focus.

Relational Trust. Teachers were asked a series of questions about their relationships with parents, the principal, and other teachers. The number of questions in this series grew from 14 in 1991 to 29 in 1997. With respect to the measure *teacher-parent trust,* teachers reported on the level of respect and personal regard that existed between teachers and parents and the degree to which they perceived that parents had confidence in teachers' expertise. In all years, teachers reflected on their working relationship with the school principal. The measure *teacher-principal trust* combines questions about the principal's openness to discuss worries and frustrations, the mutual respect and personal regard between the teachers and principal, and whether they thought the principal valued their expertise. In 1994 and 1997, we added survey items on the relational trust among teachers at the school, thereby forming the measure *teacher-teacher trust.* The questions followed similar themes: openness to discussing worries and frustrations with one another and personal regard and mutual respect. In addition, there was a question about respecting teachers who take the lead in improvement efforts.

In 1991 *teacher-parent trust* and *teacher-principal trust,* along with reports of the school-community relationship, loaded onto a single factor, *Trust.* In 1994 and 1997, *teacher-parent trust, teacher-principal trust,* and *teacher-teacher trust* also formed a single factor, *Trust.*

The full psychometric properties of these measures at both the individual and school levels are detailed in "Survey Measures, Factors, Composite Variables, and Items used in Organizing Schools for Improvement" (http://ccsr.uchicago.edu/publications/measures_in_organizing_schools.pdf).

APPENDIX D PROBABILITY EXPERIMENT TO EVALUATE RESULTS PRESENTED IN FIGURE 3.3

Taking a relatively conservative posture, we assumed in this experiment that the underlying misclassification rate due to all three sources (including indicator unreliability, construct under-representation, and temporal instability) was 8 percent. How many misclassifications might we expect due to these measurement artifacts, and how likely is it that the few anomalous results seen in figure D.1 simply reflect this?

We used a simple application of probability theory to examine this question. Specifically, suppose that for each school and outcome there is a .08 probability of being incorrectly classified as demonstrating improvement on that outcome when our organizational indicators do not predict that this should be the case. Clearly, we would expect that a certain number of schools might well be misclassified due to measurement errors. Binomial probability theory provides us with an expected distribution for the number of such cases that might occur, given the overall fallibility of the indicator system and the fallibility of the productivity trends as well. Formally, we assumed a Bernoulli trial with $p = .08$ and $n = 18$. We chose an n of 18 as an average school count, partway between the high of 23 schools for the leadership indicator and a low of 12 schools for the alignment measure in figure 3.3.

These expected outcomes appear as the black bars in figure D.1. The probability experiment predicts that in only 23 percent of the random samples that we might draw would we expect to see no schools in this category. We should expect a single false report in 35 percent of the draws, two false reports in a quarter of the experiments, three false reports 12 percent of the time, and four or more incorrect classifications in about 4 percent of the samples. The left-leaning cross-hatched bars in figure D.1 represent the actual observed results from the 15 separate findings in figure 3.3. Since there is some question about the essentiality of all 5 supports for the attendance improvement index, we also present the

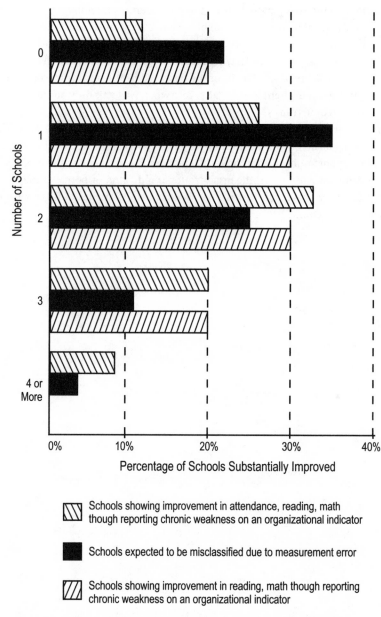

Figure D.1. Comparing observed improvement rates with expected misclassification rates (based on $p = .08$, $n = 18$).

results for just the 10 separate findings for reading and mathematics productivity (these are the right-leaning cross-hatched bars). In both instances, the observed number of anomalous cases appears reasonably consistent with those that we would expect to see, if the underlying measurement processes created a misclassification probability of .08. The fit of the observed results to those predicted in the probability experiment is especially close when we focus only on the reading and math outcome trends.

In sum, it is quite plausible that the small number of schools that appear to be improving on an outcome indicator yet have reports of chronic weakness in an essential support indicator might simply reflect measurement errors associated with the outcome indicator, the organizational indicator, or both. Although we cannot formally prove that this is the case, our results are certainly consistent with such an account.

INTERVIEW QUESTIONS FROM THE PROJECT ON HUMAN DEVELOPMENT IN CHICAGO NEIGHBORHOODS

Collective Efficacy Measure[1]

Residents were asked if it is very likely, likely, neither likely nor unlikely, unlikely, or very unlikely that their neighbors could be counted on to intervene in various ways if

(1) children were skipping school and hanging out on a street corner;
(2) children were spray-painting graffiti on a local building;
(3) children were showing disrespect to an adult;
(4) a fight broke out in front of their house; and
(5) the fire station closest to their home was threatened with budget cuts.

Using a five-point scale, the second set of questions asked how strongly residents agreed or disagreed that

(1) people around here are willing to help their neighbors;
(2) this is a close-knit neighborhood;
(3) people in this neighborhood can be trusted;
(4) people in this neighborhood generally don't get along with one another; and
(5) people in this neighborhood do not share the same values.

Religious Participation Measure[2]

(1) Have you or a household member talked to a local religious leader to help with a neighborhood problem?
(2) Do you or other household members belong to a religious organization?
(3) Is the religious organization in the neighborhood?
(4) About how many people in this neighborhood are religious or attend church regularly?

APPENDIX F COEFFICIENTS FROM ANALYSES OF LEADERSHIP IN CHAPTER 4

TABLE F.1. Coefficients from HMLM analyses predicting change in each essential support with leadership in the base year

	Change in essential support from 1991 to 1994			
	Professional Community	Work Orientation	Parent Involvement	Safety & Order
Intercept	−0.034	−0.033	−0.027	−0.025
Leadership base year [1]	0.720***	0.690***	0.539***	0.151*
Change in leadership	0.693***	0.671***	0.524***	0.248***
Essential support, base year	0.149**	0.088	0.097	−0.342***
Stability	0.094*	0.144**	0.117*	0.121*
Racially integrated	−0.065	0.023	0.071	0.289***
Predominantly minority	−0.033	−0.047	0.056	0.146**
Predominantly Latino	−0.083	0.008	0.089	0.195**
Racially mixed	−0.009	0.013	0.131*	0.137*
Small school	0.036	0.081	0.118*	0.133**
Neighborhood crime	−0.004	0.032	−0.110	−0.022
Neighborhood social status	0.014	0.038	0.035	−0.074
Neighborhood poverty	0.018	−0.059	−0.059	−0.090

	Change in essential support from 1994 to 1997				
	Professional Community	Work Orientation	Parent Involvement	Safety & Order	Curriculum Alignment
Intercept	−0.018	−0.010	−0.016	−0.032	0.012
Leadership base year [1]	0.674***	0.549***	0.478***	0.162**	−0.062
Change in leadership	0.700***	0.619***	0.559***	0.090	−0.075
Essential organizational support, base year	0.294***	0.277***	0.271***	0.209**	0.185
Stability	0.004	0.045	0.091*	0.182***	−0.092
Racially integrated	0.016	0.079	0.040	0.300***	−0.025
Predominantly minority	−0.013	0.056	−0.055	−0.008	0.030
Predominantly Latino	0.049	0.054	0.050	0.141**	0.042
Racially mixed	−0.017	0.063	0.016	0.155**	0.050
Small school	0.021	0.021	0.007	0.039	0.141*
Neighborhood crime	0.052	−0.024	0.015	−0.079	−0.089
Neighborhood social status	−0.003	−0.024	−0.028	0.032	0.049
Neighborhood poverty	0.060	0.051	−0.113*	−0.060	0.011

[1]This coefficient serves as the basis for the bars in figure 4.19. The coefficient was multiplied times the value of leadership in 1991 or 1994 at the 25th percentile or the 75th percentile to determine the size of the bars in the figure.

*$p < 0.05$, **$p < 0.01$, ***$p < 0.001$.

TABLE F.2. Raw regression coefficients and standard errors (in parentheses) for leadership predicting the other essential supports in figure 4.20

	Curriculum Alignment 1997	Professional Community 1997		Safety and Order 1997		Parent-Community Involvement 1997		Work Orientation 1997	
Intercept	0.61 (0.06)	0.02 (0.07)	−3.36** (0.88)	5.94*** (0.03)	5.21*** (0.32)	0.04 (0.06)	−0.89* (0.39)	0.06 (0.07)	−2.47** (0.76)
Base state, 1994									
Curriculum Alignment	0.14 (0.09)								
Professional Community		0.64*** (0.07)	0.33** (0.10)						
Safety and Order				0.20*** (0.03)	0.17*** (0.04)				
Parent-Community Involvement						0.54*** (0.07)	0.42*** (0.08)		
Work Orientation								0.58*** (0.07)	0.39*** (0.09)
Context controls									
Small school	0.32*** (0.09)	−0.11 (0.21)	−0.12 (0.21)	−0.09 (0.10)	−0.09 (0.09)	−0.04 (0.20)	−0.06 (0.19)	−0.03 (0.22)	−0.03 (0.21)
Crime rate	0.006 (0.03)	−0.06 (0.08)	−0.03 (0.08)	−0.08* (0.04)	−0.07* (0.04)	−0.01 (0.07)	−0.01 (0.07)	−0.15 (0.08)	−0.13 (0.08)
Social status	0.07 (0.04)	−0.06 (0.10)	−0.03 (0.09)	0.02 (0.04)	0.01 (0.04)	−0.08 (0.09)	−0.07 (0.09)	−0.09 (0.10)	−0.04 (0.10)
Concentration of poverty	0.003 (0.04)	−0.02 (0.10)	0.01 (0.10)	−0.13*** (0.04)	−0.13*** (0.04)	−0.30*** (0.10)	−0.32*** (0.10)	−0.08 (0.10)	−0.07 (0.10)

Leadership variables									
Prin. instructional leadership			0.25** (0.09)						
Prin. inclusive leadership							0.14* (0.06)		
Program Coherence			0.25 (0.14)						0.35* (0.14)
LSC Contribution			0.11 (0.07)						0.16* (0.07)
Teacher Influence					0.14* (0.06)				
School improvement plan									
R-squared	0.12	0.36	0.42	0.42	0.44	0.40	0.42	0.33	0.37

* $p < 0.05$, ** $p < 0.01$, *** $p < 0.001$.

APPENDIX G **VALUE-ADDED REPLICATION RESULTS FOR 1997 THROUGH 2005**

Between 1997 and 2005, the Consortium on Chicago School Research (CCSR) conducted surveys of all CPS schools every two years. The frequent survey indicators over this period provided more time-sensitive measures of the essential supports than were available to us during the decentralization reforms, when the Consortium was first forming.

In addition, new statistical methods allowed us to develop a separate value-added estimate for each school, each year. Formally, the CCSR deployed a cross-random effects model consisting of repeated measures on students as they cross school grades and possibly different schools over time (from 1997 through 2005). School-level value-added effects for these models were estimated using the HCM2 program in HLM.[1]

By linking together these year-by-year value-added estimates and the biannual school surveys, we were able to investigate how base levels on the essential supports, and changes in them over time, related to school change in their value-added to student learning. Specifically, we began with the school-level value-added estimate in each survey year (1997, 1999, 2001, and 2003) as a baseline for each school. We then compared these against the value-added estimates two years later in the next survey year (1999, 2001, 2003, and 2005, respectively). To examine the effects of the essential supports in these new data, we then asked two questions. First, does a strength in an essential support at the beginning of the period (say, survey year 1997) predict an improved value-added in the subsequent survey year (in this case 1999). Second, do changes in the essential support indicator between the first and second survey administration link with improvement in the value-added measure over the same period? For example, do changes in the survey reports between 1997 and 1999 correlate with changes in the value-added estimates over the same two years? We probed these two

TABLE G.1. Average effects of the essential supports on value-added measures, Chicago elementary schools, 1997–2005 (in standard deviation units)

Essential support measure	Base strength on the measure predicting subsequent value-added to learning	Improvement on the measure predicting improved value-added to learning
School Leadership		
Principal instructional leadership	0.184***	0.096**
Program coherence	0.154***	0.098**
Parent-Community Ties		
Parent involvement in the school	0.340***	0.137***
Professional Capacity		
Reflective dialogue	0.028	0.017
Collective responsibility	0.219***	0.112**
Orientation toward innovation	0.213***	0.083*
School commitment	0.288***	0.151***
Student-Centered Learning Climate		
Safety	0.429***	0.166***
Trust		
Teacher-parent trust	0.288***	0.169***
Teacher-teacher trust	0.166***	0.065
Teacher-principal trust	0.183***	0.098*

*$p < 0.05$, **$p < 0.01$, ***$p < 0.001$.

questions for four periods: 1997 to 1999, 1999 to 2001, 2001 to 2003, and 2003 to 2005. A summary of the effects over these four periods is presented in the table above for the subset of organizational indicators where comparable measures were collected over the entire duration, from 1994 through 2005.

APPENDIX H EFFORTS OF THE CONSORTIUM ON CHICAGO SCHOOL RESEARCH TO BUILD MORE PRODUCTIVE TIES BETWEEN RESEARCH, PRACTICE, AND POLICY TO IMPROVE PRACTICE

When we began the Consortium on Chicago School Research (CCSR) in 1990, a broad base of community organizations as well as civic and philanthropic leadership was deeply engaged in reforming Chicago's schools. We confronted considerable skepticism, however, about the role that researchers could play in this process. While local foundations, for example, were directly supporting school improvement efforts, it was not easy making the case for the Consortium's mission of "informing reform" with objective evidence from high-quality research. Could such activity really play a constructive role in these processes? These doubts were quite reasonable in that there was little precedent at that time for a place-based research network making such a contribution. In the intervening years, the CCSR's engagement within Chicago as well as with external public policy audiences has deepened and expanded, leading to broad public awareness of the CCSR and an increased appreciation of its novel role in informing reform.

From its inception, the CCSR built its work around a distinctive vision and value set regarding the role that applied research could and should play in public problem solving. This public philosophy guided the original investigations on which this book is based, and remains vital today in the CCSR's ongoing efforts. The vision and values are organized on three core principles.

First, the CCSR anchors its efforts on a premise that the relationship of social science to social problem solving in a democratic society is best viewed as an educational one. In the broadest sense, the CCSR aims to educate the public about the improvement of public education. Our stance here drew heavily on insights from John Dewey's classic work, *The Public and Its Problems,* and on the more recent development of these ideas in the scholarship of Benjamin Barber and Charles Lindblom.[1] This line of scholarship argues that democratic decision making involves a competition of ideas in the public policy arena. Consequently, our role as applied social scientists is to bring the best empirical evidence to bear on these discussions. This is quite different from the more conventional role of public policy analysis acting as "advisor to the prince."

Along closely related lines and complementing this normative perspective on how applied social research *should* relate to democratic decision making, we also attended to writings by Carol Weiss, David Cohen, Robert Stake, and others as to how applied social inquiry is *actually used* in public problem solving.[2] Their research documents that direct, instrumental use of research findings to change a specific policy is at best occasional. However, these studies also point out that important contributions can be made by reshaping the conceptual terms that frame policy debates. In particular, providing a coherent, empirically grounded account of action often provides a very useful frame for subsequent policy conversations. In this regard, our research plans take a mid- to long-term view of the major issues confronting urban school district reform. If we identify important concerns on or near this horizon for policy action, and bring useful evidence to bear on these concerns, our research will eventually find its way into subsequent reform activity.

Consequently, CCSR seeks to identify critical issues that need to be addressed if Chicago schools are to substantially improve, and to collect and examine objective evidence of what is or is not occurring in the schools. While individual CCSR researchers might on occasion advise system leaders on a particular reform, and as individual private citizens we might personally advocate for particular improvement activities, we deliberately crafted an organization and operating norms for the Consortium that eschewed taking advocacy stances or arguing for particular policy solutions.

Second, our vision and values were also strongly influenced by writings from the late 1970s by Robert Stake, Michael Patton, and others[3] on the design and conduct of stakeholder-based evaluations. This line of applied scholarship encouraged us to embrace an ethical responsibility to seek out actively the diverse interests operative in school reform, and assure that a wide range of questions was continually addressed. This principle had direct implications in the financing of CCSR, in crafting our relationship to the Chicago Public Schools, and in assuring multipartisan representation in the ongoing process of establishing our research agenda. In each of these regards, we sought to assure that the agenda would not be beholden to any one group.

More specifically, the CCSR deliberately seeks to activate a diverse set of viewpoints about reform; seriously consider the concerns and questions that various stakeholders might have about these activities; assure that an appropriate array of data are collected vis-à-vis these concerns; and make certain that CCSR investigators engage these diverse perspectives as they analyze results and interpret findings. As projects proceed, these stakeholder dialogues often result in our undertaking additional analyses on questions not previously examined and consideration of alternative possible explanations for emerging findings. Key in this activity is the critical advice of a standing multipartisan steering committee that meets six to eight times a year. The composition of this committee has gradually evolved as we deliberately recruit a diverse set of both proponents and critics of current reforms. The steering committee functions as a social proof network that constantly challenges preliminary findings and interpretations and in the end makes our final reports much stronger.

Third and counterbalancing our deep engagement with a democratic social proof network is a commitment to scientific rigor. Drawing on James Coleman's writing on pluralist policy research,[4] the work of individual CCSR researchers, as well as our internal collective review processes, is directed at technical quality in the conceptualization, design, and conduct of each study. While not every piece of research necessarily finds its way into peer review journals, that standard is our standard. Although ideas from various stakeholders infuse the process from beginning to end, the technical day-to-day work is governed by norms of disciplined inquiry. In joining a commitment to strong internal standards in the conduct of our research with a vigorous, democratic social proof network, the social organization of the Consortium affords strong safeguards for the overall integrity of our findings.

Taken together, these principles shape a distinctive role for us as researchers. Each civic stakeholder in school reform occupies a specific social position in the overall ecology of urban district practice and improvement and, as a result, offers a particular lens into school practice. In addition, these differences in perspective are often amplified by differences in preexisting beliefs and understandings rooted in personal background and experiences. As a result, each individual may bring unique insights suggesting distinctive questions to examine and evidence to gather. As one scans the extraordinary diversity of ideas that such multipartisan participation cultivates, many potential inquiries suggest themselves. Our role as researchers entails bringing some coherence to this cacophony of concerns. We constantly ask ourselves and test with our various stakeholders, What are the major underlying themes pulsing through these conversations? Once identified, we then engage in a scientific study about them. Applied social inquiry is a scarce social resource; consequently, critical allocation decisions must constantly be made as to which questions the CCSR will pursue. Our responsibility in these stakeholder consultations is to keep the overall research agenda-setting process centered on fundamental issues that materially affect the improvement of schooling, teaching, and learning.

These principles also reframe the social arrangements surrounding our work as applied social scientists. We now sit within a dynamic, place-based social network, consisting of the local education leaders, other researchers, practitioners, policy advocates, and interest groups. These ties in turn coexist with our more traditional memberships in academic disciplines and problem-centered informal research networks. Through the multitude of day-to-day social exchanges that occur within our place-based network, we gain much deeper insights into the school reform problems under our investigation. Perhaps even more significantly, our membership in this place-based network substantially enhances the opportunities for social learning among local researchers, policy makers, and practitioners that extend well beyond the more conventional strategies of publishing reports and the attendant press conferences and media coverage.[5] At work here is a core mechanism for broader community education about the problems of improving public education in the city of Chicago.

In sum, the CCSR seeks to neither prescribe nor endorse any particular program or reform activity. Rather, it seeks to build civic capacity for school reform by identifying focal problems that need policy and practice attention in order to increase student success and further advance school improvement. Toward this end, the CCSR conducts a diverse array of activities. These include creating critical indicators to chart progress; conducting theory-driven inquiries to identify how programs and policies are working, facilitating the engagement of a larger community of researchers in such activity; and working directly with the CPS to enhance their internal analytic capabilities.

In terms of the research reported in this book, embedding this work in a broader school reform community helped us to conduct higher-quality research while simultaneously facilitating local engagement with our findings. In the end, this results in a broad use of these findings in guiding subsequent school district actions while also creating general contributions to the literature on urban school improvement. In our view, these are the primary aims for applied social inquiry in public problem solving.

NOTES

Prologue

1. We thank Ms. Sparks (not her real name), who wrote this poem during a literacy professional development session. We include her poetry here to give the history of the neighborhood from the point of view of a teacher who grew up there and eventually returned to teach in the elementary school she had attended. There were several such teachers in both of the schools described in the prologue.
2. The two schools described here are actual public elementary schools in the city of Chicago. Pseudonyms are used for names of the neighborhoods, the schools, and the individuals in key leadership roles. A few peripheral facts have also been altered to assure anonymity. All statistical information presented in the prologue and in subsequent chapters are the actual data from these two schools.
3. The account presented here is a retrospective case study of an improving school. The development of this case is based on interviews with the school principal and other key faculty leaders about the history of their efforts. Our account has been corroborated against observations made by several external agents who worked in this school throughout the 1990s. "Hancock" was also the subject of a journalistic report by *Catalyst Chicago*, an independent monthly newsmagazine focused exclusively on analyzing and reporting on school reform efforts in the Chicago Public Schools. Our description is consistent with their findings as well.
4. Allington and Cunningham (1996); Sigmon (1997).
5. DeMoss and McCullough (2001), p. 3.
6. Although this may seem like a small point, it is actually not. Ethnographic accounts by Charles Payne have documented how highly dysfunctional schools generally reject such resources, regardless of their quality. The title of his essay, "I don't want your nasty pot of gold," is highly indicative in this regard. See Payne (2008).
7. DeMoss and McCullough (2001), p. 17.
8. Unlike the description of Hancock, which is largely a retrospective reconstruction of a reform history based largely on the recollections of key informants, the events at Alexander were extensively documented as they occurred. Alexander has been the subject of two previously published case studies. See Rollow and Bryk (1994); chap. 3 in Bryk, Sebring, Kerbow, Rollow, and Easton (1998); and a master's thesis by Moultrie (1992). We have relied heavily on these primary materials in developing this school reform vignette.
9. Moultrie (1992), p. 38.
10. This was Betty Green's characterization of her own role at Alexander. Rollow and Bryk

(1994). For a more general discussion of this role of principal as a maternal leader, see chap. 3 in Bryk, Sebring, Kerbow, Rollow, and Easton (1998).

11. Moultrie (1992), p. 31.

12. For a further analysis of this school-university partnership, see Rollow and Bryk (1994).

13. Moultrie (1992), p. 46.

14. Ibid., p. 20.

Introduction

1. For a more detailed account of the mobilization for reform in Chicago, including its intellectual and social context, see chap. 1 in our earlier volume, *Charting Chicago School Reform: Democratic Localism as a Lever for Change.* The summary presented draws extensively from this text. Our remarks here are not heavily referenced, since documentation already exists elsewhere.

2. See Wilson (1987).

3. Storey, Easton, Sharp, Steans, Ames, and Bassuk (1995).

4. In fact, the poverty rates in Chicago exceeded those in New York and Los Angeles, which were 35 percent and 33 percent, respectively, at the same point in time. See ibid.

5. Bryk, Sebring, Kerbow, Rollow, and Easton (1998).

6. A word of clarification on this point is in order. Although the legislation was originally passed in 1988, its implementation was deferred until the summer of 1989. Most of the first year was taken up with organizing council elections, training council members for their new roles, and establishing the rules by which they would actually work. Toward the end of that first year, half the school communities were required to make a decision about their principal (i.e., whether to retain their current principal on a new four-year performance contract or to hire a new one). The other half of the schools made that decision the following year. It wasn't until after a council was in place and had selected a principal that reform actually began in a school community. In practical terms, then, by the spring of 1993, when we closed data collection for *Charting Chicago School Reform: Democratic Localism as a Lever for Change,* about half the schools had three years to initiate improvements, while the rest had only two.

7. For a further elaboration of this argument see Bryk, Sebring, Kerbow, Rollow, and Easton (1998), p. 31ff.

8. These are considerably lower and presumably a more accurate reflection of the base state of student performance in Chicago than the earlier test scores had indicated. CPS had used the exact same form of the Iowa Tests of Basic Skills for over ten years, and the reference norms were also more than ten years old. Both of these factors contribute to the inflated test scores.

9. The standard deviation in school-level achievement as measured by the percentage of students scoring at or above national norms increased in a steady, monotonic fashion in both reading and math between 1990 and 1996.

10. In order to avoid capitalizing on chance, we computed an actual improvement trend for each school rather than just using the differences from 1990 to 1996. Specifically, we conducted biweighted regression analyses for each school (Tukey 1977), using the percentage of students scoring at or above national norms as the dependent variable,

and year, with values from 1990 to 1996, as the independent variable. The regression coefficient in reading and math for each school represents the average amount of change in the percentage of students scoring at or above national norms per year. We then ranked the schools—separately by subject—on the basis of these regression coefficients. The 25 percent of schools with the highest coefficients were placed in the top group, and the 25 percent with the lowest coefficients, including negative ones, were placed in the bottom group. The data presented in figures I.2 and I.3 are the average yearly test scores for schools in these two groups.

11. Don Moore, another Chicago researcher, studied test score improvements among schools that were low-achieving in 1990 (that is, schools with fewer than 40 percent of their students achieving reading scores at or above the national average). He estimated that by 1997, 26 percent of the schools in need of improvement had reading scores that were "substantially up" (a seven-year pattern of gains of 10.5 percent or more), and another 17 percent were "tending up" (a seven-year pattern of gains of between 7.0 and 10.5 percent). See Designs for Change (1998).

12. See Wilson (1987).

13. See Poinsett (1990).

14. Address information was provided by the Chicago public school system for each student and school. These data were geocoded to allow us to merge them with other geocoded databases that offer much more context detail.

15. A school neighborhood was operationalized as the census block group in which a school was located. Similarly, a student's neighborhood was defined as the census block group in which the student lived.

16. The percentage was calculated by dividing the number of people receiving public aid in a census tract in June 1994 by the number of people who lived in the census tract in 1990. Although the percentage may be somewhat distorted by population changes, the measure of public assistance highly correlated with socioeconomic status measures created using U.S. Census data, and significantly predicted academic outcomes.

17. For a vivid description of the problems associated with raising children in such a context, see Kotlowitz (1991).

18. See Sampson, Raudenbush, and Earls (1997).

19. For a further discussion of this idea of appropriating extant social networks as a resource for new social action, see McAdam (1999) and McAdam, McCarthy, and Zald (1996).

20. Within the literature, such neighborhoods are described as having both strong "bonding social capital" among its residents and strong "bridging social capital" from the neighborhood out to the larger civic society. For further discussion see Saegert, Thompson, and Warren (2001).

21. Later the Center for School Improvement was folded into the Urban Education Institute at the University of Chicago.

22. See Bilcer, Luppescu, Sebring, and Thum (1996) for details.

23. See Bilcer (1997) for details.

24. The Project on Human Development in Chicago Neighborhoods was funded by a partnership of public and private agencies. Based in Chicago and administered through the Harvard University School of Public Health in Boston, it brought together scientists from diverse disciplines and institutions around the country. The study examined

community, family, peer, and individual characteristics to offer a comprehensive understanding of human social behavior and the environments in which it plays out. The project followed some 7,000 individuals and 80 communities in a coordinated effort to study the many intricate developmental pathways toward social competence and antisocial behavior. See www.icpsr.umich.edu/PHDCN/about.html

25. The Chapin Hall Center for Children at the University of Chicago conducts policy research to bring sound information and analysis to bear on the policies and programs affecting children. See www.chapinhall.org.

Chapter one

1. Hein (1982).

2. B. Smith (1998); Stevenson and Stigler (1992); National Education Commission on Time and Learning (1994); Schmidt, McKnight, Cogan, Jakwerth, Houang (1999); Borg (1980); Carroll (1963); Gettinger (1984); Walberg (1986); Rossmiller (1986); Fisher and Berliner (1985); Stallings (1975); Denham and Lieberman (1980).

3. Entwisle, Alexander, and Olson (1997); Heyns (1987).

4. Unfortunately, CPS did not maintain a central database on individual student attendance in its elementary schools. It did this only for high school students. Thus, we could not estimate each school's value-added indicator of student attendance and how this might change over time, as we did for our indicators of student reading and mathematics achievement. Such an indicator requires student-level data on attendance.

5. To make these adjustments, we first calculated the average achievement on the Iowa Tests of Basic Skills (ITBS) of students in each residential block group. Average achievement was computed using test data from 1992 for students in grades 3 through 8. These scores were adjusted for the percentage of students in that block group at each grade. In this way, block groups that might have a disproportionate number of primary-grade children were evaluated in the same way as block groups with equal representation of children of all ages. Since the CPS does not have individual-student-level data on attendance to directly measure attendance by residential block group, these measures of block group mean achievement were used as an instrumental indicator of the propensity of students from that neighborhood to put forth effort in school.

We then used this instrumental measure of residential block group attendance to adjust each school's attendance trend for changes in the residential composition of students entering kindergarten in each year. For example, if a larger proportion of a school's kindergarten students entered from a high-achieving neighborhood in 1996 than in 1990, that school's attendance trend would be adjusted downward to account for that demographic change. We also adjusted for possible differences over time in the students entering and leaving the school in grades other than kindergarten. For this purpose, we used students' actual test scores as instruments for their individual attendance rate.

Formally, these adjusted attendance trends were computed in a two-level Hierarchical Linear Model (HLM). Level 1 was a repeated measures model of attendance rate over years (1990-96), where a linear trend was estimated for each school. We introduced a set of time-varying covariates at level 1 to control for changes in achievement levels associated with the differential residential contexts of the new children entering the school in kindergarten, and for the actual achievement levels of children leaving the school each year. The random adjusted attendance trends for each school, estimated at level 2, became our outcome indicator for the analyses reported in chapters 3 and 4.

6. There are some exceptions to this policy. Some bilingual and special-education students are not tested. Many others in these two categories are tested on the ITBS, but their results are excluded from system reporting. For analyses conducted in this study, we adjust for changes over time in the school system's test inclusion policy, making the criteria for exclusion constant throughout the period of the study. For further details on the procedures used here, see Easton, Rosenkranz, Bryk, Jacob, Luppescu, and Roderick (2000).

7. For a detailed illustration of this, see Bryk, Thum, Easton, and Luppescu (1998).

8. To carry this discussion a bit further, a system of test score reporting that uses multiple thresholds—e.g., the percentage in various quartiles of a nationally norm-referenced test—would be preferable to a single threshold indicator. Even here, however, information on the progress of students within quartiles is still being thrown away. Moreover, to obtain the full power of the analysis methods used in chapter 3 and subsequent chapters, a continuous rather than a categorical indicator of school performance is preferable.

9. It has been shown that in some cases, average annual test score reports for a school can indicate declining student achievement, even though the school is having a very positive impact on the learning of the children it has the opportunity to educate. See Meyer (1996), who examined the accuracy of efforts to judge school improvement from only cross-sectional data.

10. For further details on this study, see Bryk, Thum, Easton, and Luppescu (1998), p. 11.

11. For details on the Rasch model, see Wright and Stone (1979). A fuller explanation of the equating process can be found in chap. 2 of Luppescu (1996).

12. The equating study included ITBS form 7, which was used continuously by the CPS for over ten years until 1989. Because the same form had been in such continuous use, the data prior to 1990 looked anomalous, even after equating. Thus, in our study we used the test results from only 1990 forward.

13. For a complete explanation of the reading and math content scales created through Rasch analysis see Bryk, Thum, Easton, and Luppescu (1998).

14. The dependent variable in this study—the overall academic productivity indicator—is the residual from a regression equation modeling the empirical Bayes estimate of the gain trend as a function of the initial status, the initial gain, and the input trend. These were computed separately for each grade and then averaged to produce an overall school index.

15. For each grade, we averaged the empirical Bayes estimates of the initial status, initial gain, input trend, and gain trend for top- and bottom-quartile schools on the school productivity trend indicators in reading and math. We then used these average estimates to plot the aggregate displays in figures 1.3 through 1.6.

16. The LGIs are based on the estimated gain trends from our fitted multilevel models for each school and grade. These are more precise estimates than a simple raw comparison of the observed 1990 and 1996 gains.

17. The average base learning gain (in grade equivalents) in the CPS, averaged for 1990–91 and 1991–92, in reading and mathematics at all elementary grade levels was 0.87 and

0.82, respectively. Applying the percentage improvements to these base gains and then accumulating these effects over eight grades result in the numbers reported here.

18. In figure 1.7, the boxes include the middle 50th percentile of schools. The top of each box represents the 75th percentile, and the bottom shows the 25th percentile. The lines or "whiskers" extending up and down from the box show the range of improvement (or decline) in schools in the top and bottom quartiles, excluding a few outliers.

19. For a general discussion of these issues, see Bryk (2003). For explicit details on the indicator of cheating, see Jacob and Levitt (2003), who document that cheating by principals and teachers on the ITBS increased by 50 percent with the introduction of the high-stakes testing program post-1996. Moreover, their results are best read as a lower boundary for the actual incidence of cheating. Jacob and Levitt's simulations indicate that while they had high power to detect extensive cheating by teachers, more modest amounts of classroom cheating were likely to go undetected. In addition, their analysis focuses on only one form of cheating, the filling in of extra answer bubbles for children (or erasing and correcting answers). They did not estimate, for example, the prevalence of allowing students extra time during testing, prepping children explicitly on the particular items that would appear on the test, or numerous other creative ways that one could cheat once incentives to do so exist.

In terms of evidence of increased "test gaming," see Jacob (2002), who analyzed students' actual item-level test score results. Jacob demonstrates that, following the introduction of the high-stakes reforms, students became much more likely to complete the test rather than leaving a string of blank responses at the end. Since there is no penalty for guessing on the ITBS, even a random bubbling of responses as time is running out is likely to improve a student's test score. These results support field accounts that test prep activity exhorting test completion became common place post-1996 in the CPS.

On the changes in test inclusion policy post-1996, see Easton, Rosenkranz, Bryk, Jacob, Luppescu, and Roderick (2000). Also on this point, see Easton, Rosenkranz, and Bryk (2001).

Chapter two

1. The standard process for CCSR studies involves extensive interactions with the Steering Committee in research agenda setting, the design of specific studies within this agenda, feedback on research in progress, and extensive commentary and subsequent revisions on draft reports. Although individual Steering Committee members can have substantial impact on the conduct of study, final editorial authority for each report rests with the report authors. Typically, there is no "endorsement" by the Steering Committee as a body, and individual members are free to disagree with some aspects of some reports, and often have. Only on two occasions over eighteen years has the committee taken the rare step of unanimously endorsing the conclusions of a report. The *State of Reform* is one of these (see Bryk, Easton, Kerbow, Rollow, and Sebring [1993]).

2. She also invited representatives from the CCSR and the Center for School Improvement at the University of Chicago, the Chicago Panel on Public School Policy, Designs for Change, and the North Central Regional Education Laboratory. Together participants developed a series of research-based guidelines that schools could use in planning for their improvement. The result was the first version of the essential supports for student

learning and an official Chicago Public Schools document, *Pathways to Achievement: Self-Analysis Guide,* which was distributed to all schools.

3. Edmonds (1979), Good and Brophy (1986), and Purkey and Smith (1983).

4. Its name was eventually changed to the Center for Urban School Improvement, and it was later folded into the Urban Education Institute.

5. See, for example, Newmann and associates (1996). Subsequently, both Fred Newmann and Valerie Lee, another coprincipal investigator in CORS, undertook research projects in Chicago, respectively on ambitious instruction and social support and academic press for student learning.

6. For this imagery, we are indebted to Paul Romer's work on new growth theory in economics, as recounted in Warsh (2006), p. 9ff.

7. The ideas in this report were subsequently elaborated in our book *Democratic Localism.* Also of value to us, Designs for Change (1993) had undertaken an independent review of the school reform literature and published its own report, which identified five areas for school improvement that closely complemented the CCSR's findings. This review provided some independent validation for the general directions we were pursuing.

8. The 1988 Chicago School Reform Act was specifically designed to reconnect local school professionals with the parents and communities that the school was supposed to serve. In this regard, the reform drew inspiration from the urban school improvement efforts of James Comer, who argued that the social misalignment that often exists between poor parents and urban school professionals constitutes a major barrier to improved learning for students. See Comer (1995).

9. CCSR first made this observation in Chicago in 1991 in its report, *The Teachers' Turn.* We noted in our initial survey of teachers that while a majority felt that their school was improving under the 1988 Reform Act, substantially less than half reported any changes in their classroom instruction. We wondered aloud, how, then, would student achievement improve, if classroom teaching remained unchanged?

10. See Elmore, Peterson, and McCarthey's (1996) volume on school restructuring for a detailed account on this point.

11. See Cohen and Ball (1999), p. 3.

12. Carroll (1963); Gettinger (1984); Porter and Brophy (1988); Stallings (1980); Stevenson and Stigler (1992); Schmidt, McKnight, Cogan, Jakwerth, and Houang (1999); and Walberg (1986).

13. See B. Smith (1998). Smith and other CCSR researchers observed fifteen Chicago public schools for three years, starting in 1994–95. They found that most teachers had trouble meeting the 300 minutes of daily instruction mandated by the state in a 330-minute school day. Instead, even in well-managed classrooms, at least 90 minutes each day were lost to noninstructional activities: classroom management, transitions, preparation activities, or simply waiting and doing nothing; as many as 134 minutes a day were lost in poorly managed classrooms, which Smith estimated constitute up to half the CPS classrooms. Additionally, the researchers' findings showed that out of the 180 school days provided, fewer than 125 are fully devoted to grade-level, academic work. Disruptive start-up routines, special programs and events, holiday slowdowns, test preparation periods, and a steep drop in academic work during the last six weeks of the school year contributed to the loss of instructional time.

14. It should be noted that all of this, as well as students' prior knowledge and skill, is

shaped by earlier instructional experiences. For the purposes of the organizational theory development in this chapter, we treat these as exogenous factors. If one were advancing a dynamic theory of learning—an instructional treatment regime that students experience over time as they go through schooling—then all of this would have to be more explicitly represented within the theoretical model. This would add further complexity to figure 2.2 as a dense set of intertemporal relationships that would have to be added within the Dynamics of Student Learning box. However, the basic organizational arguments advanced in this chapter would still apply.

15. On how the organization of schools can affect student motivation for learning, see, for example, the account by Bryk, Lee, and Holland (1993) on urban Catholic high schools. For a similar and more recent account in the context of middle schools, see the evaluation report by David, Woodworth, Grant, Guha, Lopez-Torkos, and Young (2006) on the power of the normative environment inside KIPP Academy schools.

16. B. Smith (1998).

17. J. Smith, Smith, and Bryk (1998).

18. Ibid.

19. For a recent attempt to raise public awareness about these issues, see National Center on Education and the Economy (2006).

20. National Commission on Excellence in Education (1983).

21. For a popular account of these developments, see Friedman (2005).

22. Levy and Murnane (2005).

23. The labor economists Levy and Murnane (ibid.) refer to these educational objects as expert thinking and complex communication skills. For a recent policy manifesto that builds on this research, see National Center on Education and the Economy (2006). We note that this development also has profound implications for social mobility in our society. This is the "new educational equity frontier"—an education system that aspires for all students to develop a command of basic cultural knowledge and skills while at the same time nurturing their capacity to solve unstructured problems; to communicate persuasively through written, oral, and multimedia means; and to work effectively with diverse others. As Lisa Delpit has forcefully argued: "[If] minority people are to effect the change which will allow them to truly progress, we must insist on skills *within the context* of critical and creative thinking." See Delpit (1986), p. 384.

24. See, for example, the arguments on this account set out in Dewey (1916).

25. Newmann and his colleagues refer to this idea as authentic instruction. Of special significance, Newmann found that students performed better on both basic skill and higher cognitive tasks when they had been exposed to more authentic pedagogy. Similarly, Lee, Smith, and Croninger's research revealed that students who attended schools with a greater emphasis on authentic instruction learned 78 percent more math between the eighth and tenth grades than did students at other schools. See Newmann, Bryk, and Nagaoka (2001); Newmann and associates (1996); and V. Lee, Smith, and Croninger (1995).

26. A diverse educational scholarship appears on this topic. See, for example, Newmann and associates (1996); Cohen, McLaughlin, and Talbert (1993); McLaughlin and Shepard (1995); Porter (1994 and 2002); Porter and Smithson (2001); and Stevenson and Stigler (1992).

27. When the technical core of instruction is not clearly articulated and defined across the faculty as a whole, teachers tend to determine their own objective and enact instruction accordingly, leading to variation within the same school. CCSR research has documented large "teacher effects" in this regard; see, for example, Newmann, Lopez, and Bryk (1998); and Roderick, Engel, Nagaoka, and others (2003). This is consistent with more general findings in the field that the overall variation in student learning is typically greater between classrooms within the same school than among schools. See Rowan, Correnti, and Miller (2002).

28. For further discussions on this point, see Seashore Louis, Kruse, and Bryk (1995); Newmann and associates (1996); and McLaughlin and Talbert (2006).

29. Darling-Hammond (1997), Ferguson (1991), and Smylie (1995).

30. Bryk and Schneider (2002), pp. 78, 137–38, 143.

31. Darling-Hammond and Ball (1998), Darling-Hammond and McLaughlin (1995), Lieberman (1995), National Staff Development Council (1995).

32. Smylie, Allensworth, Greenberg, Harris, and Luppescu (2001).

33. Hansen (1995). See also Bryk, Lee, and Holland (1993).

34. Rowan (1990).

35. See Bryk, Camburn, and Seashore Louis (1999); Seashore Louis, Kruse, and Bryk (1995); Newmann and associates (1996); and McLaughlin and Talbert (2006). Also, for closely related ideas on communities of practice, see Wenger (1999).

36. For a good elaboration of this perspective on teachers' work, see Huberman (1993).

37. For a further elaboration on the rationale for this specific conceptual definition of professional community, see Seashore Louis, Kruse, and Bryk (1995).

38. This idea of shared norms as an effective mechanism of social control is central to theories of social capital—see Coleman (1988)—and in the organizations' literature under ideas associated with organic management. See, for example, Burns and Stalker (1961), Lawrence and Lorsch (1967), Rowan (1990), and Miller and Rowan (2006).

39. This perspective draws on organizational contingency theory. Miller and Rowan (2006) have detailed how this theory may generally apply to the social organization of teachers' work and classroom instruction. They cite several studies supporting the idea that such "organic management" may be more important in the context of literacy versus mathematics instruction.

40. McLaughlin (1993). Also see Spillane and Thompson (1997).

41. See, for example, Ponisciak, Allensworth, and Coca (2006).

42. Formally, there are two separate subsystems here: the school's ties to parents and to its community. For simplicity in our work, we have collapsed them together. Others whose principal interest is just this topic would typically be inclined to separate these two subsystems.

43. Clark (1983), Epstein and Dauber (1991), Lareau (1989), and Muller (1993).

44. Rosenholtz (1989) found this to be a significant difference between schools that were "stuck" and schools that were "moving." Teachers in stuck schools assumed that nothing could be done to encourage parent activity.

45. Furstenberg, Cook, Eccles, Elder, and Sameroff (1999) found that modest and low-income families in Philadelphia could better manage their children's development when there were strong schools and other institutions within the community. The authors urged schools to make serious efforts to reach out to families and make them aware of their programs and resources.

46. Epstein, Coates, Salinas, Sanders, and Simon (1997). The authors have outlined a set of tools and strategies to help schools promote these roles among their parents, and she and her colleagues have founded the National Network of Partnership Schools to conduct further research and develop strategies to strengthen the connections between families and schools. See also Fullan (2001).

47. See Steinberg (1996). Steinberg argues that family, peer, and institutional forces are often big impediments to school improvement.

48. See, for example, the accounts offered by Chicago teachers of their relations with parents in Bryk and Schneider (2002).

49. On balance, this element could equally well appear as a subcomponent of human resources and professional development within the professional capacity system. We chose to locate it here because of its special salience in the context of improving disadvantaged urban schools where extant school communities tend to be weak and the breach between home and school especially wide. This placement also allows us to frame teachers' knowledge of student and community context as a distinct subelement for measurement purposes rather than just embedding it within a larger knowledge and skill framework essential for quality teaching.

50. See Delpit (1996). Delpit argues that misunderstandings between white, middle-class educators and minority students and their families create an imbalance of power in schools. For example, students' cultural differences are often misperceived as behavioral problems or learning disabilities, leading teachers to hold lower expectations for these students.

51. Braddock and McPartland (1993).

52. See the discussion in Bryk, Sebring, Kerbow, Rollow, and Easton (1998), pp. 241ff., on the important role played by external school connections in actively restructuring schools in Chicago.

53. Riehl (2000).

54. Patillo-McCoy (1999), p. 206.

55. McLaughlin, Irby, and Langman (1994).

56. Establishing environmental order was a major priority for many schools during the first two years of reform in Chicago. Parent and community members on Local School Councils often played a major role in mobilizing other institutions and individuals to press for improvements in basic child safety concerns. See Bryk, Sebring, Kerbow, Rollow, and Easton (1998), chaps. 3 and 6.

57. In the context of the effective schools literature, see Edmonds (1979), Good and Brophy (1986), Purkey and Smith (1983), and Phillips (1997). For a more general treatment of the effects of teacher expectations on student learning and behavior, see Raudenbush (1984) and Rosenthal (1995).

58. McDill, Natriello, and Pallas (1986).

59. Lyon (1998) and Snow, Burns, and Griffin (1998). Going back to the progressive education movement in the 1940s, social support has been recognized as a key ingredient of cognitive learning. Personal relationships with adults foster motivation and heighten students' confidence that they can master content, develop skills, and hone their higher-order thinking. See also Bryk and Driscoll (1988); V. Lee and Smith (1999); V. Lee, Smith, Perry, and Smylie (1999); Dorsch (1998); and Noddings (1988).

60. This basic idea was first set out in Bryk, Lee, and Holland's (1993) study of the effectiveness of urban Catholic high schools in educating disadvantaged youth. Shouse (1996) more fully developed this theoretical framework and provided further empirical evidence of its effects on student learning. CCSR studies have also demonstrated the power of the combination of high expectations and a caring, personalized environment. Neither academic press nor social support by itself has as powerful an impact. In fact, in the lowest-performing schools in Chicago, we found that students rated these schools about the same as other schools with respect to the personal concern of teachers, but they did not perceive a strong press toward academic achievement. Sebring, Bryk, Roderick, Camburn, Luppescu, Thum, Smith, and Kahne (1996); V. Lee and Smith (1999); V. Lee, Smith, Perry, and Smylie (1999).

61. On this concept of culture formation in the context of urban Catholic schools, see Bryk, Lee and Holland (1993). The motto "Work hard. Be nice" is an organizing element in the KIPP school culture. For a supportive field account in this regard, see David, Woodworth, Grant, Guha, Lopez-Torkos, and Young (2006). It is important to note that the KIPP Foundation invests a substantial amount in the professional development and socialization of their new school leaders, and a major aspect of this leadership development work centers on school culture formation.

62. See, for example, Purkey and Smith (1983).

63. It is worth noting that effective school management receives little attention in the current reform literature, which tends to be dominated by concerns about the other two dimensions of leadership. In reality, it is the most basic prerequisite for school improvement. It is difficult for most any reform to achieve traction in a school with weak managerial expertise. Although this subdimension was not part of the initial conceptualization of the essential supports, its salience became especially manifest beginning in the mid-1990s as the school system, working with an array of external partners, took on the task of intervening in highly troubled schools. We are indebted on this point to observations from the clinical staff of the Center for Urban School Improvement at the University of Chicago, especially its former associate director for leadership programs, Albert Bertani.

64. This is another key element in actively restructuring schools that we identified in our earlier volume. See Bryk, Sebring, Kerbow, Rollow, and Easton (1998).

65. For discussions of the role of principal leadership in the transformation of instruction, see Leithwood, Begley, and Cousins (1994); Seashore Louis and Miles (1990); and Elmore (2002).

66. See Elmore, Peterson, and McCarthey (1996); Blase and Kirby (1992); and Sebring, Bryk, Easton, Luppescu, Thum, Lopez, and Smith (1995).

67. On the lack of coherence in school reform efforts, see our discussion of "Christmas-tree" schools in Bryk, Easton, Kerbow, Rollow, and Sebring (1993) and its further elaboration in Bryk, Sebring, Kerbow, Rollow, and Easton (1998). See also Fullan (1999) and Schlecty (1997).

68. For a field account of using power to lead in the early context of Chicago's school reform, see chap. 6 in Bryk, Sebring, Kerbow, Rollow, and Easton (1998).

69. This subdimension is also sometimes referred to as transformative leadership. See, for example, Sergiovanni (2000).

70. See Bryk, Sebring, Kerbow, Rollow, and Easton (1998), p. 230.

71. On this account, see Bryk and Schneider (2002), chap. 6.

72. See Sergiovanni (2000). He likens the principal to a midwife who enables the staff to

bring forth a transformed environment for teaching and learning. Mohrman, Wohl-stetter, and associates (1994) claim that principals must empower their constituencies to achieve high involvement. Bolman and Deal (1997) discuss how leaders empower staff and build political links to key stakeholders. Also, see Elmore (2002) and Knowles (2002) on the development of instructional leadership.

73. The effects of teacher influence on teacher retention in schools were first documented by Ingersoll (2001). These findings have recently been cross-validated in Chicago by Kapadia, Coca, and Easton (2006) using CCSR data.

74. This encompasses supporting parental role, such as offering parent-training classes. It also means teaching parents ways to monitor homework and reinforce learning at home, involving them as advisors and decision makers, and recruiting them as volunteers. See Epstein, Coates, Salinas, Sanders, and Simon (1997).

75. Bryk, Sebring, Kerbow, Rollow, and Easton (1998), chap. 6.

76. Teacher leaders often exercise leadership from a point of view different from the administration. See Spillane, Halverson, and Diamond (2001). Similarly, Ogawa and Bossert (1995) write that leadership flows broadly through social networks. Smylie and Hart (1997) see leadership as an interactive relationship between leaders and followers, or a negotiated order.

77. This is a basic tenet of systems theory. For a classic exposition on this topic, see von Bertalanffy (1969).

78. Mr. Kotsakis suffered a fatal heart attack in 1994. We dedicated our first book, *Democratic Localism*, in his honor.

79. See, for example, Burns and Stalker (1961) and Lawrence and Lorsch (1967).

80. For a further discussion of applications of contingency theory in the context of educational organizations, see Rowan (1990, 2002a, and 2002b).

81. See Miller and Rowan (2006), p. 219.

82. To reiterate, as noted earlier, we do expect that the relationship of the essential supports to math and reading improvement may be somewhat different as a result of differences in the nature of teaching in these two subject areas. According to contingency theory, and some extant research evidence, the essential supports may be more significant for reading improvement, because of the ambiguous nature of this instruction, as compared to mathematics, where teaching tends to be somewhat more standardized.

83. Bryk and Schneider (2002).

84. Kerbow (1996).

85. Pribesh and Downey (1999).

86. Anthony S. Bryk was also the director of the Center for School Improvement at the University of Chicago, subsequently named the Center for Urban School Improvement. Pilot work on many of the survey scales used in this study was initiated in CSI schools, where we had the benefit of extensive independent clinical accounts about school change processes. Literally, the words and concerns raised in this clinical activity became the basis for numerous CCSR survey items.

87. See earlier work on this in the context of our volume on democratic localism: Bryk, Sebring, Kerbow, Rollow, and Easton (1998). Additionally, in personal communication with the authors, Charles Payne, who had been studying the implementation of the Comer Initiative in Chicago, noted that he had undertaken an independent assessment which affirmed the validity of the measures against blind field reports.

88. Our early field studies focused on identifying the distinctive characteristics of improving schools. This lens directed our attention to the significance of both instructional and inclusive-facilitative principal leadership in mobilizing improvement. In contrast, the managerial dimension became more visible when we shifted attention, post-1996, to interventions in nonimproving schools. Such schools were often deeply troubled organizations where many of the basics of routine school operations just did not work very well. The importance of these daily routines and basic services, which we simply take for granted most of the time, become highly salient in their absence. This dimension of leadership plays a role similar to order and safety within the student-centered learning climate subsystem. While it does not guarantee an improving school, a sustained problem here is likely to be highly predictive of stagnation.

89. The significance of this concept was clear early in our work, but we were simply unable to develop an adequate indicator for it. While we did attempt to measure the number and types of external school ties, these data failed to capture the quality dynamic at work here. Simply reporting a large number of external programmatic connections told us relatively little about the amount and quality of the services actually provided and whether the school was able to weave these together into a coherent plan of student and family support. In the most extreme cases, which we dubbed Christmas-tree schools, the presence of a multitude of external programs proved to be a powerful indicator of the absence of any systemic local school improvement plan. See Bryk, Sebring, Kerbow, Rollow, and Easton (1998), pp. 123–24.

90. While these elements change over time within schools, the strength of each in any given year is correlated with its strength during the previous and subsequent survey years.

91. Orfield, Woolbright, and Kim (1984).

92. Bryk, Sebring, Kerbow, Rollow, and Easton (1998), pp. 160–66.

93. We note that the data collected from students generally proved less useful in distinguishing among schools than was the case for the teacher survey data. While for some teacher measures, 20 percent or more of the variance was between schools, on the student measures only 5 percent or less of the variability was typically between schools. We eventually came to conclude that students may not be especially reliable informants about their schools, because they lack a sufficient frame of reference for judging quality. The safety measure, however, was a notable exception in this regard. This measure does substantially distinguish among schools and correlates well with police-beat crime statistics. In one study we found that the correlations ranged from −0.42 to −0.60. See Sebring, Bryk, Roderick, Camburn, Luppescu, Thum, Smith, and Kahne (1996), p. 84, footnote 30.

94. An alternative measurement strategy would have focused on trying to directly assess the instructional resources provided by the school and the presence of any school-based accountability policies and routines, such as pacing guides and walk-through processes, to monitor instructional practices. Although we made some preliminary efforts along these lines, none of them ever culminated in reliable and valid measures.

Chapter three

1. See Cohen, Raudenbush, and Ball (2003) on resources for student learning. Within their framework, our five essential supports remain one step removed from the active resources used in classrooms as direct instruments of student learning.

2. We note that this is formally analogous to arguments offered by Cronbach and Meehl (1955) on the ultimate test for construct validity. See also Cronbach (1985).

3. At least one measure representing each support met these criteria, with the exception of student-centered learning climate. We had one core measure of school leadership, parent-community involvement, and instructional guidance in both years. For student-centered learning climate, we used measures that were similar, but not exactly the same, for each year; in 1994 we had a measure of safety and order, while in 1997 we just measured safety. Two factors existed for professional capacity. We chose to display just one—work orientation—but the results were the same using the other: professional community. See chapter 2 for a description of each measure and factor. For details on measures, factors, and items, see appendix C.

4. All the results presented in this chapter were also cross-validated with the 1997 data. In fact, many of our findings were even stronger in 1997. We chose to focus attention in this chapter on only the essential support indicators from 1994, since this was midway through the period of our study and represented a more conservative test of the hypothesized statistical associations.

5. The number of schools in each category: school leadership—weak 53, strong 53; parent involvement—weak 52, strong 52; work orientation—weak 53, strong 53; safety and order—weak 55, strong 56; curriculum alignment—weak 49, strong 56.

6. Note that schools with strong curriculum alignment in mathematics were more likely to improve in both mathematics and reading. This suggests that schools that work to align mathematics instruction with established standards also pay attention to such alignment in other subjects.

7. As we subsequently demonstrate, the core indicators show a more similar pattern of differentiation across the three outcomes when we switch from predicting improvement to predicting stagnation. Since schools with stagnant attendance trends are not near the "improvement ceiling," this statistical artifact does not constrain the relationship between weak essential supports and stagnation in attendance.

8. Analytic techniques are available that allow for at least a partial adjustment for this problem. The resulting statistical evidence is a bit more complicated to summarize, however. Since this evidence would not significantly alter the basic argument presented here, we rely on these simple percentage statistics in the interest of clarity of presentation.

9. The actual reliabilities for each measure are presented in "Survey Measures, Factors, Composite Variables, and Items Used in Organizing Schools for Improvement" (http://ccsr.uchicago.edu/publications/measures_in_organizing_schools.pdf).

10. Two sources of measurement error affect the misclassification of schools as being in the bottom quartile on an essential support while also appearing in the top quartile on productivity. First, a school may be misclassified as being in the bottom quartile on the support when the true school practice is actually better than that. Similarly, we may misclassify a school as improving on productivity when the true outcomes would not support this. If we assume that the both the productivity measures and the organizational indicators have a reliability of .90, and that the errors of measurement in both are independently and normally distributed, we can estimate the probability of a school being misclassified. First, for each case in the sample, we construct a probability distribution around the observed productivity score. We then compare these

distributions across cases to examine the extent of overlap among pairs. This allows us to compute the probability that an order reversal might occur in a way that would move a nonimproving school erroneously into the top quartile. The probability of misclassification derived from this exercise was 2.1 percent. We note that this misclassification probability would be greater if the measurement reliability were actually lower than assumed in this exercise.

Similarly, some schools may have been erroneously classified as being low-support schools, due to unreliability on the organizational indicators, when they actually were not. Applying the same logic as above, we expect about 2.1 percent of schools to be misclassified as low-support schools (i.e., in the bottom quartile). Assuming that the sources of measurement error in the organizational indicators and the productivity trends are independent, we can use these results to infer the probability of a correct joint classification and thereby the probability of misclassifications. Specifically, the probability of improving schools being correctly classified is 0.979. Similarly, the probability of a school weak on an essential support as being correctly classified is also 0.979. Thus, the probability of a correct joint classification is 0.958 (i.e., $.979 \times .979$). Correspondingly, the probability of a misclassification is 0.042.

11. For our sample of 390 elementary schools, 177 had student survey data, and 188 had teacher data for both 1994 and 1997.

12. The number of schools in each category is for school leadership—23, parent involvement—19, work orientation—18, safety and order—19, curriculum alignment—12.

13. If we assume that the five organizational supports are independent, then the probability of strength on one of the four other core indicators can be determined from a simple evaluation of the binomial distribution, where the probability of a success on each of the four trials is 0.25.

14. One alternative explanation for these data is that school staff holds a generic view of their school as either "good" or "bad" and applies this perspective to any question asked about their school regardless of the specific content of the questions. Such a phenomenon, if true, would also tend to produce a clustering in the indicator reports. This seems implausible, given that the survey questions focus on several different role classes (principals, teachers, parents, and the local community), and many items were posed in explicit behavioral terms (e.g., how frequently did certain behaviors occur).

15. In preliminary analyses, we attempted a range of latent class models to see if we could identify more distinct improvement profiles displayed by schools. Schools with multiple strengths and those with multiple weaknesses clearly differentiated themselves. The "middle patterns" were more mixed, but included one group of schools that were strong on parent-community ties but weak in school leadership and professional community, and another group that had weak instructional guidance despite strength in other organizational supports. We eventually decided to use the simple profile scoring method reported here, because levels of improvement in these "middle pattern" schools were between those of "high"- and "low"-support schools. In chapter 4, we provide more nuanced analyses of the supports' interactive relationships with improvements in academic productivity and attendance.

16. The number of schools in each category is for weak in most supports—40, weak in few supports—51, neutral—28, strong in few supports—52, strong in most supports—41.

Chapter four

1. Local hiring of teachers, without regard to system seniority rights, was a key provision in the 1988 reform legislation. We documented in our earlier volume, *Democratic Localism*, that leadership in actively restructuring schools made good use of this reform provision to initiate change in their buildings. See Bryk, Sebring, Kerbow, Rollow, and Easton (1998), chaps. 3 and 4.

2. This approach is quite different from the typical effective schools study. In this latter line of research, strong and/or improving schools are identified and common characteristics of these schools enumerated. The true discriminating power of these factors, however, is never examined. Might these factors, for example, also be present in nonimproving schools? In a formal statistical sense, effective schools research looks at only a quarter of the evidence presented here—the extent to which organizational strengths correlate with improvement. In contrast, we consider both improvement and stagnation and the nature of the associations between both strengths and weaknesses on the indicators, with both organizational consequences. As such, this is a "complete account" in that all the evidence from Chicago's natural experiment in school reform is considered here.

3. CHAID stands for Chi-square Automatic Interaction Detection, a data-mining technique that evaluates interactions among the independent variables to find the best fit for modeling the dependent variable.

4. We could not achieve an exact cross validation in every instance, as the available data in 1994 and 1997 differed for some of the indicators. When this occurred we examined whether closely related indicators offered an account similar to the effects identified in the 1994 data. The caption for each figure in this chapter identifies the data sources used for the indicators displayed there. Any caption that reads "all indicators from 1994" means that the same indicators were available in 1997 and that comparable results occurred.

5. This classification of schools as stagnant or substantially improving is based on the bottom and top quartiles on our indicators of school improvement; this is why the expectation for each comparison is 25 percent.

6. Again, as we noted in chapter 3, the substantive significance of this, if any, is unclear, as there is a natural ceiling effect (around 95 to 96 percent) associated with student attendance, which cautions against any strong interpretation here.

7. These safety and order effects are in line with more general educational research findings that students who feel ill at ease at school often respond with absences, class cutting, and tardiness. See, for example, Bowen and Bowen (1999); DeLuca, Pigott, and Rosenbaum (2002).

8. For an account of qualitative fieldwork on such instruction in Chicago, see J. Smith, Smith, and Bryk (1998).

9. Ibid.

10. See the study by Shernoff, Schneider, and Csikszentmihalyi (2001).

11. See the conclusion in the CCSR report by Newmann, Lopez, and Bryk (1998) on ambitious intellectual instruction in the Chicago Public Schools. This research demonstrates that ambitious intellectual work already occurs in a substantial number of Chicago classrooms with highly disadvantaged students. With well-reinforced instruction, these Chicago students rose to the expectations set out for them. The authors concluded that

disadvantaged urban students can clearly do the work; the problem is developing and supporting teachers to organize and manage such instruction.

12. Noticeably absent from this summary is any discussion of the role of academic press and classroom personalism. Although some supportive evidence on this account can be found in prior CCSR research by Lee, Smith, Perry, and Smylie (1999), the results from the analyses undertaken for this chapter were inconclusive. While findings did emerge on this point in the 1997 data, they were not replicated in 1994. For this reason, we have not discussed them in the text.

13. See on this point research by Spillane and Thompson (1997) on the efficacy of professional development schools.

14. See the seminal contributions on this point by Stodolsky (1988).

15. See Miller and Rowan (2006).

16. We note that large-scale, comprehensive data on teacher quality remain elusive.

17. See Kapadia, Coca, and Easton (2007); Ingersoll (2001 and 2004); DeAngelis and Pressley (2007). For the influence of certification requirements and salaries, see Murnane, Singer, and Willett (1991).

18. Other researchers using these same data to examine differences among classrooms have found stronger gains in student achievement associated with applications-oriented instruction. See J. Smith, Lee, and Newmann (2001), who found that on average, teachers who made frequent use of basic, skill-oriented didactic instruction were likely to produce reading and math gains that were 5-percent lower than average from one year to the next. Frequent use of more interactive, applications-oriented instruction, however, led to student learning gains about 4-percent higher than average. These results emerged from hierarchical linear model analyses that took into account students' race, gender, and history of retention; characteristics of classrooms; and characteristics of schools. In addition, Newmann, Bryk, and Nagaoka (2001) determined that teachers who gave more intellectually challenging assignments than average contributed to higher gains for their students on the Iowa Tests of Basic Skills and the Illinois Goals Assessment Program.

19. It is important to keep in mind that the focus of this book is on the school organizational supports for improving student learning. In this regard, we concentrate here on the core elements that define an instructional guidance system rather than how instruction is actually carried out in each classroom under such a guidance framework. We have evidence from Chicago studies, including Newmann, Lopez, and Bryk (1998); Newmann, Bryk, and Nagaoka (2001); and Roderick, Engel, Nagaoka, and others (2003), that when authentic instructional tasks are well taught in classrooms, significant student learning occurs. See also Newmann and associates (1996). The main point of the findings here, however, is that a successful orchestration of authentic instruction takes genuine expertise and surely involves more than just doing a lot of projects, hands-on activities, student group work, and so on. Such pedagogies are simply means to a valued educational end: students' deep intellectual engagement with ideas.

20. To utilize fully all the data collected over time and across measures, analyses were performed using a hierarchical multivariate linear model (HMLM) with missing data and a latent variable regression. In brief, all schools that participated in the CCSR surveys at any one of the three time points (1991, 1994, and 1997) were included in the analysis. The HMLM routine generates maximum likelihood estimates of the latent

multivariate distribution among the variables based on all extant data. Unlike traditional methods where units with less-than-complete data are deleted from the analysis (so-called listwise deletion), all units with any data are included in the HMLM, since they contain at least some information about the underlying multivariate distribution that generated these data. Also of note, the HMLM estimates in this case are subject to the less restrictive assumption known as the MAR (missing-at-random conditional on what has already been measured), rather than the much more restrictive requirement of MCAR (missing completely at random), which is required under listwise deletion. Subsequently, latent variable regression models were posed based on this estimated variance-covariance structure. Specifically, each essential support in the "outcome year" was regressed against the base-year level of that same essential support, the base-year level of leadership, the change in leadership between the two time points, school size, enrollment stability, racial composition, and school SES. Change in leadership was also included as a control. For further technical details on the model and estimation procedures employed here and their rationale, see Raudenbush and Bryk (2002), chap. 11.

21. We note that these are actually conservative tests for leadership effects. Any effect that leadership may have had on school development before the base year of 1991 and 1994, respectively, was removed by including the base level of each support as a covariate in the analysis. Thus, we estimated here only the incremental effects on organizational functioning over a three-year period and not the "total effect."

22. Between August 1993 and July 1994, there was a major turnover in school principals. In 1993, one hundred principals took early retirement. By spring 1994, the first round of four-year principal performance contracts came up for review and renewal, and a second round of early retirement offers was also extended. The joint effects of early retirement and contract decisions led to another round of significant change in school leaders.

23. Because the indicators were standardized within each year before the analysis, the average change for the system was set at zero.

24. See Diamond (2007); Sergiovanni (2000), chap. 9; Smylie and Hart (1997); and Smylie, Mayrowetz, Murphy, and Seashore Louis (2007).

Chapter five

1. For a further elaboration of the theory of relational trust, summarized in this section, see chap. 2 in Bryk and Schneider (2002).

2. See Seashore Louis, Kruse, and associates (1995) for a discussion of the role of trust in the formation of a school-based professional community.

3. See, for example, the three case studies in Bryk and Schneider (2002). Also, Charles Payne conducted a validation study of the CCSR's survey measures against double-blind field observations and found high agreement between the trust survey measures and what field staff actually observed in these schools. See Payne (2008).

4. Unfortunately, curriculum alignment was not measured before 1994. As a result, a 1991 to 1994 change analysis was not possible for this organizational indicator.

5. To utilize fully all the data collected over time and across measures, analyses were performed using a hierarchical multivariate linear model (HMLM) with missing data and a latent variable regression. In brief, all schools that participated in the CCSR surveys at

any one of the three time points (1991, 1994, and 1997) were included in the analysis. The HMLM routine generates maximum likelihood estimates of the latent multivariate distribution among the variables based on all extant data. Unlike traditional methods, where units with incomplete data are deleted from the analysis (so-called listwise deletion), all units with any data are included in the HMLM estimation, since they contain at least some information about the underlying multivariate distribution that generated these data. Also of note, the HMLM estimates in this case are subject to the less restrictive assumption known as MAR (missing at random conditional on what has already been measured), rather than the much more restricted requirement of MCAR (missing completely at random), which is required under listwise deletion. Subsequently, latent variable regression models were posed based on this estimated variance-covariance structure. Specifically, each essential support in the "outcome year" was regressed against the base-year level of that same essential support, the base-year level of trust, the change in trust between the two periods, school size, enrollment stability, racial composition, and school SES. For further technical details on the model and estimation procedures employed here and their rationale, see Raudenbush and Bryk (2002), chap. 11.

6. See note 5 above for a description of the statistical methods.

7. See chap. 6 in Bryk and Schneider (2002).

8. The CCSR found, in its very first report published in 1991 (see Easton, Bryk, Driscoll, Kotsakis, Sebring, and van der Ploeg), that a positive initiation of local school reform was more likely in small elementary schools. This was one of the first empirical studies done by the CCSR that reported that school size might actually affect a school's capacity to improve.

9. Bryk and Driscoll (1988) documented the positive effects of small school size on student engagement and teacher commitment. See also Bryk, Lee, and Holland (1993) for research on the effectiveness of urban Catholic high schools. Small school size was identified as a key facilitating factor in the early implementation of Chicago school reform. See Easton and Storey (1994); Bryk, Easton, Kerbow, Rollow, and Sebring (1993); and Sebring, Bryk, Easton, Luppescu, Thum, Lopez, and Smith (1995). It has also been documented as a key structural feature supporting successful school restructuring (Newmann and Wehlage [1995]). See also V. Lee and Smith (1999).

10. See Moultrie (1992).

11. See chap. 2 in Bryk and Schneider (2002).

12. For an ethnographic account of the interpersonal distrust that afflicts communal life in disadvantaged Chicago neighborhoods, see Alex Kotlowitz's *There Are No Children Here* (1991). In a most telling line on this point, one of the two children in the story, Pharaoh, declares, "I have no friends, only associates."

13. The analyses for curriculum alignment occurred only during the second time period, as curriculum alignment was not measured before 1994.

14. In estimating the overall effects of size and enrollment stability, we did not include the trust measure in this round of analyses. The mediating effects through trust, reported in the next section, replicate these models but with trust added as an additional predictor.

15. We note that the effects estimates presented in this section, especially for the 1994 to 1997 period, are relatively conservative in that these analyses remove any prior effects

that stability or size might have had on the base state of each essential support. For example, in assessing the effect of school size on change in an essential support from 1994 to 1997, the reported results are net of any previous effects accruing from a small school that are already represented in the base level of that support in 1994. That is, our analyses only estimate the incremental effect above and beyond that base.

16. For further details on our research into the initiation phase of this decentralization reform, see Bryk, Sebring, Kerbow, Rollow, and Easton (1998).

17. For a review of the accumulated empirical evidence and clinical wisdom on this account, see Fullan (2001).

Chapter six

1. For a further discussion of the political theory undergirding democratic localism as a lever for change, see chap. 2 in Bryk, Sebring, Kerbow, Rollow, and Easton (1998).

2. See ibid.

3. We note that the recent research published on the effects of charter schools (see Betts and Tang 2008) is also reporting great variability in charter school effects. For a report on Chicago charters, see Booker, Gill, Zimmer, and Sass (2008). Again as a local/decentralized initiative, this is precisely what we should expect.

4. Our analysis occurs at a macro level, where the unit of analysis is schools, and not individual students, teachers, and principals. Other scholars have developed theoretical tools and empirical data about the cultural capital that different poor and minority students bring to school, which competent educators can utilize to improve classroom instruction and student support. This line of inquiry has been exceedingly valuable in rooting out stereotypic thinking and providing guidance for effective educational interventions for students of color who are from low-income families. See, for example, C. Lee, Spencer, and Harpalani (2003); Nasir and Saxe (2003); and Orellana and Bowman (2003).

5. These categories were developed by the CCSR in collaboration with the Chicago Public Schools and are now used as standard reporting elements by both organizations.

6. The one exception is a school that is mostly African-American with a large percentage of first-generation students from China.

7. These patterns are consistent with William Julius Wilson's research in Chicago. Particularly for African-American residents, the loss of hundreds of thousands of jobs during the 1970s and 1980s, coupled with the migration of the middle class from the West and South sides of Chicago, left many communities with a greater concentration of poverty. Between 1980 and 1990, for example, Chicago witnessed 62-percent increase in the number of ghetto census tracts, even though there was only a small increase in the number of poor persons (Wilson 1996, chap. 1). Latino communities, on the other hand, were not as affected by the economic changes connected to the decline of the manufacturing industry. In 1980, for example, 21 percent of blacks but only 7.9 percent of all Mexican immigrants lived in tracts with poverty rates of 30 to 39 percent. Mexican immigrants were more likely to have small businesses and social services in their communities, whereas blacks in poverty were more isolated from commercial activity and jobs. See ibid., pp. 51–52.

8. The full details for the classification of schools by race-ethnicity and social class are presented below.

Truly disadvantaged	These schools were located in neighborhoods with extreme poverty—more than 1 standard deviation (SD) below average on our measure of SES. They were also racially segregated—at least 90-percent African American, and most were 100-percent African American.
African American, low-SES	These were schools in high-poverty areas, ranging from 1 to .25 SDs below the mean on SES. All were over 85-percent African American, and most were 100-percent African American.
African American, moderate-SES	These schools had moderate to low levels of poverty, ranging from .25 SD below the mean on SES to almost 2 SDs above the average. All were 85-percent or more African American.
Predominantly minority	These schools had a mix of African American and Latino students, with the two groups together totaling at least 85 percent of the school population. Economically, these schools served students in the midrange—from just under 1.5 SD below average to 1 SD above the mean.
Predominantly Latino	These schools were at least 85-percent Latino, and served students with moderate economic levels (between −1 and .5 SD on our SES scale).
Racially diverse	These schools were 15- to 29-percent white/Asian, and served students whose SES was above average (.5 SD above the system mean, on average).
Racially integrated	These schools were at least 30-percent white/Asian and served students with the highest SES levels—on average almost 1 SD above the system mean.

9. The percentage below the poverty line was calculated for the neighborhoods in which students live as well as the neighborhood surrounding the school. See appendix A.
10. Sampson, Raudenbush, and Earls (1997).
11. Coleman (1988), p. S100.
12. McAdam (1999).
13. Putnam (1993).
14. Sampson, Raudenbush, and Earls (1997).
15. Wilson (1987).
16. Ibid., Wilson (1996).
17. Putnam (2000), pp. 35–36, quoted in Noguera (2001).
18. Warren, Thompson, and Saegert (2001).
19. Since 1964, Chicago's Fourth Presbyterian Church has operated Chicago Lights, a program matching students from the Cabrini-Green community and other neighborhoods in the city with volunteer tutors for weekly one-to-one study sessions.
20. Warren, Thompson, and Saegert (2001), p. 15.
21. Ibid.
22. See Katz (1992) and Fung (2004), chap. 7.
23. Putnam (2000), p. 23, quoted in Noguera (2001).
24. For a detailed ethnographic account of the role of black churches in the community life

of "Groveland" (a pseudonym for an actual Chicago neighborhood), see Patillo-McCoy (1998).

25. Ibid., p. 782.

26. In general, churches and church-based organizations have long been working to orga-nize and empower people in poor communities. Examples include the Industrial Areas Foundation, which exists in at least sixty American communities, and a similar group in Chicago, the Gamaliel Foundation. For more details, see Foley, McCarthy, and Chaves (2001).

27. Lincoln and Mamiya (1990), quoted in Warren, Thompson, and Saegert (2001).

28. An immediate question was whether nonparental guardianship was in fact a good proxy for the proportion of students in a school who were in foster care. By merging our data with student-level social services files from the Chapin Hall Center for Chil-dren, we were eventually able to obtain a much more precise measure of the number of foster-care children being educated in each school. Although the absolute numbers changed, the basic pattern of results remained the same.

29. Courtney, Roderick, Smithgall, Gladden, and Nagaoka (2004) and Smithgall, Gladden, Howard, Goerge, and Courtney (2004).

30. No regular Chicago public school had more than 6 percent of its students in foster care. For further details, see ibid.

31. For a moving ethnographic account in this regard, see for example Kidder (1989). Also see Baldacci (2004).

32. Courtney, Roderick, Smithgall, Gladden, and Nagaoka (2004) and Smithgall, Gladden, Howard, Goerge, and Courtney (2004).

33. Many elementary schools in Chicago share a single school social worker with another school. In contrast, in neighborhood suburban communities, with arguably a smaller density of these problems, significantly more school social-work services exist.

34. PHDCN organized the 847 census blocks within the city of Chicago into 343 relatively homogenous neighborhood clusters. Each community cluster consisted of about 8,000 residents. Interviews were then conducted in a random sample of households within each neighborhood cluster. Overall, 8,732 Chicago residents were interviewed in 1994–95 about the social conditions in their community. By using the geocoded school address information in the CCSR data files, we were then able to match each school to its PHDCN neighborhood cluster data. For further description of the study, go to http://www.icpsr.umich.edu/PHDCN/. Also see http://www.webapp.icpsr.umich.edu/cocoon/ICPSR-SERIES/00206.xml.

35. Sampson, Raudenbush, and Earls (1997).

36. First a scale was created representing the total incidence of crime in the neighbor-hood around each school. This was the weighted sum of log rates of murder, robbery, assault, burglary, auto theft, theft, drugs, vice, arson, weapons, and other crimes. The weights were produced by factor analysis. Similarly, a scale representing the means of the total incidence of these same crimes in students' neighborhoods was also calcu-lated. The school and student neighborhood scales were subsequently combined. Thus, for each school there is a scale representing the "average" crime rate for the school and neighborhoods where students live. Data were furnished by Richard Lock of Loyola University, and the Chicago Alternative Policing Strategy Program of the Chicago Police Department.

37. We have theorized that the prevalence of crime may inhibit the voluntary associa-

tion among school community members to address local school problems. The social network of concern here involves both school parents and community leaders in the neighborhood immediately surrounding the school. Since not all students who attend a given CPS elementary school live in the same neighborhood as their school, it seemed important to take into account both the crime rates surrounding the school and the crime rates where students actually live. A high prevalence of crime in either context should weaken the propensity of parents and community leaders to join together in solving school problems.

38. The index used in our analysis is based on averaged percentage across these six years and then converted to the log odds of the percentage. While only 1995–96 data technically fall within our study period, we found that the correlation between a school's rate for that single year and the average for the subsequent five-years was 0.97. In order to generate the most stable statistic possible for all school communities, we decided in the end to simply average the reports from all six years. (Good data were not available on this problem before 1995.) It is important to note in this regard that reports in any given year capture events of abuse and neglect that actually occurred at some earlier time in a child's life. That is, it may take repeated events before a problem actually comes to light, and there is a process for inquiring and reviewing evidence before determining that any reported incident be classified as a documented case of abuse or neglect. In short, administrative records of abuse and neglect in any given year actually document events that occurred at some earlier time. As a result, many of the cases appearing in administrative records in the years post our study frame may actually reference traumatic events that occurred during the time of our study.

39. This is a simple result of the fact that we defined the improving category as the top quartile of schools on each trend indicator, and stagnating schools as consisting of the bottom quartile of schools on each outcome. For a further discussion of the justification for these cut points, see chapter 2.

40. These results are based on the following number of school communities: For the religious participation index, 57 weak and 49 strong communities; for collective efficacy, the corresponding counts were 50 and 47; for outside connections, it was 48 and 55; for the crime rate, it was 59 high-crime and 54 low-crime communities; and for the density of abused or neglected students, 55 high-density and 48 low-density schools, respectively.

41. In general, prior CCSR research has found a moderate to strong correlation between students' survey reports about school safety and the neighborhood crime rate as calculated from police beat crime statistics. These correlations range from −0.42 to −0.60, depending on the crime crate category. See Sebring, Bryk, Roderick, Camburn, Luppescu, Thum, Smith, and Kahne (1996), p. 84 n. 30.

42. For these analyses, we combined the neighborhood crime data with the local religious participation and collective efficacy indicators to form a composite indicator on bonding social capital.

43. These are the ratios of the odds, not the ratios of the probabilities. For example, the probability of substantial improvement in reading for integrated schools is 42 percent, so the odds of substantial improvement are 0.724. The corresponding probability of substantial improvement in reading for truly disadvantaged schools is 15 percent (figure 6.5), so the odds are 0.176. The ratio of the odds for truly disadvantaged schools (0.176)

compared with integrated schools (0.724) is about 0.2, which is the number displayed in figure 6.11.

44. These results are based on the following number of school communities: For the religious participation index, 57 weak and 49 strong communities; for collective efficacy, the corresponding counts were 50 and 47; for outside connections, it was 48 and 55; for the crime rate, it was 59 high-crime and 54 low-crime communities; and for the density of abused or neglected students, 55 high-density and 48 low-density schools, respectively.

45. The composite variable for community conditions is made up of an equally weighted combination of collective efficacy, religious participation, outside connections, crime (combined school and student neighborhood and coded negatively), and proportion of students who have been abused or neglected.

46. The number of schools in communities with high social capital/low crime, abuse, or neglect rates in each essential support category is as follows: weak—9, average—27, strong—38. In communities with low social capital/high crime, abuse, or neglect rates, the number in each category is as follows: weak—30, average—25, strong—10.

47. See, for example, chap. 19 in Reeves (2000) that describes a set of schools with 90-percent low-income students and 90-percent minority enrollment that still manage to achieve 90-percent student success rates. Such studies focus on the common characteristics of "good schools" but do not consider the full range of possible different conditions under which 90-percent low-income and 90-percent minority schools might be operating. A more nuanced view of the "90/90" schools problem emerged in our research, because we were able to actually study the school development process over time across a broad spectrum of such schools.

48. Warren (2005); Tough (2004).

49. One example of this in the Chicago community context is the Logan Square Neighborhood Association (LSNA). LSNA was able to convince Chicago's school system to build annexes for five elementary schools and two new middle schools. As part of its leadership development program, LSNA also trained parent mentors, who were hired to work in classrooms.

Summary and conclusions

1. See, for example, Hanushek (1992), who reports that students taught by better-quality teachers learn significantly more than students taught by teachers who are near the bottom. This finding has been replicated in several research studies, which have documented that teacher effects vary greatly among teachers within schools as well as between schools. See Rivkin, Hanushek, and Kain (2005); Kane, Rockoff, and Staiger (2006); Nye, Konstantopoulos, and Hedges (2004). Technically, these estimated effects are for classroom-teachers. That is, these value-added analyses estimate larger- (or smaller-) than-expected increments to learning associated with a particular classroom-teacher in a given year. While the analysis models generally control in different ways for prior *individual* achievement, any composition effects associated with a particular grouping of students are part of the classroom-teacher effect. Regardless, it is generally assumed in this research that these observed differences are largely a consequence of teacher effects.

2. See Hackel, Koenig, and Elliot (2008); Decker, Mayer, and Glazerman (2004); Boyd, Lankford, Loeb, and Wykoff (2005).

3. We note that there is another policy approach for improving schools that has found increasing interest given these results. Basically, this argument goes as follows. Teacher quality matters a whole lot, but we do not know how to identify it in terms of credentials, degrees, experiences, or even practices observed in the classroom. Therefore, we should rely on student outcomes as the indirect indicator (i.e., some estimate of the value-added to student learning associated with each teacher). Specifically, we should give enhanced salaries to those who consistently do well in this regard and fire the lowest achievers (e.g., the bottom 10 percent each year). Over time, assuming an adequate continuing supply of teacher candidates, the overall effectiveness of teachers will improve without our having to know what actually contributes to this improvement and how to teach others to accomplish the same. There is much to commend in the overall logic of the general argument. The big issues, as is typically the case, are associated with the details of implementation and the possible (serious) unintended side effects that might also accrue. Since this proposed policy has never been tried in any sustained fashion anywhere to the best of our knowledge, there is simply no empirical evidence available to evaluate the "what would happen if" question here.

4. See, for example, Rowan, Correnti, and Miller (2002), who report findings that the variability in effects on student learning was actually greater among teachers within schools than between schools.

5. See Kerbow (1995) and Kerbow (1996).

6. On this idea of inert school resources for improving student learning, see Cohen, Raudenbush, and Ball (2003).

7. As a point of clarification, we note that a stable, well-functioning school may be able to sustain its efficacy for some time with a weak leader; but fundamental improvements in a weak organization are unlikely to occur under these conditions. Moreover, even in good schools, we would expect organizational effectiveness to decline eventually if weak leadership persists for a long period.

8. See Newmann, Smith, Allensworth, and Bryk (2001a and 2001b), where instructional program coherence was first presented. See Bryk and Schneider (2002) for a discussion of the role of principal leadership in establishing relational trust; this argument was first articulated there.

9. Note that this problem is not peculiar to schools but represents a more general organizational consideration. One can envision an extraordinary strategic plan but lack the human resources necessary to execute it. See, for example, Bossidy and Charan's (2002) discussion of this problem in the business sector.

10. By this we mean using a set of practices and routines to teach specific subject matter and skills to a group of students with particular background characteristics and interests.

11. For detailed, case-based accounts of the processes of school trust formation, see Kochanek (2005).

12. For a further elaboration of these ideas, see ibid.

13. See Gwynne and Easton (2001) and Roderick, Engel, Nagaoka, and others (2003).

14. The Harlem Children's Zone, led by Geoffrey Canada, comes to mind in this regard. One pillar of this initiative is to rebuild the community by developing a critical mass of

leaders, thus contributing to community social capital. Another pillar is "starting early and never letting up." This principle is manifest in a coordinated set of educational programs that begin in infancy and continue through college preparation, including an extended school day and school year. Wrapped around this is a highly intentional effort at forming a peer culture, where students exert positive influence on one another. Finally, undergirding this is a panoply of physical and mental health services, and other services like emergency aid. See Fulwood, Paynter, and Livingston (2007); Pitts (2007).

15. For efforts along this line, see for example the work of the SEED Foundation. See www .seedfoundation.com.

A more delimited approach, sans the residential component, has been pursued by KIPP Academies. They operate an extended school day and year, their teachers are available to students for most of their waking hours, and they deliberately cultivate new peer norm formation aimed at "be nice, work hard" (Tough 2006; Web site: www.kipp .org). Along similar lines, see also the charter school development initiatives sponsored by the Urban Education Institute (formerly the Center for School Improvement) at the University of Chicago. See http://uei.uchicago.edu/work/education.shtml.

16. See the classic text by Shadish, Cook, and Campbell (2002) in this regard. See also Shavelson and Towne (2002).

17. We are indebted on this account to a long-standing observation made by Fred Mosteller, who was an early champion for the use of RCT in applied social and biomedical research. A significant part of Fred's argument was predicated on this observation.

18. For a further elaboration of this idea, see Shavelson and Towne (2002).

19. John Easton (unpublished analysis) found large differences between CPS students' performance on the Illinois Standards Achievement Test (ISAT) and the National Assessment of Educational Progress (NAEP). He compared trends in reading from 2002 to 2005 for CPS elementary school students on the ISAT to trends for Chicago students on the NAEP. On both tests, the nominal percentage of students meeting standards increased. However, the fraction of students meeting or exceeding expectations differed markedly. In 2005, 48 percent of students met or exceeded standards in reading on the ISAT, while only 16 percent of them were deemed proficient or better on the NAEP. In mathematics between 2003 and 2005, there also was improvement in the percentage of students meeting or exceeding standards on both tests, but in 2005, 48 percent of students met or exceeded the ISAT standards, while only 12 percent were considered proficient or better on the NAEP exam. Klein, Hamilton, McCaffrey, and Stecher (2000) discovered similar differences in Texas between the state test and the NAEP results.

20. Jacob (2002); Jacob and Levitt (2003); Bryk (2003).

21. The comments on Chicago school reform, referenced in this closing chapter, draw on results established in a ten-year research program of the Center for School Improvement at the University of Chicago and the Consortium on Chicago School Research. For a summary of what was learned during the first phase of Chicago school reform (up through the mayoral takeover in 1995–96), see Bryk, Sebring, Kerbow, Rollow, and Easton (1998). Related findings can also be found in Hess (1995).

22. For a further elaboration of these ideas, see our earlier volume: Bryk, Sebring, Kerbow, Rollow, and Easton (1998).

23. The contrasts presented at Ridgeway and Holiday schools in Bryk and Schneider (2002) illustrate why this was the case. Key is how the newfound local power established in

1988 reform was eventually utilized. The expanded local authority at Holiday led to a deepening of ties among school staff, parents, and the local community. No similar efforts occurred at Ridgeway, and the social resources to support improvement remained limited.

We note that Bryk, Sebring, Kerbow, Rollow, and Easton (1998) identified a second pattern of dysfunctional local politics. In contrast to the adversarial politics at Ridgeway, some school communities were characterized by consolidated principal power. Relational trust remained weak in these schools, too, as principals exercised authoritarian control and undermined any incipient efforts by parents, staff, or community leaders to collectively advance reform. In essence, democratic localism was never implemented in these sites.

24. It is worth noting that elementary schools with a stronger base of essential supports also fared better under some of the centrally developed initiatives. Schools with greater capacity were taken off probation sooner, for example. See Gwynne and Easton (2001).

25. Note that many of the schools that stagnated under decentralization continued to stagnate during the centralized reforms of 1997 through 2001 as well. Centralization alone provides little assurance of equity in outcomes.

26. See Hill (2008) for a further elaboration of this idea of zones of wishful thinking in school reform.

Appendix B

1. For purposes of a school productivity analysis, we only include those students who were actually enrolled in a particular school for most of the academic year. Specifically, we used the October snapshot from the CPS master files to identify each student's school enrollment as of early October. Only students who were tested at the same school the following spring count for purposes of computing the school's learning gains that year. Students who transferred midyear were excluded from the gain score results, since it is ambiguous as to which school should be held accountable in this regard. Given the relatively high mobility among the Chicago public school students, this reduces the amount of data available in some schools by as much as 15 percent.

Appendix C

1. Orfield, Woolbright, and Kim (1984).

2. Bryk, Sebring, Kerbow, Rollow, and Easton (1998), pp. 160–66.

3. An alternative measurement strategy would have focused on trying to directly assess the instructional resources provided by the school and the presence of any school-based accountability policies and routines, such as pacing guides and walk-through processes, to monitor this. Although we made some preliminary efforts along these lines, none of them ever culminated in reliable and valid measures.

Appendix E

1. The reliability of this measure ranged from 0.80 for neighborhoods with 20 respondents to 0.91 for neighborhoods with 50 respondents.

2. These items formed a Rasch measure.

Appendix G

1. Raudenbush, Bryk, Cheong, and Congdon (2004). See also Ponisciak and Bryk (2005).

Appendix H

1. Dewey (1927); Barber (1984); and Lindblom (1990).
2. See, for example, articles by Weiss, Cohen, and Stake in a volume edited by Bryk (1983). Also notable is Weiss and Bucuvalas (1980).
3. Stake (1980); Patton (1978); and Weiss (1972).
4. Coleman, Bartot, Lewin-Epstein, and Olson (1979).
5. The Chicago Public Schools made the essential supports results central to the school improvement planning process carried out every two years. At first, the essential supports provided the structure for the Self-Analysis Guide. In 2007, the system created a framework, which it called the "Five Fundamentals," that was based on the five essential supports. In the planning process, schools are asked to assess their strengths and weaknesses on practices associated with each essential support domain. Evidence comes from confidential reports of student and teacher survey results that schools receive from the CCSR. Improvement plans address areas of weakness. In addition, the Chicago Principals and Administrators Association based its Leadership Standards on the essential supports. Beyond adoption by the school system, the essential supports research guides professional development provided by the Illinois Network of Charter Schools; it is used to train new principals by the Center for School Leadership at the University of Illinois at Chicago; and it guides the Chicago Public Education Fund in evaluating leadership programs in which The Fund invests.

REFERENCES

Allington, Richard L., and Patricia M. Cunningham. 1996. *Schools that work: Where all children read and write*. New York: HarperCollins.

Baldacci, Leslie. 2004. *Inside Mrs. B.'s classroom: Courage, hope, and learning on Chicago's South Side*. New York: McGraw-Hill.

Barber, Benjamin. B. 1984. *Strong democracy: Participatory politics for a new age*. Berkeley and Los Angeles: Univ. of California Press.

Bertalanffy, Ludwig von. 1969. *General system theory: Foundations, development, and applications*. New York: George Braziller.

Betts, Julian, and Y. Emily Tang. 2008. *Value-added and experimental studies of the effect of charter schools on student achievement: A literature review*. Seattle: Center for Reinventing Public Education, Univ. of Washington.

Bilcer, Diane K. 1997. *Improving Chicago's schools: Teacher and student surveys. User's manual, version 1*. Chicago: Consortium on Chicago School Research at the Univ. of Chicago.

Bilcer, Diane King, Stuart Luppescu, Penny Bender Sebring, and Yeow Meng Thum. 1996. *The charting reform survey series: Public use data on compact disc*. Chicago: Consortium on Chicago School Research at the Univ. of Chicago.

Blase, Joseph, and Peggy Kirby. 1992. *Bringing out the best in teachers: What effective principals do*. Thousand Oaks, CA: Corwin Press.

Bolman, Lee G., and Terrence E. Deal. 1997. *Reframing organizations: Artistry, choice and leadership*. 2nd ed. San Francisco: Jossey-Bass.

Booker, Kevin, Brian Gill, Ron Zimmer, and Tim R. Sass. 2008. *Achievement and attainment in Chicago charter schools*. Santa Monica, CA: RAND.

Borg, Walter R. 1980. Time and school learning. In Denham and Lieberman 1980, 33–63.

Bossidy, Larry, and Ram Charan. 2002. *Execution: The discipline of getting things done*. New York: Crown Business.

Bowen, Natasha K., and Gary L. Bowen. 1999. Effects of crime and violence in neighborhoods and schools on the school behavior and performance of adolescents. *Journal of Adolescent Research* 14 (3): 319–42.

Boyd, Donald, Hamilton Lankford, Susanna Loeb, and James Wyckoff. 2005. Explaining the short careers of high-achieving teachers in schools with low-performing students. Papers and Proceedings of the One Hundred Seventeenth Annual Meeting of the American Economic Association, Philadelphia, January 7–9, 2005. *American Economic Review* 95 (2): 166–71.

Braddock, Jomills H., II, and James McPartland. 1993. Education of early adolescents. *Review of Research in Education* 19:135–70.

Bryk, Anthony S., ed. 1983. *Stakeholder-based evaluation: New directions for program evaluation,* no. 17. San Francisco: Jossey-Bass.

———. 2003. No child left behind, Chicago style. In *No child left behind? The politics and practice of school accountability,* ed. Paul E. Peterson and Martin R. West, 242–68. Washington, DC: Brookings Institution.

Bryk, Anthony S., Eric Camburn, and Karen Seashore Louis. 1999. Professional community in Chicago elementary schools: Facilitating factors and organizational consequences. *Educational Administration Quarterly* 35:751–81.

Bryk, Anthony S., and Mary E. Driscoll. 1988. *The school as community: Theoretical foundations, contextual influences, and consequences for students and teachers.* Madison, WI: National Center on Effective Secondary Schools.

Bryk, Anthony S., John Q. Easton, David Kerbow, Sharon G. Rollow, and Penny Bender Sebring. 1993. *A view from the elementary schools: The state of reform in Chicago.* Chicago: Consortium on Chicago School Research at the Univ. of Chicago.

Bryk, Anthony S., Valerie E. Lee, and Peter B. Holland. 1993. *Catholic schools and the common good.* Cambridge, MA: Harvard Univ. Press.

Bryk, Anthony S., and Steven W. Raudenbush. 1992. *Hierarchical linear models: Applications and data analysis methods.* Newbury Park, CA: Sage Publications.

Bryk, Anthony S., and Barbara L. Schneider. 2002. *Trust in schools: A core resource for improvement.* New York: Russell Sage Foundation.

Bryk, Anthony S., Penny Bender Sebring, David Kerbow, Sharon Rollow, and John Q. Easton. 1998. *Charting Chicago school reform: Democratic localism as a lever for change.* Boulder, CO: Westview Press.

Bryk, Anthony S., Yeow Meng Thum, John Q. Easton, and Stuart Luppescu. 1998. *Academic productivity of Chicago public elementary schools.* Chicago: Consortium on Chicago School Research at the Univ. of Chicago.

Bryk, Anthony S., and Herbert I. Weisberg. 1977. Use of the non-equivalent control group design when subjects are growing. *Psychological Bulletin* 84 (5): 950–62.

Burns, Tom, and George M. Stalker. 1961. *The management of innovation.* London: Tavistock Publications.

Carroll, John B. 1963. A model for school learning. *Teachers College Record* 64 (8): 723–33.

Clark, Reginald M. 1983. *Family life and school achievement: Why poor black children succeed or fail.* Chicago: Univ. of Chicago Press.

Cohen, David K. 1983. Evaluation and reform. In Bryk 1983, 73–81.

Cohen, David K., and Deborah Loewenberg Ball. 1999. *Instruction, capacity, and improvement.* CPRE Research Report no. RR-043. See http://cpre.wcervw.org/#.

Cohen, David K., Milbrey W. McLaughlin, and Joan E. Talbert. 1993. *Teaching for understanding: Challenges for policy and practice.* San Francisco: Jossey-Bass.

Cohen, David K., Stephen Raudenbush, and Deborah Loewenberg Ball. 2003. Resources, instruction, and research. *Educational Evaluation and Policy Analysis* 25 (2): 119–42.

Coleman, James S. 1988. Social capital in the creation of human capital. *American Journal of Sociology* 94:S95–S120.

Coleman, James S., Virginia Bartot, N. Lewin-Epstein, and L. Olson. 1979. *Policy issues and research design.* Washington, DC: National Center for Education Statistics.

Comer, James. 1995. *School power: Implications of an intervention project.* New York: Free Press.

Courtney, Mark E., Melissa Roderick, Cheryl Smithgall, Robert M. Gladden, and Jenny K. Nagaoka. 2004. *Issue brief: The educational status of foster children*. Chicago: Chapin Hall Center for Children.

Cronbach, Lee J. 1985. Construct validity after thirty years. Paper presented at the symposium "Intelligence: Measurement, Theory and Public Policy," Urbana, IL, May 1.

Cronbach, Lee J., and Paul E. Meehl. 1955. Construct validity in psychological tests. *Psychological Bulletin* 52:281–302.

Darling-Hammond, Linda. 1997. *The right to learn: A blueprint for creating schools that work*. San Francisco: Jossey-Bass.

Darling-Hammond, Linda, and Deborah L. Ball. 1998. *Teaching for high standards: What policymakers need to know and be able to do*. New York: Consortium for Policy Research in Education; Philadelphia: National Commission on Teaching and America's Future.

Darling-Hammond, Linda, and Milbrey W. McLaughlin. 1995. Policies that support professional development in an era of reform. *Phi Delta Kappan* 76 (8): 597–604.

David, Jane L., Katrina Woodworth, Elizabeth Grant, Roneeta Guha, Alejandra Lopez-Torkos, and Viki M. Young. 2006. *Bay Area KIPP schools: A study of early implementation. First Year Report 2004–2005*. Menlo Park, CA: SRI International.

DeAngelis, Karen J., and Jennifer B. Pressley. 2007. *Leaving schools or leaving the profession: Setting Illinois' record straight on new teacher attrition*. Policy Research Report IERC 2007–1. Edwardsville: Illinois Education Research Council.

Decker, P. T., D. P. Mayer, and S. Glazerman. 2004. *The effects of Teach for America on students: Findings from a national evaluation*. Princeton, NJ: Mathematica.

Delpit, Lisa. 1986. Skills and other dilemmas of a progressive black educator. *Harvard Educational Review* 56 (4): 379–85.

——. 1996. *Other people's children: Cultural conflict in the classroom*. New York: New Press.

DeLuca, Stefanie, Terri Pigott, and James E. Rosenbaum. 2002. Are dropout decisions related to peer threats, social isolation, and teacher disparagement across schools? A multilevel approach to social climate and dropout. Paper presented at the annual meeting of the American Educational Research Association, New Orleans.

DeMoss, Karen, and Ruanda Garth McCullough. 2001. A closer look: Literacy instruction in improving Chicago schools serving African American students of low-income backgrounds. Paper presented at the annual meeting of the American Educational Research Association, Seattle.

Denham, Carolyn, and Ann Lieberman, eds. 1980. *Time to learn*. Washington, DC: National Institute of Education.

Designs for Change. 1993. *Creating a school community that reads*. Chicago: Designs for Change.

——. 1998. *What makes these schools stand out?* Chicago: Designs for Change.

Dewey, John. 1916. *Democracy and education*. New York: Macmillan.

——. 1927. *The public and its problems*. Troy, MT: Holt, Rinehart & Winston.

Diamond, John B. 2007. Cultivating high expectations in an urban elementary school: The case of Kelly School. In *Distributed leadership in practice*, ed. James P. Spillane and John B. Diamond, 63–84. New York: Teachers College Press.

Dorsch, Nina G. 1998. *Community, collaboration, and collegiality in school reform: An odyssey toward connections*. Albany: State Univ. of New York Press.

Easton, John Q., Anthony S. Bryk, Mary E. Driscoll, John G. Kotsakis, Penny A. Sebring, and

Arie J. van der Ploeg. 1991. *Charting reform: The teachers' turn.* Chicago: Consortium on Chicago School Research at the Univ. of Chicago.

Easton, John Q., Todd Rosenkranz, and Anthony S. Bryk. 2001. *Annual CPS test trend review, 2000.* Chicago: Consortium on Chicago School Research at the Univ. of Chicago.

Easton, John Q., Todd Rosenkranz, Anthony S. Bryk, Brian A. Jacob, Stuart Luppescu, and Melissa Roderick. 2000. *Annual CPS test trend review, 1999.* Chicago: Consortium on Chicago School Research at the Univ. of Chicago.

Easton, John Q., and Sandra L. Storey. 1994. The development of local school councils. *Education and Urban Society* 26 (3): 220–37.

Edmonds, Ronald. 1979. Effective schools for the urban poor. *Educational Leadership* 37: 15–24.

Elmore, Richard F. 2002. *Bridging the gap between standards and achievement: The imperative for professional development in education.* New York: Albert Shanker Institute.

Elmore, Richard F., Penelope L. Peterson, and Sarah J. McCarthey. 1996. *Restructuring in the classroom: Teaching, learning, and school organization.* San Francisco: Jossey-Bass.

Entwisle, Doris R., Karl L. Alexander, and Linda Steffel Olson. 1997. *Children, schools, and inequality.* Boulder, CO: Westview Press.

Epstein, Joyce L., Lucretia Coates, Karen C. Salinas, Mavis G. Sanders, and Beth S. Simon. 1997. *School, family and community partnerships: Your handbook for action.* Thousand Oaks, CA: Corwin Press.

Epstein, Joyce L., and Susan L. Dauber. 1991. School programs and teacher practices of parent involvement in inner city elementary and middle schools. *Elementary School Journal* 91 (3): 289–305.

Ferguson, Ronald. 1991. Paying for public education: New evidence on how and why money matters. *Harvard Journal on Legislation* 28 (2): 465–98.

Fisher, Charles W., and David C. Berliner, eds. 1985. *Perspectives on instructional time.* New York: Longman.

Foley, Michael W., John D. McCarthy, and Mark Chaves. 2001. Social capital, religious institutions, and poor communities. In Saegert, Thompson, and Warren 1983, 215–45. New York: Russell Sage Foundation.

Friedman, Thomas L. 2005. *The world is flat: A brief history of the twenty-first century.* New York: Farrar, Straus, and Giroux.

Fullan, Michael. 1999. *Change forces: The sequel.* London: Falmer Press.

———. 2001. *The new meaning of educational change.* 3rd ed. New York: Teachers College Press.

Fulwood, Sam, III, Bob Paynter, and Sandra Livingston. 2007. Central Harlem program combines leadership, commitment to rebuild a community. *Plain Dealer,* December 13, 2007. www.Cleveland.com.

Fung, Archon. 2004. *Empowered participation: Reinventing urban democracy.* Princeton, NJ: Princeton Univ. Press.

Furstenberg, Frank F., Jr., Thomas D. Cook, Jacquelynne Eccles, Glen H. Elder Jr., and Arnold Sameroff. 1999. *Managing to make it.* Chicago: Univ. of Chicago Press.

Gettinger, Maribeth. 1984. Individual differences in time needed for learning: A review of the literature. *Educational Psychologist* 19 (1): 15–29.

Good, Thomas L., and Jere E. Brophy. 1986. School effects. In Wittrock 1986, 570–602.

Gwynne, Julia, and John Q. Easton. 2001. Probation, organizational capacity and improving student achievement. Paper prepared for the annual meeting of the American Educational Research Association, Seattle.

Hackel, Milton D., Judith Anderson Koenig, and Stuart W. Elliot. 2008. *Assessing accomplished teaching: Advanced-level certification programs.* Washington, DC: National Academies Press.

Hansen, David T. 1995. *The call to teach.* New York: Teachers College Press.

Hanushek, Eric A. 1992. The trade-off between child quantity and quality. *Journal of Political Economy* 100 (1): 84–117.

Harris, Chester W., ed. 1963. *Problems in measuring change.* Proceedings of a conference sponsored by the Committee on Personality Development in Youth of the Social Science Research Council. Madison, WI: Univ. of Wisconsin Press.

Hein, Margaret G. 1982. Attendance policy. In *Encyclopedia of Educational Research,* ed. Harold E. Mitzel, 1:173–79. 5th ed. New York: Free Press.

Hess, G. Alfred, Jr. 1995. *Restructuring schools: A Chicago perspective.* New York: Teachers College Press.

Heyns, Barbara L. 1987. Schooling and cognitive development: Is there a season for learning? *Child Development* 58 (5): 1151–60.

Hill, Paul T. 2008. Spending money when it is not clear what works. *Peabody Journal of Education* 83 (2): 238–58.

Hoy, Wayne K., and Cecil G. Miskel, eds. 2002. *Research and Theory in educational administration.* 7 vols. Greenwich, CT: Information Age.

Huberman, Michael. 1993. The model of the independent artisan in teachers' professional relations. In Little and McLaughlin 1993, 11–50.

Ingersoll, Richard M. 2001. Teacher turnover and teacher shortages: An organizational analysis. *American Educational Research Journal* 38 (3): 499–534.

——. 2004. Why do high poverty schools have difficulty staffing their classrooms with qualified teachers? Paper prepared for the conference "Renewing our schools, securing our future: A national task force on education." Washington, DC: Center for American Progress/Institute for America's Future.

Jacob, Brian A. 2002. Accountability, incentives and behavior: The impact of high-stakes testing in the Chicago Public Schools. Working Paper 8968, National Bureau of Economic Research.

Jacob, Brian A., and Steven Levitt. 2003. Rotten apples: An investigation of the prevalence and predictors of teacher cheating. *Quarterly Journal of Economics* 118 (3): 843–78.

Kane, T. E., J. E. Rockoff, and D. O. Staiger. 2006. What does teacher certification tell us about teacher effectiveness? Evidence from New York City. Working Paper 11844, National Bureau of Economic Research.

Kapadia, Kavita, and Vanessa Coca; with John Q. Easton. 2007. *Keeping new teachers: A first look at the influences of induction in the Chicago Public Schools.* Chicago: Consortium on Chicago School Research at the Univ. of Chicago.

Katz, Michael B. 1992. Chicago school reform as history. *Teachers College Record* 9 (1): 5672.

Kerbow, David. 1995. Pervasive student mobility: A moving target for school improvement. Chicago: Chicago Panel on School Policy and Center for School Improvement.

——. 1996. Patterns of urban student mobility and local school reform. *Journal of Education for Students Placed at Risk* 1 (2): 147–69.

Kidder, Tracy. 1989. *Among schoolchildren.* Boston: Houghton Mifflin.

Klein, Stephen P., Laura S. Hamilton, Daniel F. McCaffrey, and Brian Stecher. 2000. *What do test scores in Texas tell us?* Santa Monica, CA: RAND.

Knowles, Timothy. 2002. The principal and the academic imperative. PhD diss., Harvard Univ.

Kochanek, Julie R. 2005. *Building trust for better schools: Research-based practices.* Thousand Oaks, CA: Corwin Press.

Kotlowitz, Alex. 1991. *There are no children here.* New York: Doubleday.

Lareau, Annette. 1989. *Home advantage: Social class and parental intervention in elementary education.* London: Falmer Press.

Lawrence, Paul R., and Jay W. Lorsch. 1967. *Organization and environment.* Cambridge, MA: Harvard Univ. Press.

Lee, Carol D., Margaret Beale Spencer, and Vinay Harpalani. 2003. "Every shut eye ain't sleep": Studying how people live culturally. *Educational Researcher* 32 (5): 6–13.

Lee, Valerie E., and Julia B. Smith. 1999. Social support and achievement for young adolescents in Chicago: The role of school academic press. *American Educational Research Journal* 36 (4): 907–45.

Lee, Valerie E., Julia B. Smith, and Robert G. Croninger. 1995. Another look at high school restructuring: More evidence that it improves student achievement and more insight into why. *Issues in Restructuring Schools* 9:1–10.

Lee, Valerie E., Julia B. Smith, Tamara E. Perry, and Mark A. Smylie. 1999. *Social support, academic press, and student achievement: A view from the middle grades in Chicago.* Chicago: Consortium on Chicago School Research at the Univ. of Chicago.

Leithwood, Kenneth, Paul T. Begley, and J. Bradley Cousins. 1994. *Developing expert leadership for future schools.* London: Falmer Press.

Levy, Frank, and Richard. J. Murnane. 2005. *The new division of labor: How computers are creating the next job market.* Princeton, NJ: Princeton Univ. Press.

Lieberman, Ann. 1995. Practices that support teacher development. *Phi Delta Kappan* 76 (8): 591–96.

Lincoln, C. Eric, and Lawrence H. Mamiya. 1990. *The Black church in the African-American experience.* Durham, NC: Duke Univ. Press.

Lindblom, Charles E. 1990. *Inquiry and change.* New Haven, CT: Yale Univ. Press.

Little, Judith W., and Milbrey W. McLaughlin, eds. 1993. *Teachers' work: Individuals, colleagues, and contexts.* New York: Teachers College Press.

Luppescu, Stuart. 1996. Virtual equating: An approach to reading test equating by concept matching of items. PhD diss., Univ. of Chicago.

Lyon, G. Reid. 1998. *Overview of reading and literacy initiatives.* Prepared statement to the Committee on Labor and Human Resources, U.S. Senate, April 28.

McAdam, Doug. 1999. *Political process and the development of black insurgency, 1930–1970.* 2nd ed. Chicago: Univ. of Chicago Press.

McAdam, Doug, John D. McCarthy, and Mayer N. Zald, eds. 1996. *Comparative perspectives on social movements: Political opportunities, mobilizing structures, and cultural framings.* Cambridge: Cambridge Univ. Press.

McDill, Edward L., Gary Natriello, and Aaron M. Pallas. 1986. A population at risk: Potential consequences of tougher school standards for student dropouts. *American Journal of Education* 94 (2): 134–81.

McLaughlin, Milbrey W. 1993. What matters most in teachers' workplace context? In Little and McLaughlin 1993, 79–103.

McLaughlin, Milbrey W., Merita A. Irby, and Juliet Langman. 1994. *Urban sanctuaries: Neighborhood organizations in the lives and futures of inner-city youth.* San Francisco: Jossey-Bass.

McLaughlin, Milbrey W., and Lorrie A. Shepard. 1995. *Improving education through standards-based reform.* Stanford, CA: National Academy of Education, Stanford Univ.

McLaughlin, Milbrey W., and Joan E. Talbert. 2006. *Building school-based teacher learning communities: Professional strategies to improve student achievement.* New York: Teachers College Press.

Meyer, Robert H. 1996. Value-added indicators of school performance. In *Improving America's schools: The role of incentives,* ed. Eric A. Hanushek and Dale W. Jorgenson, 197–223. Washington, DC: National Academy Press.

Miller, Robert J., and Brian Rowan. 2006. Effects of organic management on student achievement. *American Educational Research Journal* 43 (Summer): 219–53.

Mohrman, Susan A., Priscilla Wohlstetter, and associates, eds. 1994. *School-based management: Organizing for high performance.* San Francisco: Jossey-Bass.

Moultrie, Lisa. 1992. School reform left behind: The case of John Alexander School. Master's thesis, Univ. of Chicago.

Muller, Chandra. 1993. Parent involvement and academic achievement: An analysis of family resources available to the child. In *Parents, their children, and schools,* ed. Barbara Schneider and James S. Coleman, 77–113. Boulder, CO: Westview Press.

Murnane, Richard, Judith D. Singer, and John B. Willett. 1991. *Who will teach? Policies that matter.* Cambridge, MA: Harvard Univ. Press

Nasir, Na'ilah Suad, and Geoffrey B. Saxe. 2003. Ethnic and academic identities: A cultural practice perspective on emerging tensions and their management in the lives of minority students. *Educational Researcher* 32 (5): 14–18.

National Center on Education and the Economy. 2006. *Tough choices or tough times: The report of the New Commission on the Skills of the American Workforce.* San Francisco: Jossey-Bass.

National Commission on Excellence in Education. 1983. *A nation at risk: The imperative for educational reform.* Washington, DC: U.S. Government Printing Office.

National Education Commission on Time and Learning. 1994. *Prisoners of time.* Washington, DC: U.S. Government Printing Office.

National Staff Development Council. 1995. *Standards for staff development: Elementary school edition.* Oxford, OH: National Staff Development Council.

Newmann, Fred M., and associates. 1996. *Authentic achievement: Restructuring schools for intellectual quality.* San Francisco: Jossey-Bass.

Newmann, Fred M., Anthony S. Bryk, and Jenny K. Nagaoka. 2001. *Authentic intellectual work and standardized tests: Conflict or coexistence?* Chicago: Consortium on Chicago School Research at the Univ. of Chicago.

Newmann, Fred M., Gudelia Lopez, and Anthony S. Bryk. 1998. *The quality of intellectual work in Chicago schools: A baseline report.* Chicago: Consortium on Chicago School Research at the Univ. of Chicago.

Newmann, Fred M., BetsAnn Smith, Elaine Allensworth, and Anthony S. Bryk. 2001a. Instructional program coherence: What is it and why it should guide school improvement. *Educational Evaluation and Policy Analysis* 23 (4): 297–322.

Newmann, Fred M., BetsAnn Smith, Elaine Allensworth, and Anthony S. Bryk. 2001b. *School instructional program coherence: Benefits and challenges.* Chicago: Consortium on Chicago School Research at the Univ. of Chicago.

Newmann, Fred M., and Gary G. Wehlage. 1995. *Successful school restructuring: A report to the public and educators.* Madison, WI: Center on Organization and Restructuring of Schools.

Noddings, Nel. 1988. An ethic of caring and its implications for instructional arrangements. *American Journal of Education* 96 (2): 215–31.

Noguera, Pedro A. 2001. Transforming urban schools through investments in the social capital of parents. In Saegert, Thompson, and Warren 2001, 189–212.

Nye, Barbara, Spyros Konstantopoulos, and Larry V. Hedges. 2004. How large are teacher effects? *Educational Evaluation and Policy Analysis* 26 (3): 237–57.

Ogawa, Rodney T., and Steven T. Bossert. 1995. Leadership as an organizational quality. *Educational Administration Quarterly* (31) 2: 224–43.

Orellana, Marjorie F., and Phillip Bowman. 2003. Cultural diversity research on learning and development: Conceptual, methodological, and strategic considerations. *Educational Researcher* 32 (5): 26–32.

Orfield, Gary, Albert Woolbright, and Helene Kim. 1984. Neighborhood change and integration in metropolitan Chicago: A report of the Leadership Council for Metropolitan Open Communities. Chicago: Leadership Council for Metropolitan Open Communities.

Patillo-McCoy, Mary. 1998. Church culture as a strategy of action in the black community. *American Sociological Review* 63 (6): 767–84.

———. 1999. *Black picket fences: Privilege and peril among the black middle class.* Chicago: Univ. of Chicago Press.

Patton, Michael Q. 1978. *Utilization-focused evaluation.* 1st ed. Newbury Park, CA: Sage Publications.

Payne, Charles M. 2008. *So much reform, so little change: The persistence of failure in urban schools.* Cambridge, MA: Harvard Education Press.

Phillips, Meredith. 1997. What makes school effective? A comparison of the relation of communitarian climate and academic climate to math achievement and attendance during middle school. *American Educational Research Journal* 34 (4): 633–62.

Pitts, Leonard, Jr. 2007. Harlem program forms a circle of success for kids. *Miami Herald,* January 29, 2007. www.Miami.com.

Poinsett, Alex. 1990. School reform, black leaders: Their impact on each other. *Catalyst* 1 (May): 7–11.

Ponisciak, Stephen M., Elaine Allensworth, and Vanessa Coca. 2006. Teacher mobility in the Chicago Public Schools. Paper presented at the annual meeting of the American Educational Research Association, San Francisco.

Ponisciak, Stephen M., and Anthony S. Bryk. 2005. Value added analysis of the Chicago Public Schools: An application of hierarchical models. In *Value added models in education: Theory and applications,* ed. Robert Lissitz, 40–79. Maple Grove, MN: JAM Press.

Porter, Andrew C. 1994. The uses and misuses of opportunity-to-learn standards. *Educational Researcher* 24 (1): 21–7.

———. 2002. Measuring the content of instruction: Uses in research and practice. *Educational Researcher* 31 (October): 3–14.

Porter, Andrew C., and Jere E. Brophy. 1988. Synthesis of research on good teaching: Insights from the work of the Institute for Research on Teaching. *Educational Leadership* 45 (8): 74–85.

Porter, Andrew C., and J. L. Smithson. 2001. Are content standards being implemented in the classroom? A methodology and some tentative answers. In *From the Capitol to the classroom: Standards-based reform in the states—One hundredth yearbook of The National Society for the Study of Education, part 2*, ed. S. H. Fuhrman, 60–80. Chicago: Univ. of Chicago Press.

Pribesh, Shana, and Douglas B. Downey. 1999. Why are residential and school moves associated with poor school performance? *Demography* 36 (4): 521–34.

Purkey, Stewart C., and Marshall S. Smith. 1983. Effective schools: A review. *Elementary School Journal* 83 (4): 427–54.

Putnam, Robert D. 1993. *Making democracy work: Civic traditions in modern Italy*. Princeton, NJ: Princeton Univ. Press.

———. 2000. *Bowling alone: Collapse and revival of American community*. New York, NY: Simon and Schuster.

Raudenbush, Stephen W. 1984. Magnitude of teacher expectancy effects on pupil IQ as a function of the credibility of expectancy induction: A synthesis of findings from 18 experiments. *Journal of Educational Psychology* 76 (1): 85–97.

Raudenbush, Stephen W., and Anthony S. Bryk. 2002. *Hierarchical linear models: Applications and data analysis methods (advanced quantitative techniques in the social sciences, no. 1)*. Thousand Oaks, CA: Sage Publications.

Raudenbush, Stephen W., Anthony Bryk, Yuk F. Cheong, and Richard Congdon. 2004. *HLM6: Hierarchical linear and nonlinear modeling*. Chicago: Scientific Software International.

Reeves, Douglas B. 2000. *Accountability in action: A blueprint for learning organizations*. Denver: Advanced Learning Press.

Riehl, Carolyn J. 2000. The principal's role in creating inclusive schools for diverse students: A review of normative, empirical, and critical literature on the practice of educational administration. *Review of Educational Research* 70 (1): 55–81.

Rivkin, Steven G., Eric A. Hanushek, and John F. Kain. 2005. Teachers, schools, and academic achievement. *Econometrica* 73 (2): 417–58.

Roderick, Melissa, Mimi Engel, and Jenny Nagaoka; with Brian A. Jacob, Sophie Degener, Alex Orfei, Susan Stone, and Jen Bacon. 2003. *Ending social promotion: Results from Summer Bridge*. Chicago: Consortium on Chicago School Research at the Univ. of Chicago.

Rogosa, David R., David Brand, and Michele F. Zimowski. 1982. A growth curve approach to the measurement of change. *Psychological Bulletin* 90:726–48.

Rogosa, David R., and John B. Willett. 1985. Satisfying a simplex structure is simpler than it should be. *Journal of Educational Statistics* 10 (2): 99–107.

Rollow, Sharon G., and Anthony S. Bryk. 1994. Catalyzing professional community in a school reform left behind. In Seashore Louis, Kruse, and associates 1995, 23–45.

Rosenholtz, Susan J. 1989. *Teachers' workplace: The social organization of schools*. New York: Longman.

Rosenthal, Robert. 1995. Critiquing Pygmalion: A 25-year perspective. *Current Directions in Psychological Science* 4 (6): 171–72.

Rossmiller, Richard A. 1986. *Resource utilization in schools and classrooms: Final report*. Program Report 86–7. Madison: Wisconsin Center for Education Research, Univ. of Wisconsin.

Rowan, Brian. 1990. Commitment and control: Alternative strategies for the organizational design of schools. *Review of Research in Education* 16: 353–89.

———. 2002a. Teachers' work and instructional management, part 1: Alternative views of the task of teaching. In Hoy and Miskel 2002, 1:129–49.

——. 2002b. Teachers' work and instructional management, part 2: Does organic management promote expert teaching? In Hoy and Miskel 2002, 1:151–68.

Rowan, Brian, R. Correnti, and R. J. Miller. 2002. What large-scale, survey research tells us about teacher effects on student achievement: Insights from the *Prospects* study of elementary schools. *Teachers College Record* 104 (8): 1525–27.

Saegert, Susan, J. Phillip Thompson, and Mark R. Warren, eds. 2001. *Social capital and poor communities.* New York: Russell Sage Foundation.

Sampson, Robert J., Stephen W. Raudenbush, and Felton Earls. 1997. Neighborhoods and violent crime: A multilevel study of collective efficacy. *Science* 277 (5328): 918–24.

Seashore Louis, Karen, Sharon D. Kruse, and associates. 1995. *Professionalism and community: Perspectives on reforming urban schools.* Thousand Oaks, CA: Corwin Press.

Seashore Louis, Karen, Sharon D. Kruse, and Anthony S. Bryk. 1995. Professionalism and community: What is it and why is it important in urban schools? In Seashore Louis, Kruse, and associates 1995, 3–22.

Seashore Louis, Karen, and Matthew B. Miles. 1990. *Improving the urban high school: What works and why.* New York: Teachers College Press.

Schlecty, Phillip C. 1997. *Inventing better schools: An action plan for educational reform.* San Francisco: Jossey-Bass.

Schmidt, William H., Curtis McKnight, Leland Cogan, Pamela Jakwerth, and Richard Houang. 1999. *Facing the consequences: Using TIMSS for a closer look at United States mathematics and science education.* Dordrecht, The Netherlands: Kluwer Academic.

Sebring, Penny Bender, Anthony S. Bryk, John Q. Easton, Stuart Luppescu, Yeow Meng Thum, Winifred A. Lopez, and BetsAnn Smith. 1995. *Charting reform: Chicago teachers take stock.* Chicago: Consortium on Chicago School Research at the Univ. of Chicago.

Sebring, Penny Bender, Anthony S. Bryk, Melissa Roderick, Eric Camburn, Stuart Luppescu, Yeow Meng Thum, BetsAnn Smith, and Joseph Kahne. 1996. *Charting reform in Chicago: The students speak.* Chicago: Consortium on Chicago School Research at the Univ. of Chicago.

Sergiovanni, Thomas J. 2000. *The lifeworld of leadership: Creating culture, community, and personal meaning in our schools.* San Francisco: Jossey-Bass.

Shadish, William, Thomas D. Cook, and Donald P. Campbell. 2002. *Experimental and quasi-experimental designs for generalized causal inference.* Boston: Houghton Mifflin Company.

Shavelson, R. J., and Lisa Towne, eds. 2002. *Scientific research in education.* Washington, DC: National Academy Press.

Shernoff, David J., Barbara Schneider, and Mihaly Csikszentmihalyi. 2001. An assessment of multiple influences on student engagement in high school classrooms. Paper presented at the annual meeting of the American Educational Research Association, Seattle.

Shouse, Roger. 1996. Academic press and sense of community: Conflict and congruence in American high schools. *Research in Sociology of Education and Socialization* 11:173–202.

Sigmon, Cheryl M. 1997. *Implementing the 4-blocks literacy model.* Greensboro, NC: Carson-Dellosa.

Smith, BetsAnn. 1998. *It's about time: Opportunities to learn in Chicago's elementary schools.* Chicago: Consortium on Chicago School Research at the Univ. of Chicago.

Smith, Julia B., Valerie E. Lee, and Fred M. Newmann. 2001. *Instruction and achievement in Chicago elementary schools.* Chicago: Consortium on Chicago School Research at the Univ. of Chicago.

Smith, Julia B., BetsAnn Smith, and Anthony S. Bryk. 1998. *Setting the pace: Opportunities to learn in Chicago's elementary schools.* Chicago: Consortium on Chicago School Research at the Univ. of Chicago.

Smithgall, Cheryl, Robert Matthew Gladden, Eboni Howard, Robert M. Goerge, and Mark E. Courtney. 2004. *Educational experiences of children in out-of-home care.* Chicago: Chapin Hall Center for Children.

Smylie, Mark A. 1995. Teacher learning in the workplace: Implications for school reform. In *Professional development in education: New paradigms and practices,* ed. Thomas R. Guskey and Michael Huberman, 92–112. New York: Teachers College Press.

Smylie, Mark A., Elaine Allensworth, Rebecca C. Greenberg, Rodney Harris, and Stuart Luppescu. 2001. *Teacher professional development in Chicago: Supporting effective practice.* Chicago: Consortium on Chicago School Research at the Univ. of Chicago.

Smylie, Mark A., and Ann W. Hart. 1997. School leadership for teacher learning and change: A human and social capital development perspective. In *Handbook of educational administration,* ed. Joseph Murphy and Karen S. Louis, 421–41. New York: Longman.

Smylie, Mark A., David Mayrowetz, Joseph Murphy, and Karen Seashore Louis. 2007. Trust and the development of distributed leadership. *Journal of School Leadership* 17 (4): 469–503.

Snow, Catherine E., M. Susan Burns, and Peg Griffin, eds. 1998. *Preventing reading difficulties in young children.* Washington, DC: National Research Council.

Spillane, James P., Richard Halverson, and John B. Diamond. 2001. Investigating school leadership practice: A distributed perspective. *Educational Researcher* 30 (3): 23–28.

Spillane, James P., and C. Thompson. 1997. Reconstructing conceptions of local capacity: The local education agency's capacity for ambitious instructional reform. *Educational Evaluation and Policy Analysis* 19 (2): 185–203.

Stake, Robert E. 1980. Program evaluation, particularly responsive evaluation. In *Rethinking Educational Research,* ed. W. B. Dockrell and D. Hamilton, 72–87. London: Hodder and Stoughton.

——. 1983. Stakeholder influence in the evaluation of Cities-in-Schools. In Bryk 1983, 15–30.

Stallings, Jane. 1975. Implementation and child effects of teaching practices in follow through classrooms. *Monographs of the Society for Research in Child Development* 40: 7–8.

——. 1980. Allocated academic learning time revisited, or beyond time on task. *Educational Researcher* 9 (11): 11–6.

Steinberg, Laurence. 1996. *Beyond the classroom: Why school reform has failed and what parents need to do.* New York: Simon & Schuster.

Stevenson, Harold W., and James W. Stigler. 1992. *The learning gap: Why our schools are failing and what we can learn from Japanese and Chinese education.* New York: Summit Books.

Stodolsky, Susan S. 1988. *The subject matters: Classroom activity in math and social studies.* Chicago: Univ. of Chicago Press

Storey, Sandra L., John Q. Easton, Thomas C. Sharp, Heather Steans, Brian Ames, and Alicia Bassuk. 1995. *Chicago's public school children and their environment.* Chicago: Chicago Public Schools.

Tough, Paul. 2004. The Harlem Project. *New York Times Magazine,* June 20, 2004. www.nytimes.com/2004/06/20/magazine/20HARLEM.html?ei=5. Accessed June 29, 2004.

——. 2006. What it takes to make a student. *New York Times Magazine,* November 26, 2006. www.nytimes.com.

Tukey, John W. 1977. *Exploratory data analysis.* Reading, MA: Addison-Wesley.

Walberg, Herbert J. 1986. Syntheses of research on teaching. In Wittrock 1986, 214–39.

Warren, Mark R. 2005. Communities and schools: A new view of urban education reform. *Harvard Education Review* 75 (2): 133–75.

Warren, Mark R., J. Phillip Thompson, and Susan Saegert. 2001. The role of social capital in combating poverty. In Saegert, Thompson, and Warren 2001, 1–30.

Warsh, David. 2006. *Knowledge and the wealth of nations: A story of economic discovery.* New York: Norton.

Weiss, Carol H. 1972. *Evaluation research: Methods for assessing program effectiveness.* Englewood Cliffs, NJ: Prentice Hall.

———. 1983. The stakeholder approach to evaluation: Origins and promise. In Bryk 1983, 3–14.

Weiss, Carol H., and Michael J. Bucuvalas. 1980. *Social science research and decision making.* New York: Columbia Univ. Press.

Wenger, Etienne. (1999). *Communities of practice: Learning, meaning, and identity.* Cambridge: Cambridge Univ. Press.

Willett, John B. 1989. Questions and answers in the measurement of change. *Review of Research in Education* 15 (1988–89): 345–422.

Wilson, William Julius. 1987. *The truly disadvantaged: The inner city, the underclass, and public policy.* Chicago: Univ. of Chicago Press.

———. 1996. *When work disappears: The world of the new urban poor.* New York: Knopf.

Wittrock, Merlin C., ed. 1986. *Handbook of research on teaching.* 3rd ed. New York: Macmillan.

Wong, Kenneth K., and Sharon G. Rollow. 1990. From mobilization to legislation: A case study of the recent Chicago school reform. *Administrator's Notebook* 34 (5 and 6).

Wright, Benjamin D., and Mark H. Stone. 1979. *Best test design.* Chicago: MESA Press.

INDEX

Note: Italicized page numbers indicate illustrations.

absenteeism. *See* attendance
abused children. *See* students living under extraordinary circumstances
academic engagement measure, 74, 236, 240
academic goals of instruction, 53–54; in instructional guidance subsystem, 50, 52; and student-centered learning climate, 60. *See also* Academic Support and Press indicator
academic productivity, 31–38; academic productivity profile, 33–38, 225–30; estimating trends in, 228–30; first look at overall trends in, 39–41; improvements as inequitably distributed, 160–61; problems with public statistics for judging improved, 31–32; variation by race, ethnicity, and class, 164–68
Academic Support and Press indicator, 74; components of, 74, 240; at Hancock School versus Alexander School, 76, *76*, 77; interrelationships among essential supports, 77, 78; and negative student-centered learning climate in context of poor adult relations as impediment to improvement, 123–25, *124*; percentage of schools showing improvement in attendance, by essential supports, *100*; percentage of schools showing improvement in mathematics, by essential supports, *111*; percentage of schools showing improvement in reading, by essential supports, *109*; percentage of schools showing stagnation in attendance, by essential supports, *101*; percentage of schools showing stagnation in mathematics, by essential supports, *112*; percentage of schools showing stagnation in reading, by essential supports, *110*; for probing organizational mechanisms, 97; relatively weak effects associated with, 202–3; and student engagement with learning, 273n12
academic support systems, 49, 205–6
accountability: academic productivity improvements and, 40, 215; of local school professionals, 221; in school-site decision making and school-based management, 217; secondary, 217
active student applications emphasis. *See* Applications Emphasis indicator
African-American low SES school communities: accounting for improvement in, *184*, 186; accounting for stagnation in, *185*; criteria for classification of, 276n8; school community indicators for different subgroups of schools, *175*, *176*; summary statistics on racial-SES classification of school communities, *165*; variation in academic productivity by race, ethnicity, and class, *166*, *167*, *167*
African-American moderate SES school communities: accounting for improvement in, *184*, 186; accounting for stagnation in, *185*; criteria for classification of, 276n8; school community indicators for different subgroups of schools, *175*, *176*; summary statistics on racial-SES classification of school